FORTUNE, MISFORTUNE, FORTIFIES ONE

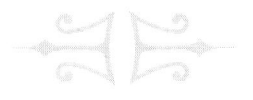

FORTUNE, MISFORTUNE, FORTIFIES ONE

Margaret of Austria, Ruler of the Low Countries, 1507-1530

SHIRLEY HARROLD BONNER

Copyright by Shirley Harrold Bonner 1981
All rights reserved.

ISBN: 150768861X
ISBN 13: 9781507688618

With deepest gratitude, this book is dedicated to my daughter, Margaret Lizabeth Bonner, without whose skills and suggestions it never would have become a reality.

AND many thanks to my steadfast husband, Joe, and son, Jeb for his translation help; also to my cousin, Dr. Sarah Gustafson who showed it could be done; and to the staff at Lighthouse Pointe, my home.

TABLE OF CONTENTS

	Preface	ix
Chapter 1	Margaret's Early Life and Education	1
Chapter 2	"Fortune, Misfortune, Strengthens a Woman"	20
Chapter 3	Sovereign of the Low Countries	72
Chapter 4	Margaret's Involvement in the Arts and Humanities	149
Chapter 5	The Tumultuous Years of the Reformation	171
	Bibliography	281

PREFACE

I became interested in Margaret of Austria and Burgundy in a roundabout fashion. We moved to Belgium because of my husband's work in 1976, and our first year there was very difficult for me. Unable to get a job or find anything useful to do, isolated in a small provincial border town in the north, I sought help from our minister, Dr. Lawrence Schwarz. Knowing my background in religion and psychology, he suggested study at the Brussels Protestant Theological Seminary and made arrangements for an interview. My ability in French and Nederlands was passive and this precluded my taking any courses immediately, but the faculty graciously offered me the use of their valuable library for reading. Dr. R.H. Boudin, the president of the Seminary, and Dr. Andre Pieters, president of the Protestant Council of Churches in Belgium, willingly gave of their time and thoughts - Dr. Pieters gripping my arm and whispering "Bon courage!"

So, one day a week that long, cold, dreary winter, I made the two-hour trip by train and subway to the charming old houses converted to seminary use, buried myself in a comfortable chair, and browsed and read through many precious volumes in the Meyhoffer Collection. I soon found myself turning back to a volume by Ghislaine de Boom on Margaret of Austria, first regent of the Low Countries, 1507-1530. The troubles Margaret had endured touched a soft spot in my heart and her despair met my own.

Eagerly I began looking for more information in histories, only to find that the indexes often contained little or no mention of her name; her accomplishments being credited to her father Maximilian or her nephew Charles V. It struck me as unjust and even as historically irresponsible that this capable and thoughtful woman who ruled the Low Countries for 23 years, should be so summarily dismissed. A sense of mission began to possess me. I was determined to get all the information I could, soon becoming a frequent visitor at the Koninklijke Bibliotheek (Bibliothèque Royale) Albert I in Brussels, the Stadsbibliotheek in Antwerp, the Archives du Nord in Lille, France, the archives in Mechelen (Malines) and the churches there - Sts. Peter & Paul, the Cathedral of St. Romboud. Margaret's palace is in Mechelen, and a statue of her stands in the town square.

The reading, of course, was difficult and slow, but my resolve drove me. A short trip to England for texts in English of background material helped. My family, pulled into my research, spent our vacation traversing many of Margaret's old paths, and visiting places where she had lived.

In February 1979, I was accepted into the doctoral program of Foundations of Education, University of Pittsburgh. Through course work, our library here, interlibrary loans, and the encouragement and advice of Dr. Margaret Anderson and Dr. Richard Seckinger, my research has been extended and enriched. In the two other members of my committee, Dr. Paul Masoner and Dr. Louis Petrone, I have been well blessed by the interest and concern they have shown.

Chapter 1

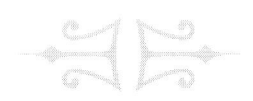

MARGARET'S EARLY LIFE AND EDUCATION

On January 10, 1480, when the long night of winter in northern Europe is just beginning to lift, there was born in the palace at Brussels a little girl named Margaret whose lifetime would span that arc of years in which the Middle Ages turned into the Renaissance. Her parents were the Archduke Maximilian of Austria and the Archduchess Mary of Burgundy who, two years earlier on July 22, 1478, had borne a son called Philip. Margaret was baptized at Saint Gudule's (St. Michael's[1]). Her godparents were Philip of Cleves, Lord of Ravenstein; Jean de Chalons, Prince of Orange; and Margaret of York, her step-grandmother. This little princess would one day rule over the Low Countries, and in her lifetime can be observed the transition from a chivalric government based on swashbuckling exploits, to the modern methods of realistic (at times cynical), patient and painstaking diplomacy and conciliation.[2]

---

1 This cathedral is now called St. Michael's, but known as Sts. Michael's and Gudule's, since the dismissal of many saints from the Catholic roster following the research done by the Bollandists, a Jesuit order specializing in hagiography and located in Brussels.

2 See Albert William Levi, Humanism and Politics (Bloomington: University of Indiana Press, 1969), pp. 41-58; Theodore K. Rabb, The Struggle for Stability in Early Modem Europe (New York: Oxford University, 1975), pp. 71-72; Nicola Abbagnano, "Humanism" trans. by Nino

The background of this biography begins in the conflict between the houses of Orleans and Burgundy over policy brought about by the recurring insanity of Charles VI (1380-1422) of France, aggravating the continuing strife between England and France known as The Hundred Years' War. In 1407 Louis of Orleans was assassinated, and was revenged in 1419 when John the Fearless was murdered at Montereau - but that was not the end of it; instead, a whole century of contention was ushered in. John's son, Philip the Good, married to Michele of France, nevertheless spent sixteen years avenging his father's death and demanded expensive and pious reparations at the Treaty of Arras in 1435. In 1451 Louis XI came to the throne of France. He was cantankerous, deceitful, avaricious, practical and wise.[3] In spite of having received the protection of Philip the Good while out of favor with his father, Louis had an undying hatred for the house of Burgundy. The territories of this powerful duchy had grown through judicious marriages to comprise not only Burgundy in France, but most of that area now known as the Low Countries and including the rich provinces of Flanders and Brabant.

Philip's son, Charles the Bold, took over the rule of Burgundy at his father's death in 1467. Charles was a man of culture and learning, skilled in government, but his vaulting ambition, obstinacy and fearful temper led him to foolhardy deeds of reckless courage in his attempts to bring outlying territories into the Burgundian sphere.[4] In order to make a corridor between Burgundy and the Low Countries, he sensibly bought

---

Langiulli, in The Encyclopedia of Philosophy (New York: The Macmillan Company, 1967),, Vol. IV, p. 71; and J.R. Hale, Renaissance Europe 1480-1520 (7th ed. London: Fontana/Collins, 1977), pp. 304-310. In view of the many wars since, many will find it difficult to give credence to this, but up to that era, conflict was resolved "by God" in hand-to-hand combat or wars. Negotiation has remained as much as an aspirational activity as a decisive or conclusive one.

3   Pierre Champion, Louis XI (Paris: Librairie Ancienne Honore Champion, 1927; Paul Murray Kendall, Louis XI (New York: W.W. Norton and Company, 1971. For a fictional account of Louis XI of France and Robert de la Marek, 11 the Wild Boar of the Ardennes, see Sir Walter Scott, Quentin Durward (Boston: Houghton, Mifflin and Company, 1900?).

4   Richard J. Walsh, "Charles the Bold and the Crusade: Politics and Propaganda" in the Journal of Medieval History 3, No.1, North Holland Publishing Company, March 1977, pp. 53-86. For a history of these times from the point of view of the Low Countries, see Henri Pirenne, Histoire de Belgique (Bruxelles: Henri Lamertin, Libraire Éditeur, 1907).

the country of Ferette and land in Alsace. He brought Gelderland under his jurisdiction in 1473 (which became a continuing headache to Margaret during her rule). He arranged to acquire the title of king through the Emperor Frederick III who, at the last moment, slipped away from Trier where the ceremonies were to be held. Perhaps he feared Charles's unbridled drive and energy. It is unfortunate that this coronation never took place for it would have served to unite these disparate provinces, some of which owed suzerainty to the Empire and some to France.

Nevertheless, Charles pressed on. His skirmishes with, his laying waste to, then a bishopric and not under his authority, and his invasions of French territory kept the country in perpetual turmoil. His brother-in-law, Edward IV of England, signed a treaty with Louis in 1475. Attacked by René of Lorraine and a confederation of the Swiss, Sigismund of Austria, and some small towns on the upper Rhine, Charles suffered three great defeats ending in his death at the battle of Nancy on January 5, 1475. Though the French forces took no part, Burgundy found itself at the mercy of Louis, and when the states of Burgundy were partitioned, France took the Duchy of Burgundy itself.

Now what a plight his wife and daughter found themselves in. On the one hand menacing Louis, and on the other, the disgruntled burghers of Flanders and Brabant who had had their fill of war,[5] and only wanted to get on with the business of life, which was business. These two women, Margaret of York (who had married Charles in 1468), and her stepdaughter Mary of Burgundy, were kept under virtual house arrest in Ghent. Secretly, they were able to send for help to Maximilian of Austria. Other husbands had been suggested for Mary, even Louis's baby son Charles, but Madame Halcwijn, Mary's governess, remarked that "what they needed was a man and not a child; her mistress was capable of bearing children, and this is what her territory needed. And this opinion prevailed."[6]

---

5 Ghislaine de Boom, Marguerite d'Autriche-Savoie et la Pré-Renaissance (Bruxelles: La Renaissance du Livre, 1946/1935), p. 8.
6 Philippe de Comines, The Memoirs of Philippe de Commynes, Vol. II, ed., Samuel Kinser; trans. by Isabelle Cazeaux (Columbia: University of South Carolina Press, 1973), p. 380.

Tentative arrangements leading to a betrothal had been made for Mary of Burgundy and Maximilian, and a proxy ceremony was held in April. Mary in a tender, pleading letter urged him to come to their relief. And did he come, this handsome prince charming? Well, yes - but not as soon as one might envision or in as dashing a way. For Maximilian, an inveterate dawdler was penniless as well. For Margaret, who had been separated from Mary, was able to arrange payment to him of a sum large enough to equip and clothe himself, his courtiers and his soldiers in suitably impressive style. But it was not until August, seven months after Charles's death that the young prince arrived at the castle in Ghent. The wedding was held secretly at night in the chapel, and the Archbishop of Trier performed the ceremony. The marriage was a happy one, and there is a woodcut of the charming pair shown sitting in the garden teaching each other languages.

In a rush of jubilation and hospitality, the town welcomed Maximilian with open arms. There is nothing more pleasant than a softly warm summer day in Flanders. Add to that colorful banners flying in a light breeze, bands playing; silks, damasks, ermine and jewels in abundance on the backs of the prosperous, gleaming armor, excited horses, rough German soldiers, a cheering peasant crowd, fountains flowing with wine, and tables loaded with grilled meats and fish, fruits and cheeses, sausages, blood pudding and sweetmeats, and all varieties of pâtés and tarts.[7] At once, we feel the spirit of it and hope the couple will live happily ever after.

But the position of France had not altered. Mary had not the strength for ruling, and Maximilian, after consulting with Margaret of York and her Flemish counselors, took charge of his wife's armies. The French had made inroads into the territories of Burgundy and the Low Countries, and finally a decisive battle was fought at Guinegate on August 7, 1479, in which Maximilian defeated the French forces. Louis continued his war covertly by fomenting and subsidizing rebellion in Gelderland and by subverting

---

[7] Scenes such as this are recreated in Belgium today, faithfully following the narrative of the chroniclers or the documents in the town archives. This generation is fortunate also in that the Breughels have left us a record in their paintings of the peasants in various occupations and celebrations.

the loyalty of the Flemish cities who detested the presence of the German soldiers and were beginning to regard Maximilian with suspicion.[8]

For a period, however, everything seemed to go well, and then tragedy struck. Mary and Maximilian set out for a hunt from their palace at Bruges one fine morning in late winter. Though Mary was an excellent horsewoman and skillful in hawking, her horse failed to jump a dike, and off-balance, stumbled and fell, throwing her to the ground. Out of modesty, she refused medical care though according to one account she suffered a broken thigh, and to another that she was pregnant and suffered a miscarriage with complications. For whatever reason, Mary died three weeks later on March 27, 1482 and was buried in The Church of Our Lady at Bruges where her tomb may still be seen. She was only twenty-five, her son Philip four, and Margaret, a two-year-old.

Any young mother's death is pathetic, and Mary's was no exception. Maximilian broke down in grief and despair and though he lived to be sixty and married once again, never quite recovered from it. However, the death of his beloved wife was not only an emotional loss for the family, but a political disaster for the Low Countries. Mary's being and presence as the native Archduchess was the tenuous glue which held those factious provinces together.

Louis XI of France, ever cunning and watchful to take advantage, concluded the Peace of Arras with the Flemish communities led by the hostile burghers of Ghent. The states of Brabant, Hainault, Holland, Zeeland, Friesland and Namur remained loyal to Maximilian, but his children were in the hands of the aldermen of Ghent.

Part of the French-Flemish agreement was a marriage contract between the little Margaret and the twelve-year-old Charles, the Dauphin of France. According to the Chronicler Comines who was himself Flemish but was employed by Louis XI, the diplomats from Ghent were inept and vengeful. Louis had wanted only the country of Artois or of Burgundy, but these "lords of Ghent (as he called them) were willing to give the countries of

---

[8] Ghislaine de Boom, Marguerite d'Autriche-Savoie et la Pré-Renaissance (Bruxelles: La Renaissance du Livre, 1946/1935), p. 7.

Charolais, Maconnais, and Auxerrois, and if they could have given all the subjects of the House of Burgundy who are French speaking to Louis, they would have done it willingly in order to weaken Maximilian."[9]

Maximilian had no voice in the matter because the aldermen of the Flemish cities were strengthened by a great many of the nobles such as the Lord of Ravenstein (who was Margaret's godfather, and who had Philip in his custody), and the Duke of Cleves. Of course the saddest result by our standards, and even deplored then, was that Margaret was to be taken to France. Mass was said in the Church of St. John at Ghent to celebrate the peace, and the fickle crowds reveled once again. But for Maximilian there was only the deepest misery.

Concerning Margaret's babyhood, one story has come down to us. She and Philip were playing a game out of doors, which involved putting a ball into a basket attached to the wall. Success meant being able to move closer to the basket. When she found herself at the basket and realized she had won, she turned and ran triumphantly into her father's arms. He laughed and hugged and kissed her.[10] That is the first instance we know of, but Margaret would spend a lifetime proving herself.

Margaret left Ghent April 26, 1483, accompanied by a brilliant escort of knights and ladies, and surrounded by men of arms not only to protect her from the dangers of the road, but to prevent her being taken away by Maximilian-

> If the Duke of Austria had been able to take her away from those who were leading her to Hesdin, he would have done so willingly before she left his territories; but those of Ghent had her well guarded. Anyway, he was beginning to lose all authority.[11]

---

9 Philippe de Comines, The Memoirs of Philippe de Commynes, Vol. II, ed., Samuel Kinser; trans. by Isabelle Cazeaux (Columbia: University of South Carolina Press, 1973), p. 412.
10 Elsa Winker, Margarete Von Österreich, Grande Dame der Renaissance (München: Verlag Georg D.W. Callwey, 1966), pp. 17-18.
11 Philippe de Comines, The Memoirs of Philippe de Commynes, Vol. II, ed., Samuel Kinser; trans. by Isabelle Cazeaux (Columbia: University of South Carolina Press, 1973), p. 413.

There is a portrait of Margaret at the Chateau of Versailles Museum showing her in a square-necked dress and wearing two delicate chains around her neck. A close-fitting cap comes down over her ears, but curly blonde hair is visible. She was a sweet-faced child with big brown eyes whose gaze seems to be turned back in on herself. The roundness of babyhood still lingered. It is thought to have been painted at Ghent in 1433 just before her trip to France to marry the dauphin.

Ghislaine de Boom writes that the dauphin of France, seated in a litter at the bosom of his wet nurse, made a "pompous" entry into the city of Lille on April 26, 1483.[12] Considering that he was twelve years old, this is certainly indicative of his condition. He was a sickly child, weak and ill formed, and a stutterer, and the Flemish ambassadors had been astute enough to ask to see him when they were at the court of Louis. Now it was the turn of the other side. Margaret's entourage rested for a short time at Lille, and then went on to the town of Hesdin near Calais. There she was met by the French ambassador and Louis's daughter Anne de Beaujeu with her husband Pierre. Margaret was undressed and examined, and all fear of physical infirmity was dispelled. On May 16, 1483 in the great hall of the Chateau at Hesdin, the dauphin Charles and Margaret were presented to each other. Madame of Ravenstein solemnly delivered up her little charge and made ready with the other Flemish to return home. If she felt any anguish at leaving Margaret in the hands of the rather cool Anne, it is not recorded. This Madame of Ravenstein was Anne of Burgundy, one of the eighteen recognized illegitimate children of Philip the Good who were reared at court, and thus a youthful great-aunt to Margaret. Secure in her own judgment, and with the presumption of an archduchess, she always bore herself as a true daughter of the house and had immense influence at court.[13] Her husband was the Lord of Ravenstein who had sided with

---

12 Ghislaine de Boom, Marguerite d'Autriche-Savoie et la Pré-Renaissance (Bruxelles: La Renaissance du Livre, 1946), p. 10.

13 Later, Anne of Burgundy became lady-in-waiting to Juana, but she visited Margaret to offer the services of her father-in-law in the matter of Margaret's future "employment." She is even referred to as the "Archduchess Madama de Ravestain." See Gomez de Fuensalida, Correspondencia ... (Madrid: Published by the Duque de Berwick y de Alba, Conde de Siruela, 1907), p. xvii.

Ghent against Maximilian. Far from feeling shame at these barbarous arrangements - even for that time - she was strong minded enough to feel she was doing the best not only for Margaret but for Flanders.

What can be said of the bewilderment and sense of loss and fright of a three-year-old whose mother has died, whose father has been forcibly separated from her, whose familiar surroundings and speech patterns have been left behind, and now whose last protector has turned to go?

In the development of Margaret's personality, she was fortunate in that she was permitted to keep her nurse, Jeanne Lejeune, and Jeanne's husband Le Veau de Bousanton, who held the post of steward, his brother plus a few other servants, all considered of little significance socially or politically, but emotionally, these familiar people were of extreme importance.[14] Furthermore, Margaret was placed under the indulgent and intelligent governance of Madame de Segré (Secret), a cheerful woman of tremendous good will and great artistic sense whom Margaret came to love with all a child's ardor.

The procession wended its way slowly and in a great estate to Paris, where in June 2, Margaret was received by cheering crowds some drunk from too much celebrating; by new masters of crafts created in her name, and by prisoners freed in honor of her arrival. After many receptions, the procession continued toward Amboise nearly a hundred miles away, arriving Sunday, June 22, 1483. According to an account by Champion in Louis XI:

> The King [Louis] published the news of the peace throughout the kingdom in the most solemn manner. He ratified the treaty of peace as the most Christian King, moved by pity and compassion "for the poor people." To the feast at Amboise, the King invited the people of his good cities ... They saw the Dauphin, who was thirteen years old, astride his palfrey... in the midst of his archers while he awaited the arrival of his betrothed. He wore a robe of crimson

---

14 They also accompanied Margaret to Spain in 1497. See Jean Molinet, Chroniques de Jean Molinet (Bruxelles: Palais des Académies, 1935), Vol. II, p. 433.

satin, lined with black velvet...The Dauphin made his reverence to the ladies then returned to a dwelling nearby the bridge where he descended and changed his clothing, putting on a long robe of cloth of gold ... Then the Dauphiness arrived within the enclosure and descended from her litter, at which time the prothonotary betrothed them. He asked the Dauphin in a loud voice if he would have Margaret of Austria in marriage. He responded "Yes." The same question was addressed to the Dauphiness two times. Then they returned to the chateau. The men of Amiens remarked that the streets of Amboise ... were hung with cloth ... and in the midst of all was a fountain in the shape of a siren whose breasts jetted white wine and red wine.[15]

The marriage took place in the chapel within the grounds of the ancient castle of Amboise. Through the centuries, many of the old "lodgings" have disappeared, and the gardens have been replaced by a tree-shaded terrace, but the lovely old chapel remains, and the castle itself still commands a magnificent view of the Loire, the town, and the countryside. And on that solemn day, ambassadors of Maximilian were present - Jean de Lannoy; Abbé de Saint Bertin, the Chancellor of the Golden Fleece; the Abbe de Saint-Pierre of Ghent; Jean de Bergues, (Berghes) Lord of Walhain (Walcheren), and Baldwin of Lannoy, Lord of Molenbaix. The cities of Flanders also sent representatives, and those from Amiens recorded:[16]

The people who had been invited to the wedding in the chateau observed the Dauphin on his way to the church, dressed in a long robe of white damask, and holding Monsieur de Beaujeu by the

---

15 Pierre Champion, Louis XI (Paris: Librairie Ancienne Honore Champion, 1927), pp. 362-363. Taken from Bibl. nat., ms. fr. 32511, fol. 398. - Une fête a lieu à Compiègne pour la paix entre le roi et le duc d'Autriche, à l'occasion du mariage du dauphin (arch. com. cc. 28 and lettre des députés de la ville d'Amiens, 22 juin 1482
(Commynes, ed. de Dupont, Preuves, III, pp. 345-349). Sur le voyage de Clabault, voir Arch. com. d'Amiens, BB. 14, fol. 98. Trans. by SHB.
16 Ibid.

hand. Two by two came clarions and trumpets, followed by the lords. On arriving at the gate of the chapel within the lower court of the castle, Madame de Segre carried the Dauphiness. The couple took the oath of marriage:[17] or better or worse ... then the Dauphin placed a ring on Margaret's finger; the mass was sung ... The King did not attend.

When the ceremony was over, the Abbé de Saint Bertin gave a sermon in honor of the peace which this marriage would ensure. Under these pathetic circumstances, he had to grope for a theme - he compared the young couple to King. Ahasuerus and Queen Esther in the Old Testament, and he dwelt at length on the glorious history of the five Margarets of Burgundy; little Margaret, now the future Queen of France, being the fifth.

Though it could be of no concern to a very young child, Margaret had not long to wait for that title, for King Louis XI died at Plessis-les-Tours, on August 30, 1483. The guardianships of Charles and Margaret were placed in the hands of Anne de Beaujeu, and she was named regent of France. She had been the favorite child of Louis who said of her, "She is the least foolish woman in the world; for there is no such thing as a wise one."[18]

Anne of France was a remarkable woman. She was bright and talented herself, and her court became a refuge for scholars, writers and artists. The imaginative Pico della Mirandola was in France between 1485 and 1488; suspected of heresy, he nevertheless found refuge.[19] It is impossible to say

---

17 Richardson explains: "There were two types of recognized contract, per verba defuturo and per verba de praesenti, depending upon the tense of the verb used in the promise. In the former, it was a convenient announcement of future intent, not a true marriage. Ordinarily this form was used when the parties were so young that the date of consummation had to remain indefinite. In contrast, the de praesenti contract was pronounced in the present tense, making it more final and obligatory. . . In both cases cohabitation sealed the union." See Walter C. Richardson, Mary Tudor: The White Queen (London: Peter Owen, 19701, p, 42. Both Margaret and Comines, the historian, believed it was a true marriage.)

18 Christopher Hare (Mrs. Marian Andrews), The High and Puissant Princess Marguerite of Austria (London: Harper and Brothers, 1907), p. 29.

19 Yvonne Labande-Mailfert, Charles VIII et Son Milieu (1470-1498) (Paris: Libraire C. Klincksieck, 1975), p.90. See note 713: Dorez et Thuasne, Pic de La Mirandole en France, 1485-1488.

what influence he had, if any; but knowing how conservative the University of Paris was,[20] and how scholars of that era gravitated to the courts, and with what honor Italian humanists were welcomed, it would be safe to conclude he was at the center of many agreeable and stimulating discussions.

Anne oversaw the education of the several children in her charge. First to Charles, belatedly, as Louis had purposely neglected his education, though perhaps through subterfuge, his mother (while she lived) and his tutor had been able to instill some information in him. Later he developed an interest in speaking Latin which was fostered by the College of Navarre, an institution he warmly supported. He also learned to read and understand Italian. Throughout his short and often unhappy life, he displayed "a curiosity of spirit with a desire for culture."[21]

As was customary at the time, the palace conducted a school for relatives, wards, and children of the nobles in the service of the court at Amboise. As Charles VIII had his own tutor, this particular school was comprised of little girls who grew up to play dominant roles in history. Besides Margaret, there was Louise of Savoy, four years older, related in the convoluted way of royalty to both Anne and her husband Pierre.[22] After the early death of her parents, she made her home at Amboise. There was also Susanne, the daughter of Anne and Pierre, much younger than the others and a frail child.

Around the court was Louis d'Orleans, now twenty-one years of age and yoked in a forced and embittered marriage with the sweet and holy, but deformed Jeanne, sister of Anne and Charles. Louis would eventually succeed Charles on the throne of France. He must have been quite taken with the lively little tot Margot, with her golden hair and her quick rejoinders to his teasing, because he ever afterwards regarded her with kindness and affection, and referred in his letters to their happy youth at Amboise.[23]

---

20 Paule Henry-Bordeaux, Louise de Savoie, "Roi" de France (1476-1531) (Paris: Librairie Académique Perrin, 1971/1954/1943), p. 280: "All the world, or nearly, is suspect at the Sorbonne."
21 Yvonne Labande-Mailfert, Charles VIII. . , p. 166.
22 First cousin of Anne and niece of Pierre.
23 Eleanor E. Tremayne, The First Governess of the Netherlands (New York: G.P. Putnam1s Sons; London: Methuen & Company, 1908, p. 5: "Years after, when Louis of Orleans was King of

11

Concerning the education of that time, research today is enriched by a little volume entitled Les enseignements (Lessons) written by Anne de Beaujeu which was first published in 1504 (though probably composed much earlier), and which fortunately has been preserved for us.[24] The dedication is to Susanne and begins:

> The perfect, natural love which I have for you, my daughter, and thoughts of the frailty of life and the innumerable great dangers of this world and sudden death that strikes at every hour, these give me courage and the desire, in spite of my poor, weak brain, to set down for you while I am still with you some little lessons, informing your ignorance and extreme youth, with the hope that at times you will remember them and be able to gain some little profit from them.[25]

Recognizing individual differences in character and abilities, she felt that education should influence the student as "good wine colors its cask."[26] She believed the foundation of true education should be based on strong religious principles as drawn from the early Fathers of the Church:

France, he refers in his letters to Margaret to their happy youth at Amboise when 'she was the second person he loved best in the world; that he desires above all things to embrace his cousin, his vassal, his first mistress, to remind her of their childish games, and after having made her blush by his compliments, to swear eternal love for her.'" See also Jean Godefroy, ed., Lettres du roy Louis XII et du cardinal d'.Amboise, avec plusieurs lettres, mémoires et instructions écrites depuis 1506 jusques et y compris 1514 (Bruxelles, 1712, 4 vols.) This anthology contains, besides the correspondence of the King of France with his representatives, the Kings of England and of Aragon, the dispatches of Austria, as well as the relations between their ambassadors. [See Ghislaine de Boom, Marguerite d'Autriche-Savoie,... p. 12 and in her bibliography, p. 111.]

24 Anne of France, Les enseignements d'Anne de France ... à sa fille Susanne de Bourbon (Moulins: C. Desrosiers, 1878).

25 Unfortunately, Susanne predeceased her mother. In the conflict to come between Francis I and Charles V. Susanne's husband Charles de Montpensier, Duke de Bourbon and Constable of France, would flee Francis and join Charles, taking with him this manuscript written by his aunt and mother-in-law, Anne de Beaujeu. From Ruth Kelso, Doctrine for the Lady of the Renaissance (Urbana: University of Illinois Press, 195b), p. 212.

26 Christopher Hare, 'The High and Puissant Princess Marguerite of Austria (London: Harper and Brothers, 907), p. 34.

St. Paul, St. Augustine, St. Bernard, St. Ambrose, and St. Thomas Aquinas the thirteenth-century theologian and philosopher. These principles were to be harmonized with lessons from the Greek philosophers Socrates, Aristotle and Plato; her belief being, however, that Christianity was the flowering of all that was best. She believed that devotions were not to be over done, and in practice, the Lord's prayer was said three times every morning and evening, as well as the Ave Maria.

The curriculum consisted of grammar, rhetoric and logic, known as the trivium, which formed the lower base of the liberal arts. Our generation wonders what rhetoric really was. It becomes clear if one thinks of it as literature and philosophy along with principles of effective self-expression both in speaking and writing. Another group known as the quadrivium consisted of arithmetic, music, geometry and astronomy, and formed the upper division of the liberal arts, but here most of the emphasis was on simple mathematics and music. Languages are not much dwelt on, but certainly Latin was taught, and perhaps even some Italian (since we know Charles had a passive knowledge of the language). Later Margaret learned to read and write Flemish though she never mastered the speaking of it, but she did become fluent in Spanish.

Moral and philosophic education was based on the ancient philosophers. Anne's emphasis was on Plato according to Boethius's[27] translation, the standard text. As the humanists gained the ascendance in the coming years, they tended to find Boethius's Latin barbaric, but for now, and since the sixth century, his works were the established authority.

---

27 Boethius, called "the last of the Romans," was born in 480, named consul in 510 and appointed to high office by Theodoric, was put to death in 524 for "magic practices." He was not able to accomplish his life's goal of translating all of Aristotle and Plato and that of their commentators into Latin, but he did accomplish a substantial amount. He also wrote a treatise on arithmetic based on Nicomachus of Gerasa, and on music. His Consolation of Philosophy was written while in prison as he tried to explain the injustice of his position. This is a testament to the moral life from a Stoic and Platonic defense of God in spite of, and through an explanation of, the existence of evil. We can see from this scant overview what an influence was brought to bear on the Middle Ages from the study of his works on Hellenic culture. They became the guideposts of humanism. A copy of Boethius's Consolations was included in each of the library collections consulted for this work. For more about Boethius, see Emile Brehier, The Middle Ages and the Renaissance (Chicago: University of Chicago Press, 1965), pp. 5-10.

According to Woodward, during this period the Doctrinale of Alexander de Villa dei - the Latin grammar in metrical form - seems to have served as the first textbook, superseded by Donatus (and others) in the case of more advanced students.[28] This seems heavy going for children, but as they copied and recopied the material, played learning games, and listened to the explanations of a kindly tutor in the scholastic methods of the day, some of the Instruction must have been absorbed, or seeds were planted for a later day. Girls of the nobility were often better educated than their brothers as learning was sometimes considered a hindrance to soldiering. At any rate, they did not take part in the jousting exercises and games felt necessary for boys - an art so necessary for the future battles which they knew would occur and to which they looked forward so eagerly. It has been said about this era that education for noblewomen was Christian and responsible, while that for men was pagan and irresponsible. Anne's work embraced a vast plan for the conduct of all the circumstances a young noblewoman would meet in life. She warned that "idleness, envy and mockery are the three sins to be avoided in herself and in her women." She despised affectation and false simplicity as being dishonest. In the attitude of the day, she believed in dressing according to one's rank in life, but with moderation. (According to the chroniclers and preachers, this was seldom done.) She believed there should be amusing pastimes between the mistress and her ladies with games to relieve low spirits and to enhance pleasant relations - though without familiarity for she saw a danger in favoring any special one for friendship, feeling that kind of closeness should be reserved to the family.

Concerning the tasks of government, she advocated following the middle way, acting always in a benign and courteous manner with friends and council alike. She warned to be on guard against those who would

---

28 William Harrison Woodward, Vittorino da Feltre and Other Humanist Educators (New York: Columbia University Teachers College, Bureau of Publications, 1963), p. 209. The Doctrinale is founded on the great work of Priscian, the sixth century Latin grammarian at Constantinople, but its metrical form made it easier to memorize. For the use of this text and that of Donatus, see Elsa Winker, Margarete Von Österreich, Grande Dame der Renaissance Verlag Georg D.W. Callwey, 1966), p. 31.

cause trouble among the people of the cities, and to govern in such a way that "you do not develop an unpleasant reputation ... and give up your sovereignty to no one. In aspect be cold and assured, constant, firm, and courageous." Anne once told Margaret, "Don't worry about anybody else but yourself."[29]

Probably Anne's own activity in government was the best guidance of all. In those days a ruler's life was not so compartmented, and as her students observed her firmness and diplomacy, her logic and skill, they too learned how to govern well. And her court with so many different people representing various cultural and intellectual opinions - rational and worldly - made an indelible impression on her charges. Both Louise of Savoy and Margaret of Austria absorbed her good advice, but neither one ever achieved that cool demeanor, each of them loving and hating warmly.

Within the text of Les enseignements is an illustrative tale.[30] It is the story of three young ladies, daughters of the Lord of Poitiers, who were very noble, powerful and of excellent beauty, renowned throughout the world. Three young princes came from Germany desiring their hands in marriage, but the first had her waist so clenched in, that her heart failed her and she fainted. The second was so inconstant and frivolous that she appeared the color of madness ... the third talked so much and especially about love that she was judged silly and not chaste of her body, and likely to die at the hour of her espousal. So the three young princes made a hasty return to their own country... and the three young ladies lost their good by their follies. So learn from this to never suffer anyone whatsoever to touch your body, press your hands, or make contacts with your feet ... guard against gushing, pinching, teasing, and be slow and cool in all your responses. Apparently. Anne did not have faith in subtle lessons.

---

29 Elsa Winker, Margarete Von Österreich, Grande Dame de Renaissance (München: Verlag George D.W. Callwey, 1966), p. 48.
30 Anne of France, Les enseignements d'Anne de France ... à sa fille Susanne de Bourbon Moulins, C. Desrosiers, 1878, p. 39.

Following the text is a "moving and patriotic" story written like a legend and patterned after one by Froissart.[31] It is much too long to relate, but the essence of it is this:

At the time of the powerful Prince of Wales, the English laid siege to the very strong chateau and the city of Brest defended by the Lord of Chastel in Lower Brittany, who was the captain of the King. During an assembly of kinsmen and friends, it was seen that there was no one to employ as hostage except his only son thirteen years of age. He is devastated because he is the cause of the surrendering of his child and wishes for death, but is grateful for the consolation of his wife who comforts him, though remarking in an aside that "it is a thing most apparent that children are more sons and daughters of their mothers." She speaks to him of faith and courage and that they will love and cherish the day he is freed, adding that "I abandon the misery to God." When the prince hears this response, he has the boy's feet and hands secured like a common malefactor, but because of his age gives him something to drink and eat. The mother faints upon hearing this, and the boy realizes what is happening and saddens at the thought of the anguish of his parents; but he makes himself ready and commits his soul to God. The swordsman in one blow beheads him.

The captain now tries to comfort his wife and the herald who brings the bad news, as this man has sought to bring the boy's body from the prince. The captain prays at the mass, "He died to save my honor ... my dear son, I pray that you will pardon me." The captain and his wife try to console each other.

In the end this terrible prince and his company set sail, but the weather is so foul that they are all lost, which was the punishment and judgment of God to one so cruel as to kill the child of the captain.

What an account of strong and courageous yet tender parenthood, and think what a lesson for all those little girls. Years later in 1526 Louise's grandchildren (the two sons of Francis) would be held hostage by Charles V (Margaret's nephew) in Spain. One can't help wondering if those two ladies remembered Anne's story. Anne's work is not entirely original. As

---

31 Ibid., pp. 137-190. Both sections greatly condensed and freely translated by SHB.

has been noted, the tale above is similar to one by Froissart. Other sections are based on the Enseignements de Saint Louis and on Le livre de la cité des dames by Christine de Pisan[32] who lived a century earlier than this period but whose works were copied widely and treasured in the libraries of many nobles.

The 1878 edition of Anne's Les enseignements contains two inventories of books,[33] dated 1507, totaling 491 volumes some of whose authors, subjects and titles are familiar to us today: Chronicles of France, Aesop's Fables, History of Troy, Knights of the Round Table, Life of St. Augustine, City of God, Works of Master Jean Gerson, Boethius, St. Thomas Aquinas, Life of St. Francis, Cicero, Life of Aristotle, Ovid, Virgil, Life of St. Paul, Petrarch, St. Catherine of Siena, Pliny, two copies of The Book of Melusine, Books of the Bible, a Life of Christ, Boccaccio, Josephus, Foissart's Chronicles of England, The Book of Merlin's Deeds, and Christine de Pisan's Le livre de la cite des dames and Le livre du tresor (two copies). Of the three libraries having the greatest influence in Margaret's life, this one from her childhood in France is the most extensive.

There was a lighter side to growing up. Writing poetry seemed to be a universal ability at the time and one that was done for amusement. Drawing and painting were taught, and judging from the household

---

32 See editorial comments on p. xxxi of Les enseignements d'Anne de France ... a sa fille Susanne de Bourbon (Moulins, C. Desrosiers, 1878) [As I saw Christine's titles appear on list after list, I began to think feminism already had a healthy start back in 1405. Le trésor de la cite des dames also called Le livre des trois vertus à l'enseignement des dames is most frequently quoted by feminists today. Anne's mother Charlotte of Savoy had Christine's works in her library which Anne inherited, Charles VIII's library contained them, as did the Burgundian library, and later (1523) three volumes by Christine were contained in Margaret's library which Mary of Hungary inherited. Christine was the daughter of Thomas de Pisan who was secretary and astrologer to Charles V of France, and the wife of Etienne Castel of Picardy, a royal secretary. When she was widowed in 1399 with three children to support, she began to write for a living, perhaps the first woman to do so. SHB]
City of Ladies defended women and female education and envisioned a very efficiently run utopian society governed entirely by women ... woman's inferior role in society reflected social custom and not native ability. See Melissa Meriam Bullard, "The Roots of Higher Education for Women" in Graduate Woman (the AAUW Journal) May/June 1979, p. 26.
33 Anne of France, Les enseignements d'Anne de France...à sa fille Susanne de Bourbon (Moulins, C. Desrosiers, 1878), pp. 213-258.

17

accounts of Anne, apparently such masters[34] as "Jean of Paris" (either Jean Perréal or Jean Hey,[35] or both) and Jean Bourdichon were teachers as well. Margaret learned sewing and embroidery,[36] and the stately dances of the court balls. Every young woman of that time learned something about pharmacy and jelly making. As little children they played with their dolls and carriages, and from the accounts of her treasurer, Louis de Brézé,[37] we know Margaret had pigeons and puppets, dogs and ponies, and a favorite parrot which had belonged to her mother.[38] They learned to play cards and chess, tell stories, to sing and play various instruments, and of course, to ride and hunt. Social gatherings gave opportunities to witness the excitement of jousts and tourneys, and to take part in the elaborate masques and feasts. For holidays such as Christmas there were intricate engineering and artistic displays.[39] Perhaps on rainy days they played in the galleries at Amboise where there was to be seen:

> ... a collection of historic armour and weapons which had belonged to the most famous kings of France or to celebrated warriors ... the axe of King Clovis, the sword of Dagobert, the dagger of Charlemagne, two axes belonging to St. Louis, the sword of Philippe-le-Bel, that of King John, two swords of Charles VII and a dagger which had belonged to Louis XI ... a three cornered ax of

---

34   Jane de Iongh, Margaret of Austria: Regent of the Netherlands (New York: W.W. Norton Company, Inc., 1953), p. 200.

35   Yvonne Labande-Mailfert, Charles VIII et Son Milieu (1470-1498) (Paris: Librairie C. Klincksieck, 1975), p. 495.

36   Margaret even found time when she became Regent of the Low Countries to make some shirts for her father Maximilian.

37   Ghislaine de Boom, Marguerite d'Autriche-Savoie et la Pré-Renaissance (Bruxelles: La Renaissance du Livre, 1946), p. 12.

38   The violent demise of this beloved parrot in 1504 was immortalized by Jean Lemaire in his poem Les Épîtres de l'Amant Vert. See the édition critique publiée par Jean Frappier (Lille: Librairie Giard; Genève: Librairie Droz, 1948).

39   In 1497 on Christmas night, the nativity was staged by Antoine 'Bryant, painter at Amboise. An idol stuffed with twelve fuses was enflamed when a thirteenth fuse was flung "from Paradise." See Yvonne Labande-Mailfert, Charles VIII et Son Milieu (1470-1498) (Paris: Librairie C. Klincksieck, 1975), p. 495.

Bertrand du Guesclin, armour worn at the coronation of Charles VII by Jeanne D'Arc; the helmet, to which is attached a gorget of mail, was gilded outside and lined with crimson satin.[40]

Thus the early years passed. If the history lesson were tilted in favor of France, If Maximillian was held in contempt, Margaret soon learned the wisdom of keeping her own counsel. She was kind to the slighted, quiet and slender Louise, and positively doted on the little Susanne whom she called her "playchild."

The agreement which sent the three-year-old Margaret to France appears to us to have been a cruel and inhuman bargain, yet the account of the first seven years of her life there refutes this; and one can't help concluding that she was better off emotionally and educationally than she would have been in Ghent. Margaret had these years of peace and kindness growing up in the chateau of Amboise where the air of Touraine and the beauty of the stimulating countryside nourished her body and her soul, just as the stimulating atmosphere of the court molded her mind. When unhappy years unfolded, she must often have looked back on this tranquil period in her life with wistfulness.

---

40 This is an extract from inventory made at Amboise on September 23, 1499. See "A Twice Crowned Queen" Anne of Brittany, by Constance, Countess De La Warr (London: Eveleigh Nash, 1906), pp. 43-44

Chapter 2

"FORTUNE, MISFORTUNE, STRENGTHENS A WOMAN"[41]

It had certainly seemed like a real wedding, that ceremony at Amboise - the young couple, Charles and, Margaret, in bridal finery, the honored words said,[42] the distinguished guests, but political expediency and a compliant pope nullified it.

In Brittany in 1488, Duke Francis II died leaving two daughters, Anne and Isabel.[43] Anne succeeded her father and continued his policy of alliance with England, Spain and Austria. But the French, taking advantage of this power vacuum Just as they had in Burgundy, forced the intrepid young Duchess to arms. Entrenched in Rennes, she sold her silver to pay for English and Spanish mercenaries. Further, by proxy, she married Maximilian who at this time was thirty-two years old - Anne was in her fourteenth year. But it was all for nothing. Anne resisted at first and hoped for rescue by Maximilian's forces, but that dilatory gentleman never

---

[41] Or Fortune, Misfortune, Fortifies One from Margaret's motto: "Fortune Infortune Fort Une"

[42] Philippe de Comines, The Memoirs of Philippe de Commynes Vol. II, ed., Samuel Kinser; trans. by Isabelle Cazeaux Columbia: University of South Carolina Press, 1973), p. 449. "… and since she was very young, there could have been no other obligations except verbal ones (but the words that were exchanged were such and so great that nothing more could have been said)."

[43] Isabel died in 1491.

made it. Overwhelmed, she ultimately acquiesced to the marriage with Charles which took place in December 1491.

Margaret at this time was a month short of twelve years of age, and was fifty-two "thumbs" (inches) tall. She was described as intelligent and humorous. Her bearing was graceful, she had thick golden hair, fine hands, and despite the prominent Habsburg chin, was described as "fraiche" and comely. The rumors of the French plans had reached her in November. She confronted Charles while he was in the midst of "designating La Trémoille as lieutenant general for the Brittany war." After "embracing and kissing him in tears, she asked him if it were true that he would marry another woman in Brittany." At which Charles responded "that the late king his father had given her as his wife, and that as long as she lived, he would have no other." (Furthermore, Charles had renewed his oath during his seventeenth year when Margaret was eight.) Erasme Brasca, the diplomat from Milan, wrote to Ludovico "of the heartbreak and despair of Margaret at Baugé in November 1491 when she learned the separation was irrevocable." Charles as well lamented the separation into which he had been forced. They had a tender regard for each other and Margaret kept the portrait of Charles painted in 1491 by Bourdichon all the rest of her life.[44] No longer queen, no longer favored, Margaret was banished to the Chateau of Melun,[45] but was permitted to take the Princess of Tarente with her as companion. That she was enraged, bitter, and grief stricken, there is no doubt. That year a cold autumn had prevented the grapes from ripening, and Margaret remarked in a play on words that Charles deserved to have the grapes (sarments de vigne) fail, because the oaths (serments) were no longer valid.[46] And Madame de Segre, trying to console and admonish commented, "Madame, you should not carry on so terribly, you

---

44 For the above paragraph, I am greatly indebted to the research of Yvonne Labande-Mailfert, Charles VIII et Son Milieu (1470-1498) (Paris: Librairie C. Klincksieck, 1975}, pp. 105-106. Trans. by SHB. Baugé is about 150 miles SW of Paris. The court had joined the army encamped there for the Brittany campaign.

45 Melun is about 25 miles SE of Paris.

46 Jean Lemaire, Oeuvres, publiées par J. Stecher, Tome IV (Genève: Slatkine Reprints, 1969), pp. 105-106. See also De Boom's Marguerite ... p. 13; and Tremayne's The First Governess .... p. 13; and Labande-Mailfert's Charles VIII ... , p. 106.

are the child of a great king and sister of a great prince, you cannot fail to be a great princess. Even though, you don't have a king now, you will find another."[47] When a possible future Spanish match was intimated she cried that "she did not wish to marry anymore."[48]

Margaret's seclusion at Melun as it continued for two years, came to feel more and more like prison. The comforts and amenities of life as she knew them dropped away, but when the companionship she held so dear was threatened, she was finally moved to protest in a letter to Anne de Beaujeu:

> Madame my good aunt, I must complain to you as to her in whom I place my hope, with regard to my cousin whom they wish to take away from me, who is all the pastime that I have, and when I shall have lost her I know not what I shall do. Therefore I pray you that you hold out your hand to me, that she be not taken from me, for greater distress they could not cause me. Lechault came and brought letters addressed to my said cousin, by which the King wrote to her that she must go away; in any case I would not suffer it until I had let you know, hoping that you would come to my help, as I have in that and in other things perfect confidence, praying you, Madame my good aunt, that wherever I may be I may not depart from your good favor, for I shall always have need of it, to which I desire strongly to recommend myself. Madame de Molitart told me that you wished me to be better treated than I was formerly, which is a thing which has greatly rejoiced me, since you still remember me. Saying à Dieu to you, Madame my good aunt, I pray that He may give you the most beloved of your desires.
>
> Written at Melun, the seventeenth day of March. Your good, humble and loyal niece, Marguerite.[49]

---

47   Ghislaine de Boom, Marguerite d'Autriche-Savoie et la Pré-Renaissance (Bruxelles: La Renaissance du LIvre, 194, p. 13.

48   Yvonne Labande-Mailfert, Charles VIII et Son Milieu (1470-1498) (Paris: Librairie C. Klincksieck, 1975), pp. 105-106.

49   Translation of this letter is strongly based on that of Christopher Hare, The High and Puissant Princess Marguerite of Austria (London: Harper and Brothers, 1907), p. 40. Original in French

The letter is very revealing of Margaret's character – her keen sense of justice, her loyalty and desire for companionship, her ability to assert herself in a kind and diplomatic way. It is not known who this "cousin" was. Margaret had no first cousins on her mother's side, and of course it may have been a courtesy title just as "my good aunt" was. On the other hand, all of these ruling families were related, Louise of Savoy was the daughter of Marguerite de Bourbon and Margaret was the granddaughter of Isabelle de Bourbon (second wife of Charles the Bold), and so Hare and Henry-Bordeaux surmise that the cousin was Louise.[50] If so, it makes an interesting twist in the stories of these two women whose lives often met and intertwined. However, from another point of view, this is highly unlikely. Louise was married to Charles, Count of Angoulême, on February 16, 1488, and though she did not go to live with him for some time, it is implausible to speculate that this period extended into three or four years. A considered guess on my part is that the companion was Charlotte, Mademoiselle de Tarente, who was a cousin of Charles VIII and who was permitted to accompany Margaret to Melun. It is known that she was a friend of "la petite reine," and in the royal accounts are listed payments for portraits of Margaret and of Charlotte made in 1491.[51] Charlotte also accompanied her to the border of France when Margaret returned home.[52]

Margaret was kept at Melun much like a hostage for two years, in spite of the terms of the original contract which stipulated she was to be returned to her father Maximilian or Philip her brother at the King's expense should the marriage "God forbid" not be consummated. If she hoped for rescue

---

found in Hare; Dennis Godefroi's Life of Charles VIII, 1684; also Max Bruchet's Marguerite d'Autriche, Duchesse de Savoie (Lille: Imprimerie L. Danel, 1927, p. 313.

50 Christopher Hare, The High and Puissant Princess Marguerite of Austria (London: Harper and Brothers, 1907), p. 40; and Paule Henry-Bordeaux, Louise de Savoie, "Roi" de France (Paris: Librairie Académique Perrin, 1943), p. 44.

51 Yvonne Labande-Mailfert, Charles VII et Son Milieu (1470-1498) (Paris: Librairie C. Klincksieck, 1975), p. 498. Tarente or Tarentaise was part of the Duchy of Savoy.

52 Max Bruchet and E. Lancien, L' Itinéraire de Marguerite d'Autriche (Lille: Imprimerie L. Danel, 1934), on page 5 it is noted that on June 15, 1493, Margaret distributed gifts to the Lord de Segre, to the Dame de Segre, to Mademoiselle de Tarente, etc.

by Maximilian, it was in vain. In one of those switch-arounds in the diplomacy of the time, Maximilian was abandoned by England, Spain and even his own States of the Holy Roman Empire. The treaty of Senlis was signed on May 23, 1493. Maximilian renounced his claims on the Duchy of Burgundy, but Franche-Comté, Charolais and Artois and the seigneurie of Noyers were returned as Margaret's dowry. Charles promised to return Margaret to the ambassadors of Maximilian as befitted her station, and she promised to renounce all pretensions to her marriage with Charles and the throne of France, swearing on a piece of the true cross, and saying that she believed "all marriages ought to be voluntary." A kind act by Anne of Brittany, now Queen of France, is mentioned by many historians. At the last moment she had presented to Margaret an embroidered coif and several valuable gold ornaments. Each of them were political pawns, but their regard for each other through the years transcended all this.

Margaret was accompanied by the French nobles who had been with her household and loyal to her for ten years, and who opposed present French policy. As she traveled back in June of 1493, the scenery must have evoked dim memories of another sad trip, for when they passed through the town of Arras, the people shouted, "Noel, Noel!" As her Burgundian spirit rose, she exclaimed, "Do not cry Noel, but long live Burgundy!"[53]

At Amiens she was coldly treated as just another foreign noble, but at Valenciennes[54] Margaret was given a brilliant reception, and she stood to give a farewell to all those who had served her so well. Many cries and sobs were heard testifying to their devotion to her, and Margaret presented many gifts, but especially to Madame de Segré whom she had loved as a mother, there was jewelry and silver. Her stepgrandmother and godmother, Margaret of York had journeyed here to meet her. If there was

---

53 Jean Molinet, Chroniques de Jean Molinet, Vol. II (Bruxelles: Palais des Académies, 1935), p. 372.

54 The formal exchange had taken place at the windmill at Vendhuile in the Cambrésis where the French delegates placed her in the hands of the ambassadors of Maximilian. See Jean Molinet, Chroniques de Jean Molinet (Bruxelles: Palais des Academies, 1935), Vol. Ii, p. 372; Ghislaine de Boom., Marguerite d'Autriche-Savoie ... (Bruxelles: La Renaissance du Livre, 1946/1935), p. 15; Yvonne Labande-Mailfert, Charles VIII ... (Paris: Librairie C. Klincksieck, 1975), p. 133.

any correspondence between these two during the years of separation, it is not recorded, but there must have been remembrance and awareness on the part of the child of the devotion which this older woman bore for her. Mons fêted her with processions and games, and her brother the Archduke, known as Philip le Beau because he was so handsome, welcomed her with great honor and then led her to Malines (Mechelen) where she was received with great joy. The little Queen of France was as before, the Archduchess of Austria and Burgundy.

The shame of the repudiation, the strain of her last two years at Melun, the ordeal of the trip back with its bravely-faced festivities may have left her filled with both relief and depression. For the next four years she made her home at Namur in the deep valley of the Meuse River with its rocky banks and its view of the Ardennes. Philip provided for her: generously, and Margaret of York, known as Madame la Grande, lavished her with attention and care.

At first it was a studious retreat as Margaret's education resumed under the direction of the strong-minded Madame Halewijn who had been governess to her mother. This good lady pressed her to learn Flemish which Margaret found fatiguing.[55] Nevertheless, she persisted, and was able in later life to understand it and to give a lecture in that language according to Lemaire.[56] To be able to write poetry was considered the mark of an educated person, and the members of the court took part in this pastime for their own as well as others' amusement. Lemaire found Margaret's prose as well as her "rhythme Gallicane" very elegant.[57] Music was a passion with the houses of Burgundy and of Habsburg, and Margaret continued the study of voice and instruments under the tutelage of Master Gomar Nepotis, organist of the archducal chapel. Madame la Grande,

---

[55] Elsa Winker, Margaret Von Österreich, Grande Dame der Renaissance (München: Verlag Georg D.W. Callwey, 1966), pp. 51-53. [Modern-day students of Flemish often echo the Archduchess's judgment.]

[56] Jean Lemaire de Belges, Oeuvres, Tome IV., ed., J. Stecher (Genève: Slatkine Reprints, 1969), p. 476. He refers to the "language thyois" which refers to Germanic tongues: German, Dutch and Flemish.

[57] Ibid. p. 111.

visiting from her home in Malines, nurtured the love of art in her godchild by encouraging her to acquire beautiful illuminated manuscripts.

As time began to assuage her sorrow, she became aware of the deep feeling and high regard with which she was held in her own country, she began to participate in the magnificent feasts, games, archery contests and ceremonies so dear to the hearts of Burgundians.

The Dowager Duchess had been in charge of Philip since the summer of 1485 when he was seven years old and when Maximilian had finally regained his custody. Olivier de la Marche relates: "The son did not know the father, but when he drew near, the father kissed the son, and the son began to cry."[58] He placed his son under the supervision of this indomitable woman in the same year that Henry VII, the first of the Tudor line, came to the throne of England. A sister of Edward IV, she carried on the War of the Roses from her estates in Malines and her court was open house to any Yorkists and their conspiracies. Her encouragement with funds and armed forces of Lambert Simnel who posed as the real Earl of Warwick (nephew of Edward IV and of Margaret of York), and later of Perkin Warbeck as Richard, Duke of York, and son of Edward IV (who had somehow been whisked away from the tower and had escaped the murderous intent of his uncle), is well documented in English history. In these schemes, she was aided and supported by Maximilian and Philip.[59]

During Margaret's years in France, Maximilian had succeeded somewhat in subduing those rebellious burghers of Flanders, and was acknowledged regent on his son's behalf. He acted without revengefulness

---

58   Christopher Hare, The High and Puissant Princess Marguerite of Austria (London: Harper and Brothers, 1907), p. 57.

59   A.F. Pollard, The Reign of Henry VII, Vol. I (New York: AMS Press, 1967), pp. 102-103. The Flanders ambassador in Flanders wrote to Duke Gian Galeazzo Sforza of Milan from 's-Hertegenbosch, February 11, 1495, contributing this racy gossip: "These last days in England, the first man [Sir Robert Clifford] who had this son of King Edward [Perkin Warbeck], when he was in England, has run away. Many were taken ... His Majesty [Maximilian] told me that this man Clifford, when he was in England, divulged that this Duke of York [Warbeck] was not the son of King Edward, but is the son of the Dowager Duchess of Burgundy and of the Bishop of Cambrai [Henri de Berghes]. His Majesty also told me that the said duke will proceed for the present to Ireland, where he has strong connections, and that island held him for its lord before he went to France, according to what the duke himself told me."

for the past deeds, altering the constitution, but still permitting the privileges of the city. He was crowned King of the Romans with the diadem of Charlemagne on April 9, 1486 at Aachen. Uneasy with the thought of the power inherent in this title, and disgusted with his undisciplined and unpaid mercenaries,[60] Ghent and Bruges rebelled again. This time Bruges held him in the town square where he was daily afforded the opportunity of seeing his men tortured and slain. When an army sent by his ailing father finally brought his release, Maximilian, sick to death of the Low Countries, a feeling which was heartily returned, mortgaged Friesland to Duke Albert of Saxony and appointed him governor over all the provinces. With that he returned to Germany and Austria. In skirmishes with the Hungarians, he regained Vienna, but the Treaty of Bratislava of November 7, 1491, made a peaceful settlement with Vladislav of Bohemia as King of Hungary, the succession reverting to the Habsburgs if he had no heir. Further, when he should have been claiming Anne of Brittany as his bride, and upholding his daughter's rights as Queen of France, he was engaged in driving the Turks from Carinthia. Brittany had by this time been overrun, but in January 1493, Maximilian defeated the French at Salins in Franche-Comté, resulting in the Treaty of Senlis.

His father, Frederick III, died that year, and Maximilian became head of the house of Habsburg. In 1494 at Innsbruck he married Bianca Maria Sforza, sister of the Duke of Milan and niece of Ludovico "the Moor." It could only have been for money and matters of state as both appeared bored with the match.[61] "The marriage was most displeasing to the princes of the Empire and to several friends ... because the lady was from a house which was not as noble as would have been suitable for him ... though she was a descendant of Duke Francesco of Milan...who was a true, good

---

60 These landsknecht's had tried to take: Margaret captive on her return from Valenciennes as ransom for their pay. See Christopher Hare, The High and Puissant Princess Marguerite of Austria (London: Harper and Brothers, 1907), p. 52.

61 Gutierre Gomez de Fuensalida, Correspondencia de Gutierre Gomez de Fuensalida, Embajador en Alemania, Flandes e Inglaterra: 1496-1509 (Madrid: Published by the Duque de Berwick y de Alba, Conde de Siruela, 1907), p. xi. According to Fuensalida, Maximilian tried to repudiate his wife because she was sterile.

prince."[62] While Maximilian had been held at Bruges, the French released Charles of Egmond who returned to his own domain of Gelderland bent on stirring up trouble. Later, in 1494 Maximilian crushed a rebellion he had caused, and then transferred the government of the Low Countries to the sixteen-year-old Philip. As he and Bianca Maria made their progress toward the Low Countries, Philip and Margaret learned of their approach, and prepared to travel to Maastricht to meet him.

When Maximilian saw them, he bowed to them and to the ladies of the company - Madame de Halewijn, Mademoiselle de Vere and several others, and they made honorable reverence to him. Their father said to them, "Welcome! My children, I have for a long time desired to see you." And with one on each arm, they entered the city in great triumph.[63]

Bianca Maria made her "joyous entries" into the cities of Malines and Antwerp where she was accompanied by –

> ...princes and lords, ladies adorned richly in the mode of Milan and Italy, entered to great triumph and rich ceremony in the most sumptuous chariots. The city of Malines which always treated the king well, made the most honorable reception possible. Historical tableaux, very well costumed, were held outside as well as inside the city, and the usual parade of all the great personages. Monday, the eighteenth of August, Maximilian, Bianca, Philip and Margaret with all the entourage, traveled to Antwerp which gave even more magnificent tableaux than Malines. Being Antwerp,[64] they had adorned their streets and hung tapestries; the ports, belfries, streets and houses were illuminated with candles, lanterns, and torches. There was great hunting in the woods of the environs of Malines,

---

62 Philippe de Comines, The Memoirs of Philippe de Commynes, Vol. II. ed., Samuel Kinser; trans. by Isabelle Cazeaux (Columbia: University of South Carolina Press, 1973), pp. 450-451.
63 Jean Molinet, Chroniques de Jean Molinet, Vol. II. (Bruxelles: Palais des Académies, 1935), p. 392.
64 Antwerp was a wide-open trading city in those days with the bars and houses of prostitution usually associated with sailors and ports, and a vigorous merchant class of parvenus who perhaps overdid things. However, Maximilian had encouraged the development of this port, and they knew how to be grateful.

FORTUNE, MISFORTUNE, FORTIFIES ONE

Antwerp and Brussels. It was in one of these woods coming upon the king accidentally, that Philip of Cleves who had been emprisoned by him in Brussels for causing trouble in Flanders and Brabant, formally asked for pardon and was graciously granted it.[65]

... Philip had come of age and on the tenth of September took the oath of Duke of Brabant at Louvain, and on the fifth day of October, the oath as Archduke in Antwerp followed by Mass in the Cathedral[66] of Our Lady the next day. Among the princes on this occasion was one whom they believed to be Richard of York, son of Edward IV.[67]

... In Brussels he received a warm reception, as much for Madame Marguerite as for him, and they did not arrive at the Cauberghe [palace] until nine in the evening.[68]

For the overextended Maximilian, one could wish that this were the end of the story - his domains in good order, his children in happiness and safety. But that would be reckoning without the French claims in Italy dating back to 1379 when the Duke of Anjou had conquered the greater part of the papal states and kept them for his own; or the vagaries of fifteenth century politics; or the very real danger of the Turks against whom Maximilian appealed for united action from all Christian sovereigns. In Antwerp in October he had joined the Crusading Order of Saint George.

Charles VIII laid claim to the Kingdom of Naples, and following the Duke of Orleans with an advance guard of the French army in July, 1494, he was received with great honor by Ludovico Sforza and the Duke of Ferrara. He marched as if on tour and found Naples an open city. Alarmed at his success, Pope Alexander VI, Naples, the Duke of Milan, Ferdinand of Aragon, the Republic of Venice, Maximilian and Henry VII formed

---

65 Molinet, Vol. II, p. 393.
66 High Church. The church was not elevated to the rank of Cathedral until 1559. Molinet or later editors have made a mistake.
67 Jean Molinet, Chroniques de Jean Molinet, Vol. II. (Bruxelles: Palais des Academies, 1935), p. 395.
68 Ibid., Vol. II, p. 418.

the Holy League. They were able to unite against Charles, but not against the threat from the East. During this period of unity, however, marriages were arranged between Maximilian's children, and a son and daughter of Ferdinand and Isabella. Philip was to marry Juana of Spain, and Margaret was to marry Juan who would be the first king of a united Spain, a goal to which his father Ferdinand of Aragon and his mother Isabella of Castile had dedicated all the thoughts, energies and resources of their reigns. One can imagine that Margaret's spirits were high at this second chance for success in a marriage which befitted her rank. Perhaps Madame de Segré had been right and there would truly be another king.

While these marriage arrangements and jealous old-world quarrels were carried on, a whole new world was being discovered by men who had the sailing techniques, tremendous drive, and economic backing of a merchant class encouraged by nobles in their quest for money, prestige and power. Columbus made his first voyage in 1492, his second in 1493. Compared to the cost of the constant wars, the money put forth for his venture was negligible, while what it held for the future was so much more promising.[69] (However, while these discoveries caused excited conversations in the courts of the day, they had little bearing on their lives at this time.) Furthermore, out of the frightful Italian campaigns arose two other auspicious developments: the spread of the renaissance from Italy to the northern countries, and the introduction of the art of diplomacy. In these fields, Margaret became one of the great proponents and negotiators. Learning as she went along, she eventually became recognized as a connoisseur in the arts, and in diplomacy as "the true grand man of the family and the founder of the House of Austria."[70]

"On the fifth day of the month of November 1495, were celebrated the solemnities of nuptials of Madame Margaret with the Prince of Castile." She was married in the church of St. Peter at Malines and was attended by her brother and the Marquis of Baden. Francisco de Rojas, who was the proxy for Juan, was attended by the Lord of Ravenstein and the Prince de

---

69 J.R. Hale, Renaissance Exploration (New York: W.W. Norton and Company, Inc.,, 1968).
70 Jules Michelet, Histoire de France, Vol. VII, p. 146. Nineteenth century French historian quoted by J. Stecher in Jean Lemaire, Oeuvres (Genève: Slatkine Reprints, 1969), p. vi.

Chimay. It was quite a grand affair and Margaret's splendid appearance in her gold robe and jeweled crown is described by Molinet.[71] She too had the Burgundian lip of her mother, and just slightly, the Habsburg chin of her father, but her eyes were soft brown, her complexion translucent, and she had heavy, pale-blond, wavy hair. She was about five feet, then thought tall, slender, and in good health. The chroniclers of the time thought she was beautiful, and so she must have been on that day.[72]

According to the custom of the houses of Austria and Burgundy, a marriage, in order to be sealed, required the proxy to lie on the bed with the lady fully dressed but with one leg bared. Francisco de Rojas was properly briefed on how to do this with delicacy. However, in ordering a robe for the occasion, he neglected to tell the tailor to make a slit on the right side so his leg could be easily exposed with modesty. As a result, his entire robe had to be pulled up, and the dignity of the occasion was lost to the smiles of the witnesses. Later, de Rojas was subjected to ribald joking, never to hear the end of it, and versions of the story have been repeated in histories ever since.[73]

Margaret returned to Namur for the winter, but at the end of the month of April in 1496, she and Philip and the Gentlemen of the Golden Fleece, along with her train and those of her chapel, left Namur to visit their father in Germany. They went through Cologne, the county of Ferrette and other cities, and were received with great festivities in Speyer by Bianca. Finally they arrived in Ulm, the next to last day of May, and the night of Pentecost, where they were welcomed by their father. They were relieved to reach their destination as, according to the chronicler, that May was such a rainy month. Besides the difficulty of travel with horses in bad weather, there were signs in the sky, and one cloudy night a figure appeared

---

71 Ibid.

72 Hannelore Sachs in The Renaissance Woman, trans. from the German by Marianne Herzfeld (New York: McGraw-Hill Book Company, 1971), has listed the attributes of the Renaissance woman, and Margaret fulfilled these standards in every way.

73 Elsa Winker, Margarete Von Österreich, Grande Dame der Renaissance (Munchen: Verlag Georg D.W. Callwey, 1966), p. 75. Eleanor E. Tremayne, The First Governess of the Netherlands (New York: G.P. Putnam's Sons; London: Methuen & Company, 1908), p. 18. See also Zurita; A.R. Villa's Life of Dona Juana la Loca.

in the heavens over Brabant.[74] Such uninterpreted omens filled them with foreboding and apprehension. In returning, the months of June and July were hot with horrible thunderstorms which destroyed crops and pasturage lands. A very hideous malady made the rounds (perhaps a severe form of smallpox). Molinet notes that "the times were marvelously strange."[75]

The delay following the proxy marriage was due to the time it took to build, assemble and man a special fleet to carry Juana to the Low Countries, and, in returning, to take Margaret to Spain. Thus it was not until autumn that Margaret again left Namur for Brussels and then to Malines to join her godmother, the Dowager Duchess Margaret. From there they traveled together to meet Juana in Antwerp.

When Juana did not come forward to greet them, Margaret was somewhat at a loss to know what to do. But after waiting for a little, Margaret went ahead to the place where Juana was lodged and found her sister-in-law lying sick on a pallet. She had had a dreadful voyage north, and there had been great loss of life and valuables as the ships were tossed by the bad weather. Juana's chamber, though, was furnished so beautifully with cloth of gold, and vessels of gold, that even Margaret, with her wealthy Burgundian background, was impressed at the richness and stateliness of all these treasures. She would soon learn that Isabella had made the same provisions for her.

The winter that year was so severe that it is said nine thousand Spanish men and sailors perished in Antwerp from the cold. Philip refused to help, or to pay Juana's household expenses, because, supposedly, Ferdinand had not fulfilled his part of the agreement. In contrast to his good looks, Philip's character left much to be desired. His upbringing had left him irresponsible, grasping and calculating,[76] and, though his sister and his

---

74 Jean Molinet, Chroniques de Jean Molinet, Vol. II, (Bruxelles: Palais des Académies, 1935), p. 427.

75 Jean Molinet, Chroniques de Jean Molinet, Vol. II, (Bruxelles: Palais des Académies, 1935), p. 427.

76 For opinions of Philip, see: Gutierre Gomez de Fuensalida, Correspondencia ... (Madrid: Published by the Duque de Berwick y de Alba, Conde de Siruela, 1907), p. xxvi; J.N. Hillgarth, The Spanish Kingdoms: 1250-1516 (Oxford: Clarendon Press, 1978), pp. 588-597; and William

wife loved him deeply. It is often difficult to see why. He was not even on hand to greet Juana when she arrived, being off in the Tyrol.

Finally, in January 1497, Margaret traveled with Philip to the Abbey of Middleburg in Zeeland with a company of lords and ladies, and ambassadors from Spain. Her faithful servants, Le Veau de Bousanton and his wife Jeanne Lejeune, Margaret's old nurse, would make the trip to Spain with her.

On the twenty-seventh of January 1497, they embarked at Vlissingen. If Juana's trip had been bad, this one for Margaret was worse. Though it was the strongest armada ever yet to leave the ports of Spain, it was no match for violent and capricious sea squalls. After one terrifying storm had abated, the ladies, giddy with relief, amused themselves by writing their own epitaphs which they rolled in wax and bound to their arms for identification just as the sailors did. Margaret's read:

Cy gist Margot la gentil' amoiselle,
Qu' ha deux marys et encor est pucelle.[77]

(Here lies Margot the gentle maiden,
Who had two husbands and is still a virgin.)

One cannot help thinking what a hardy lot they were to endure so much terror and discomfort and still retain their sense of humor. After this the ships did pull into Southampton at the beginning of February for refuge and repairs.

When the Spanish Habsburg marriage agreements were concluded, Queen Isabella had written to Henry VII of England explaining that Juana would be going to Flanders and Margaret would be coming to Spain by sea. She asked Henry to treat them as his own daughters if they were forced to shelter in England because of winter storms in the Channel.

H. Prescott; History of the Reign of Ferdinand and Isabella (Philadelphia: J.B. Lippincott & Co., 1880), Vol. II, p. 106.

77 Jean Lemaire de Belges, Oeuvres, publiées par J. Stecher, Tome IV (Genève: Slatkine Reprints, 1969), p. 106.

Unfortunately for the loving and worried Isabella, her fear was realized and each of the young women had to put into English ports. They were treated most graciously by Henry, and letters from him to Margaret are preserved. Addressing her as "Most illustrious and most excellent Princess, our dearest and most beloved cousin ...," he wrote that he was glad they had arrived in "good health and cheerful spirits."[78] He sent several of his trusted men and domestic servants to ensure their safety and comfort. He suggested they take lodgings in the town of Southampton until the weather cleared and the wind became favorable, and he also proposed to visit if they remained for a while. Henry thanked Margaret for her letter of February 2, but we have no record of the letter, and do not know if they met at this time,[79] though the fleet remained about three weeks becalmed.

Henry appended a short and cordial message to his first letter:

> Dearest and most beloved cousin. Desirous the more to assure your Excellence that your visit to us and to our realm is so agreeable and delightful to us, that the arrival of our own daughter could not give us greater joy, we write this portion of our letter with our own hand, in order to be able the better to express to you that you are very welcome, and that you may more perfectly understand our

---

78 Gustav Adolph Bergenroth, ed., Calendar of Letters, Despatches and State Papers, relating to the negotiations between England and Spain, Vol. I, (London: 1862), p. 119, August 19-20, 1496. This was pushing Henry quite a bit. He had requested in 1495 that as part of the marriage agreements, the "old Duchess (Margaret of York and Burgundy) should be sent away from Flanders. Ferdinand replied that they also had "grave complaints against her... Nevertheless, she is a woman, and it would be mean to ask or to grant her banishment. Our daughter is now going to Flanders, and when she is there the old Duchess will no longer occupy the same position nor enjoy the same authority as hitherto ... the King of England should desist from his demands." Ibid., p. 74. Part of the trouble was the dowager Duchess's support of Perkin Warbeck who continued as the Duke of York to harass Henry until he was caught and finally put to death in 1499.

79 Andre J.B. Le Glay, Maximilian I, Empereur d'Allemagne, et Marguerite d'Autriche, s a fille, Gouvernante des Pays-Bas (Paris: Chez Jules Renouard et Cie., 1839), p. 43, writes that she was received graciously at Hampton Court by Henry VII. Elsa Winker, Margarete Von Österreich, Grande Dame der Renaissance (München: Verlag George D.W. Callwey, 1966), pp. 77-79, relates that Margaret did visit and was appalled at the simplicity and poverty of Henry's court though she was impressed with the fine farmhouses. However, I cannot find any original source for this information. If it is true, it would help explain why, many years later, Margaret refused to marry Henry.

good wishes. We most earnestly entreat and beseech your Highness from the bottom of our heart, to be as cheerful as though you were with the dearest and most beloved King and Queen of Spain. In all and everything you want, do not spare us and our realms, for you will render us a great and most acceptable service by accepting anything from us.[80]

The armada set sail again in what promised to be fine weather, but it soon turned into more of what they had previously endured. They met the most violent storm in the Gulf of Gascony and did not put into the port of Santander until March 6, 1497. Only ten ships out of the imposing fleet were able to reach port. Relieved that she and her company had survived this harrowing voyage, Margaret sent word by Jacques de Croy to Ferdinand that they had arrived safely in Santander.[81] Margaret assumed responsibility on this journey for her court both in England and Spain, and, though she had just turned seventeen on January 10, she showed both a willingness and an ability to undertake the duties of her rank.

If Margaret had had apprehensions about her future life, they were soon dispelled by the beauty of the mountainous landscape and the warmth of the greeting given her by a large company of nobles, and a band of trumpets, clarions, lutes and other instruments "fort haulte, que l'on n'eust peut oyr Dieu tonner"[82] (so loud that they could not have heard God thunder). It took a train of 120 mules laden with gold and silver plate, many precious gems, tapestries, velvet carpets, bed hangings of cloth of gold and fine needlework, gold embroidered pillow covers, to carry the gifts to her.[83]

As her company set out for Burgos, they were met on the way at Reynosa by Ferdinand and Juan hurrying north to meet her. With them

---

80 Gustav Adolph Bergenroth, ed., Calendar of Letters ...Vol. I, (London: 1862), pp. 137-139.
81 Jean Molinet, Chroniques de Jean Molinet, Vol. II, (Bruxelles: Palais des Académies, 1935), p. 433.
82 Jean Molinet, Chroniques de Jean Molinet, Vol. II, (Bruxelles: Palais des Académies, 1935), p. 434.
83 Many of these would be listed later in her life in an inventory at Mechelen/Malines.

was a splendid procession of knights dressed in gold and silver. Margaret, or the Infanta as she was now called, tried to show her respect by kissing the hands of her husband and his father. They tried not to permit it, but eventually she succeeded. This little vignette seems as amusing as a vaudeville routine to us today, but such were the manners of the Spanish Court. Once again there was music of such grandeur "that one could see God tremble."[84]

Margaret made a triumphal entry into Burgos, the capital of Old Castile. The marvelous Gothic Cathedral, reminiscent more of northern architecture, seemed transplanted in the brightness of sunny Spain with its azure skies. On leaving the church, she took her place under a canopy of silk and cloth of gold carried by the governors of the city and was directed towards the palace. Isabella of Castille and her son Prince Juan waited for her under the beautiful and lacy galleries of the newly built Casa del Cordon. The Queen and her daughters and the eighty ladies of the court, all in cloth of gold, kissed the hand of Margaret. And since these joyful meetings were deemed to be inappropriate in public during Lent, the royal family moved the following day, which was Palm Sunday, to the Monastery of the Trinity where they spent a week. Juan had fallen passionately in love with Margaret,[85] and it was arranged that they should be married secretly on Monday at eight in the morning in the convent chapel,[86] with a private week for a honeymoon. The public ceremony followed a week later on April 3, 1497 in the Cathedral of Burgos, performed by the Archbishop of Toledo. It was attended by the nobility of Castile and Aragon, foreign ambassadors, and mayors of the principal cities who wore their crimson robes of office. Celebrations succeeded day after day: traditional bullfights, tilting and tourneys, feasts, processions. The ebullience of Margaret and

---

84 Ghislaine de Boom, Marguerite d'Autriche-Savoie et la Pré-Renaissance (Bruxelles: La naissance du Livre, 1946/1935) p. 19.
85 This is related in J.N. Hillgarth, The Spanish Kingdoms: 1250-1516 (Oxford: Clarendon Press, 1978), V0l. II, p. 586 following a letter of Peter Martyr d'Anghiera dated June 13, 1497.
86 Jean Molinet, Chroniques de Jean Molinet, Vol. II, (Bruxelles: Palais des Académies, 1935), p. 437.

her court at these affairs drew attention to a cultural difference in conduct. In Reyes de Aragon, Abarca writes:

> And although they left the princess all her servants, freedom in behaviour and diversions, she was warned that in ceremonial affairs she was not to treat the royal personages and grandees with the familiarity and openness usual with the houses of Austria, Burgundy, and France, but with the gravity and measured dignity of the kings and realms of Spain.[87]

Margaret, being a sensitive and proud person, living in a time when "honor" was paramount, and wanting to make a good beginning, must have felt scalded with shame at this reprimand, but her Flemish attendants were angered. Nevertheless, these fêtes initiated a happy married life. According to Juan's tutor Peter Martyr,[88] this political union became a love so passionate that it disturbed the frail health of the Prince and there was talk of separating the young couple for a time. Another chronicler wrote, "… the Prince and his wife loved each other marvelously."[89] It truly was a brilliant match of mind and heart.[90] Each of them loved music, were well-educated, honorable and capable. While he was quiet and shy, her gaiety transcended court ritual. The gentle Juan was enchanted with her and she was buoyantly happy. Her past sufferings and humiliations dwindled into insignificance.

Ferdinand and Isabella were pleased with Margaret[91] and did everything they could (short of loosening court etiquette) to ease her into this new life.

---

87 Eleanor E. Tremayne, The First Governess of the Netherlands (New York: G.P. Putnam's Sons; London: Methuen & Company, 1908), quoted on p. 25. (Abarca, Tome II, fol. 330.)
88 There are two men in history with the name Peter Martyr. This one is Peter Martyr d'Anghiera (called Anglerius) of Lombardy, 1459-1526, who lived in Spain, served as tutor to the royal children, and chronicled the discovery of America in his Decades de Orbe Novo.
89 Ghislaine de Boom, Marguerite d'Autriche-Savoie et la Pré-Renaissance (Bruxelles: La Renaissance du Livre, 1946/1935), p. 19.
90 William H. Prescott, History of the Reign of Ferdinand and Isabella (Philadelphia: J.B. Lippincott & Co., 1880), Vol. II, pp. 352-359.
91 Ibid., p. 360, Note: Zurita, Historia del Rey Hernando, tom. v. lib. 3, cap. 4.

And they were very happy for their son and hopeful for the future. As Juan and Margaret made their progress through the cities of Spain that summer, it was obvious their subjects loved them, and the months passed like a holiday. Margaret became pregnant, and with this both their personal futures and the destiny of Spain held promise.

The constant journeys and receptions did not seem to tire Margaret, but Juan, not blessed with her robust constitution, became exhausted. They were in Salamanca, a city the scholarly Juan is said to have favored because of its university, when he became ill during a great entertainment given for the bridal pair. The King and Queen were in Alcantara attending the wedding of their daughter Isabel to King Emanuel of Portugal when they were informed. Well aware of the danger of such an illness to his son's delicate health, Ferdinand raced to Juan's bedside only to learn that his condition had deteriorated, and there was no hope. With words of thanks for the rich blessings he had enjoyed in life, and with a loving farewell, Juan accepted the end with resignation, and died on October 4, 1497. Margaret's kiss was on his lips.[92]

Ferdinand, in deep distress, nevertheless contrived to send a series of messages to Isabella so that the news of Juan's death would not come as a sudden shock. When the last letter came, however, Isabella with heroic fortitude replied with these words of Scripture: "The Lord giveth and the Lord taketh away; blessed be the name of the Lord." Not for her the rage of grief, only the stillness of despair. Peter Martyr wrote: "Thus was laid low the hope of all Spain."[93]

They turned with anxious care to Margaret who, prostrate with grief, had collapsed at the sudden death. All their hopes centered on the child she was carrying. On December 8, 1497, from Alcala, Ferdinand and Isabella wrote to their ambassador Gutierre Gomez de Fuensalida at the court of Maximilian:

---

[92] Eleanor E. Tremayne, The First Governess of The Netherlands (New York: G.P. Putnam's Sons: London: Methuen & Company, 1908), p. 27; William H. Prescott, History of the Reign of Ferdinand and Isabella (Philadelphia: J.B. Lippincott & Co., 1880), Vol. II pp. J57-358. Original source Peter Martyr, opus Epistolarum, 182, 183.
[93] Ibid.

FORTUNE, MISFORTUNE, FORTIFIES ONE

> By now you have learned of the death of our son who is now in saintly glory. God wishes us to conform ourselves to his will, as is right, and even though the Catholic faith gives us much consolation, our loss is too great to be borne without distress, and this is the reason that we were not able earlier to notify our brother, the King of the Romans. Tell him thus on our part and further that without fail, we will attend to anything that touches the Princess [Margaret] or her pregnancy which adds to our concern. She is as strong and full of courage as you would wish her to be, and we try to console her, and give her rank as if nothing were lost. And if her pregnancy goes well, praise God, we hope from our misery that the fruit which she carries will be a consolation to us in our travail. We have and will have as much care for her as we would have if her husband were alive, and she will always have a place in our hearts … in that love we will hold her and tenderly care for her always.[94]

Margaret sent word to her father sometime in the December dispatches "that she is never without care, because she has their majesties, her true father and mother."[95]

Sometime between December 8, 1497 (the date of the above letter) and February 22, Margaret gave birth. According to Jean Lemaire in his Couronne Margaritique,[96] she labored for two days and two nights without intermission, without eating or sleeping, and brought forth a baby girl who lived only a few moments.

On March 23, 1498, Fuensalida wrote from Innsbruck to Ferdinand and Isabella:

> As I told you in my letter of February 22, the King of the Romans had learned that the Lady Princess had miscarried a son and

---

[94] Gutierre Gomez de Fuensalida, Correspondencia … (Madrid: Published by the Duque de Berwick y de Alba, Conde de Siruela, 1907), p. 6. Trans. SHB.
[95] Ibid.
[96] Jean Lemaire de Belges, Oeuvres, publiées par J. Stecher, Tome IV, Genève: Slatkine Reprints, 1969), pp. 15-167.

that you have declared for the inheritance the rulers of Portugal, though the King of the Romans had spoken nothing concerning this; now the 19th day of March, the King sent me to speak with a secretary who had received letters from the Princess and from his ambassador Lupian by which they were informed that the Princess had a daughter, and that though she knew that such things could not go without grief, they should consider that these things are sent by God and that He has a purpose, and that her father should conform himself to His will and give thanks for all that He made, and that in conforming herself to the loss of her Lord, the Prince, in saintly glory, nothing else could increase her sadness because she was so full of sorrow that there was no room for any more griefs...[97]

Even though this letter from Margaret comes down in history in a second-hand fashion from Fuensalida, he seems to have transmitted it faithfully. The letter has a run-on breathless quality so typical of Margaret under stress, as future letters will indicate.

Fuensalida lived on a footing of intimacy and familiarity with Maximilian, and they often spent long hours together communicating in "macarronico latin"[98] which the ambassador transcribed with fidelity and at length, and which is surprisingly easy to read. Perhaps much of diplomacy was conducted in polyglot form, and Margaret may have had to communicate in this fashion with the royal family before she learned Spanish. At any rate, the conversations of these two artful schemers - Maximilian and Fuensalida - make amusing reading. Maximilian wished Margaret to return at once, and Ferdinand wanted Margaret to remain in Spain in order to prevent her marriage with Louis XII (Charles VIII had died in April 1498) - Spain was against a strong alliance of Empire and France. Furthermore, Ferdinand and Isabella had grave doubts about

---

97 Gutierre Gomez de Fuensalida, Correspondencia ... (Madrid: Published by the Duque de Berwick y de Alba, Conde de Siruela, 1907), p. 23, Trans. SHB.
98 Ibid., Note on p. 22.

their son-in-law Philip and his influence over Juana, and holding Margaret exercised some restraint on Philip's wild life and his ambitious schemes.[99]

Fuensalida, acting on behalf of Ferdinand, was highly imaginative and intuitive in his delaying techniques, and smooth as silk in proposing them. Maximilian, fearing the use of Burgundian ships for Margaret's homecoming because they lacked experience of the sea, suggested that if the King and Queen of Spain could lend him one merchant ship and four boats that the Princess could be brought back with security.[100]

Fuensalida replied, "With such a little armada, I could not assure you of her safety, secondly the French are aware of her coming and would overcome so small a fleet; and in addition it brings no honor to your majesty that such a great princess should go so meanly attended." At another time, he also reminded the impecunious Maximilian of the expense of fitting out his own fleet. The Emperor, with growing asperity, exclaimed "This is enough for her company, and as for her security, we have no fear of the French since we have peace." After more words the King said, "There is nothing more concerning this I wish to say."[101]

On August 20, 1498, Fuensalida again wrote from Freiburg:

… A messenger has come to the King of the Romans from the Princess, and I have worked to find out why he comes, but I haven't been able to learn (in spite of many payments), except that he comes carrying a thousand complaints; and the same with Hulibet who was macebearer to the Princess and in such a mood as not to pardon anything.[102]

In spite of such chicanery, Margaret remained with Ferdinand and Isabella for two more years, their mutual grief having created an affectionate

---

99 J.N. Hillgarth, The Spanish Kingdoms: 1250-1516 (Oxford: Clarendon Press, 1978), pp. 588-591.
100 Gutierre Gomez de Fuensalida, Correspondencia … Madrid: Published by the Duque de Berwick & de Alba, Conde de Siruela, 1907), pp. 81-87.
101 Ibid.
102 Ibid. p. 87.

bond. In 1498, Isabella, their eldest daughter who had married the King of Portugal and was now heiress to the throne of Spain, died in childbirth, and the following year, her little son died. The succession then fell on Juana, wife of the Archduke Philip, and Margaret's brother. "All these great turns of fortune happened to them in the space of [11] months ... and I believe that they would have wanted God to take them away from the world because those whom they loved and treasured so much, had died."[103]

In spite of this corrosive chain of losses, the government still had to continue. An interesting sidelight to this time in Spain was a request from Queen Elizabeth of England, wife of Henry VII, to Isabella:

> The Queen and the mother of the King wish that the Princess of Wales Catherine of Aragon should always speak French with the Princess Margaret, who is now in Spain, in order to learn the language, and to be able to converse in it when she comes to England. This is necessary, because these ladies do not understand Latin, and much less, Spanish. They also wish that the Princess of Wales should accustom herself to drink wine. The water of England is not drinkable, and even if it were, the climate would not allow the drinking of it.[104]

And so Margaret became a tutor to her young sister-in-law, one day to become the bride of Henry VIII and the Queen of England.

With the closeness which had naturally developed between Margaret and the other members of the royal family, she was able to observe, learn and help where needed, and thus life for her assumed a measure of contentment. She became proficient in Spanish, and attentive of Isabella's skill in government and diplomatic affairs. Sorrow had deepened and enriched her character, but her Flemish attendants had never adjusted to

---

103 Philippe de Comines, The Memoirs of Philippe de Commynes, Vol. II ed., Samuel Kinser; trans. by Isabelle Cazeaux (Columbia: University of South Carolina Press, 1973), p. 587.
104 Gustav Adolph Bergenroth, ed., Calendar of Letters...Vol. I, (London: 1862), p. 156. This dispatch from de Puebla, July 7, 1498.

the morbidity and stiffness of the Spanish court;[105] and constantly wearied by the etiquette, they rebelled in countless ways which only caused trouble between Margaret and the King and Queen.

Pirenne describes medieval religiosity as having a "gloomy and agonized cast, a preoccupation with terror, an obsession with eternal torments."[106] While this had lifted in Italy, the Empire, France, the Low Countries and England, Spain retained this image. Therefore, it must have been a trying time for all with limited patience wearing thin. With Maximilian continuing to hear reports of all this, he urged Margaret to return to him.

Finally, after attending Catherine's proxy wedding to Arthur of England on May 19, 1499, she began to make preparations. In September 1499, laden with loving departure gifts of jewelry, gems, bolts of embroidered cloth of gold, plate engraved with her initials, great works of art (some of which she herself had commissioned while in Spain), illuminated manuscripts, tapestries, and her priceless and sentimental wedding gifts, Margaret once more turned toward home. This time, however, it was overland. Louis XII was now King of France; he remembered the little Margaret with fondness and wrote a letter offering her safe conduct through his country. And so from Bayonne, she and her company made the long trek north through France, passed her old home at Amboise and arrived in Paris in February. A messenger there informed her that Juana was expecting another child, and so she brought her visit quickly to a close and traveled on to Ghent, arriving there on March 4, 1500.

Juan's death, with no heir, followed by the deaths of young Isabella and her little son, altered the dream that Ferdinand of Aragon and Isabella of Castille had cherished for a unified kingdom of Spain, and changed the course of European history. Now the throne devolved on Juana and Philip.

Unlike Margaret's harmonious and loving marriage, Philip's was stormy. He had so many amorous adventures, and was so arrogant, callous and domineering toward his wife that even the nobles of that day, accustomed

---

105 William H. Prescott, History of the Reign of Ferdinand and Isabella (Philadelphia: J. B. Lippincott & Co., 1880), Vol. II, p. 360, footnote.
106 Henri Pirenne, A History of Europe, trans. by Bernard Miall (Wakefield, Mass: Murray Printing Company, 1956), p. 62.

to the double standard in behavior, remarked on it.[107] The unstable Juana's sensitive, passionate and possessive nature was wounded beyond bearing by his lack of loyalty, and her outbursts of bitterness caused him to avoid her as much as possible.[108] Juana must have felt she was only a stepping stone to his ambitions, and indeed she was. For him, the marriage produced a kingdom, and heirs to carry it on. For her there was only madness.

The marriage, begun so auspiciously, was lived in constant strife. Maximilian had exclaimed in the early days, "God was a very good matchmaker when he gave such a woman to such a husband, and such a husband to such a woman!"[109] Nevertheless, they had five children. The first child was a daughter, Eleanor, born in Louvain on November 16, 1498 and named for Maximilian's Portuguese mother. Their second child was a boy born February 24, 1500, who became Charles V, very unlike his great-grandfather Charles the Bold for whom he was named. The festivities surrounding his birth are chronicled nowadays at the belltower in Ghent by a narrator who leads visitors through a model of the town as it was then. Thus on March 5 eleven days after his birth and the day after Margaret's arrival, the little Charles was held in the arms of his step-great-grandmother, Madame la Grande (Margaret of York), who sat in a brocade-covered chair carried by four men on the route from the palace to the Church of St. John[110] for his baptism. At their side walked his Aunt Margaret, the other godmother, still dressed in mourning. In the soft light of a long spring evening in Flanders, the richness and colors and fabrics of the clothing made a brilliant display. The occasion was so happy, the future of this little prince so grand, that no expense was spared.

The return by candlelight at almost midnight was even more spectacular. It is said that money was thrown to the crowds and the wine flowed in the

---

107 Gutierre Gomez de Fuensalida, Correspondencia ... (Madrid: Published by the Duque de Berwick y de Alba, Conde de Siruela, 1907), p. xxvi gives reference to Henry VII, see also p. 151. Fuensalida related that each time Maximilian spoke of his son it was with a sigh. See also J.N. Hillgarth, The Spanish Kingdoms: 1250-1516 (Oxford: Clarendon Press, 1978), p. 588, quoting anonymous contemporary chronicler "nothing seemed to him better than women's pretty faces."
108 Hillgarth, p. 588.
109 Fuensalida, p. xxii.
110 Now named St. Bavo

streets that night.[111] The Flemish capacity for celebration is well known even today, and so there must have been many a groggy head the following day as they cleaned up wax from torches, paper from lanterns, and all the mess and litter of a parade.

With the birth of this baby at the beginning of a new century, a new era began; one in which, through a series of misfortunes, Charles would rule over more territory than even Charlemagne had possessed. The central figure in his life for many years would be his Aunt Margaret. For now, however, her return meant picking up the threads of her old life.

Margaret made her home at Quesnoy-le-Comte, now just over the border in France. Located in a wooded area, it had been an animal sanctuary kept by her grandfather Charles the Bold, and some of the wild animals may still have remained. It is thought however that Philip found her presence at court meddlesome. Quesnoy was not banishment - Philip even dodged council meetings in order to visit her - but it certainly was removal from the center of activity. Nor was she denied visitors. Madame of Ravenstein made a social call and brought Margaret up to date on state matters after her long sojourn in Spain. She offered the aid of her father-in-law for Margaret's future placement,[112] if she would so desire - a rather seditious and tantalizing proposal.

The Fuensalida correspondence gives ample reason to believe that Margaret's sense of propriety was offended by the chaotic conditions of the court and the government, and by her brother's behavior; that she remonstrated with him and tried to put matters right. This only raised his resentment. Nevertheless, she loved Philip and took part in some of his merrymaking activities – and this aroused the suspicions of the opposing faction which was loyal to Ferdinand and Isabella. Such is often the fate of those who try to reconcile conflicting wills and interests.

---

111 Eleanor E. Tremayne, The First Governess of The Netherlands (New York: G.P. Putnam's Sons; London: Methuen & Company, 1908), p. 33. Original source is A.R. Villa's La Reina Doña Juana La Loca.
112 Gutierre Gomez de Fuensalida, Correspondencia … (Madrid: Published by the Duque de Berwick y de Alba, Conde de Siruela, 1907), p. xvii.

Fuensalida had counseled her when she first arrived in Flanders to have nothing to do with this court; and, secondly, that she not follow the "appetites and condition of her brother."[113] Margaret offered to mediate between her brother and the Spanish rulers, but Philip rejected this. He did not want the intervention of such a third party, as she maintained herself as though she were Castillian. This observant ambassador sent all the gossip home. It was rumored that Madame la Grande through devious means and in cooperation with Madame of Halewijn and the Lords of Berghes and Molenbaix had procured the governance of the land and the custody of the children when Philip and Juana should leave for Spain. "One for all and all for one" he said. "As they are now the major part of the council, they will probably accomplish it."[114] But when he could get word to Juana, whom Philip kept isolated, he advised her not to accede to this,[115] but the Governor of her household and members of the council who double-dealt with her in the most shameful way, had created in Juana such fearfulness and distrust that "she did not dare to raise her head."[116] Fuensalida did get to see the children whom he described in the most glowing terms – they are the prettiest creatures in the world, so lively and bright; Eleanor seems like five years old and Charles so chubby and rosy now goes in a little cart and is as healthy and strong as if he were three years old.[117] He added that Juana was "very pregnant and very good, thank God."[118]

Philip was scheming with Henry's agents to have the marriage of Catherine of Aragon and Arthur set aside in favor of Margaret as this would greatly enhance trade between England and Flanders.[119] Also he was fearful Margaret would marry the King of Portugal and that those

---

113 Ibid., p. xxvii.
114 Gutierre Gomez de Fuensalida, Correspondencia ... (Madrid: Published by the Duque de Berwick y de Alba, Conde de Siruela, 1907), p. 171.
115 Ibid., p. 171.
116 Ibid., p. xxvii.
117 Ibid., pp. 138 and 182.
118 Ibid., p. 182.
119 Ibid., p. 116.

FORTUNE, MISFORTUNE, FORTIFIES ONE

two would be named successors in Spain, and he and Juana dismissed.[120] The fact that Margaret was so popular in Spain and spoke the "lengua castillana"[121] aggravated his anxiety because he didn't know "the manner of the land, nor the people, nor the way of negotiations."[122]

However, Maximilian was still the head of the house. He was against the English marriage, saw no future in the Portuguese match, and besides was busy with his own schemes for Margaret. She seems to have had some say in the matter and voiced her desire to remain with the governing of the Low Countries and to retain in her power her nephew and nieces (Isabel was born July 27, 1501 and Margaret was her godmother). The council appears to have been willing to support Margaret in this, but Philip was too jealous of his power to permit it; and since her loyalty to Philip did not inspire confidence in Ferdinand and Isabella, that meant she had no support from the Spanish party at court.

Margaret resigned herself to marriage. Her father leaned toward Saxony, but she had finally settled on Philibert of Savoy as being the best of the lot - the others being of "not much estate."[123] Fuensalida relates that Philibert had been present in secret at her homecoming, and disguised, in order to see what she looked like.[124]

And they tell me that as those here who know the will of the father and daughter, that it will be hurried on, and that they are able to demand certain lands which her mother left her and which she renounced when she was in Spain ... moreover that she does not wish to lose the estate.[125] Savoy was close enough to enable Margaret to keep abreast of matters in the Low Countries, and even after her marriage, she encouraged Madame of Halewijn and the Lords of Berghes and Molenbaix to remain with the council.[126]

---

120 Ibid., p. 153.
121 Ibid., p. 153.
122 Ibid., p. 165.
123 Ibid., p. 91.
124 Ibid., p. 153.
125 Ibid., p. 153.
126 Ibid., p. xxvii.

Fuensalida had tried fruitlessly to explain to Philip that they all must take counsel together, and that his presence was needed in council meetings,[127] but these efforts to bring Philip up to the mark earned him only hostility. Philip's court had become so inhospitable, that the ambassador made plans to go to England. He presented himself before Madame la Grande and the Princess Margaret to bid farewell. They wished him well and gave him their thanks for all his past services.[128]

In August of 1501, Margaret began preparations for herself and her party for the journey to Savoy.

As a rich young widow and daughter of the Emperor, Margaret had great matrimonial value. The nobleman who had finally been decided on, was Philibert II of Savoy, called the Handsome. In spite of Maximilian's vacillation over the proposed groom, Philibert was a great favorite of his. He had played an important part in Maximilian's campaigns in Italy and was considered a fine captain and a good companion. His duchy occupied a strategic place between Italy, Germany and France and was often pivotal - Philibert had marched with Charles VIII on his way to Naples in 1494. Now with this marriage, Savoy and Austria united, and this meant the pass to Italy would be cut off to the French.

Philibert was a widower, his wife Louise-Jolenta having passed away at a very tender age. He himself was quite young. He had been born April 10, 1480 and was thus three months younger than Margaret. His sister was Louise of Savoy with whom Margaret had been reared, and the possibility exists that they knew each other as children.[129]

---

127 Ibid., p. 157.
128 Ibid., p. xxviii.
129 Jean Molinet, Chroniques de Jean Molinet (Bruxelles: Palais des Académies, 1935), Vol. II, p. 544. "He was in his youth nourished in France at the residence of King Charles VIII." Paule Henry-Bordeaux, Louise de Savoie, "Roi" de France. (Paris: Librairie Académique Perrin, 1971/1954/1943), p. 43. "... played with Philibert, her only love." In spite of these two references, the writer is loath to say for certain that Margaret and Philibert knew each other as children. Philibert spent his early childhood in Savoy, going later (after 1491?) to the court of Charles VIII. In this case, their paths would not have crossed. In the old Chronicles such as Molinet and Lemaire, there is no allusion to their having known each other as children.

Margaret had entered the negotiations for this politically expedient marriage with no enthusiasm. At this time of her life, she wasn't strong enough to resist, but she did leave a protest of sorts in that she refused to sign the act of agreement.[130] The new marriage contract was concluded at Brussels September 26, 1501. Philip endowed his sister with 300,000 gold coins, but Margaret had to make a new renunciation to the succession of her mother and to those estates which she had not wanted to relinquish. Previous to that she had signed away any rights she had to the throne of Spain.[131] Philibert, for his part, promised that should he die before his wife, she would receive a settlement of 12,000 gold crowns from the revenues of the county of Romont and the provinces of Vaud and Faucigny.[132] In addition, she was to receive such other items to make life comfortable as tapestries works of art, jewelry, plate, etc., an important clause which enabled Margaret later to carry back to the Low Countries many important and valuable manuscripts of the library of Savoy. In addition to this, she still enjoyed a revenue from Spain as their Dowager Princess,[133] though this was often slow in coming. Margaret must have taken some sombre consolation in the fact that, even if life were to deny her happiness, her money could at least give her a measure of power, dignity and comfort. Maximilian hurried north from Innsbruck to see her before she left, and on October 22, 1501,[134] Margaret set out from Brussels accompanied by 250 Savoian knights sent by Philibert as bodyguard as well as her own entourage of churchmen, knights and ladies. Madame la Grande and Juana accompanied her to Halle where they said their good-byes, and Philip continued on a little further. The days are very short at that time of year, but many difficulties in traveling down through France were

---

130 This document is still in the Archives at Lille, France.

131 Elsa Winker, Margarete Von Österreich, Grande Dame der Renaissance (München: Verlag Georg D.W. Callwey, 1966, p. 110.

132 Romont and Vaud are now in Switzerland; Faucigny, in France.

133 Elsa Winker, Margarete Von Österreich, Grande Dame der Renaissance (München: Verlag George D.W. Callwey, 1966), p. 234. As Duchess of Burgundy, Margaret received 20,000 livres; as Dowager Princess of Spain, 12,000 gold guilders.

134 Jean Molinet, Chroniques ... p. 489.

avoided because of the hospitality of Louis XII in his regard for their old comradeship. The towns gave cordial welcomes. Molinet[135] enumerated the abundant gifts of food and puncheons of wine and hypocras[136] (a drink which sets the mouth on fire). There were offerings of venison, wild boars, partridges, rabbits, sheep, calves, capons, geese and all the good things still associated with French and Burgundian cuisine.

At Dijon, the old capital of the duchy of Burgundy, Margaret was welcomed by the lords of the city and 260 horsemen as their own princess. Mystery plays and feasts were given in her honor, and speeches on the history of her family.[137] That she regretted the loss of Burgundy is evident in the comments made later in her will, but for now, all served to relieve the tedium and discomfort of such a long journey.

On November 22, Margaret was met at Dole by Rene,[138] the Count of Villars and Bastard of Savoy who was a great favorite of his half-brother Philip. At Salins on November 28, he stood for his brother in the customary proxy wedding. She was dressed in a robe of black velour, with black lamb fur. The Bishop of Lausanne married them. After the dinner, "Madame was dressed in a robe of cloth of gold made in the fashion of Spain, with satin and a border of pearls, rubies, diamonds and other stones."[139] Following the banquets and dances, Rene carried Margaret to her bed…

> And as the custom with princes married by proxy, the Bastard of Savoy lay down near her, a leg nude on the bed in the presence of all the guests. After several gracious words were exchanged, the Bastard arose, asked Madame for a kiss which was accorded him,

---

135   Ibid., pp. 489-491.

136   James Egan, "An Old French Town That Stubbornly Defends Its Past," New York Times, Sunday, March 9, 1980, Section 10, p. 7. "I knew I was caught up in the past when I ingested the house aperitif, called hypocras. Flavored with anise, cinnamon and other mysterious herbs, it is billed on the label as 'A wine of the Middle Ages, a stimulant and digestive of the first order… prepared according to a recipe of Guillaume Taillevant, celebrated master chef of King Charles VII.' It explodes in the mouth."

137   Jean Molinet, Chroniques … p. 490.

138   Ibid., p. 491.

139   Ibid., p. 492.

FORTUNE, MISFORTUNE, FORTIFIES ONE

and this done, he rendered himself her humble servant. Madame sat up and wishing him good night, gave him a diamond ring… He gave her for the duke a very large heart-shaped pendant and a girdle composed of 26 large diamonds, three good rubies and pearls.[140]

The wedding party continued their journey, and Philibert and Margaret finally met one morning in early December at the village of Romainmoutier about two miles from Geneva, and in a remote valley of the Jura Mountains.

After the dances that evening until 11 o'clock, they retired from the chapel in order for it to be cleaned and prepared for the Mass and wedding, and then…

Madame went there with her ladies and the duke with his most private friends. The Bishop of Maurienne [Louis von Gorrevod] married them in the said monastery. The mass said, they bedded together about 12 o'clock until the day. The following day the court opened and the day passed in dancing…[141]

And so they turned to the receptions in their honor with enthusiasm. After a hard trip through ice and snowstorms so typical of the Alps in winter, they arrived in Geneva. There the rest of the family awaited them, and Margaret met Philibert's two half-brothers Charles 14, the Bishop of Savoy 10, Philibert his half-sister and his young bastard sister Claude 5, whom Margaret came to raise and love as her own and ever afterwards kept her interests close to heart.

Geneva was at this time under the jurisdiction of Savoy (as was the Piedmont area in Italy), and the city prepared a most thoughtful and extravagant reception. While she sat on a white bench under a canopy of taffeta embroidered with the arms of Burgundy and Savoy, a progression of pageants, biblical tableaus and scenes telling the history of the people and the countryside were presented. Another series of symbolic exhibits gave Margaret's genealogy and presented her ancestors as glorious warriors,

---
140 Ibid.
141 Jean Molinet, Chroniques … p. 493.

strong and good looking, powerfully armed but surrounded by flowers, culminating in the figures of Maximilian and Philip and Margaret. After this a heavy table was laid for the reunion of the family of Savoy,[142] the ambassadors from Maximilian, all the knights and ladies from the Low Countries, the gentlemen of Savoy and the knights of Geneva. Finally a series of brilliant tourneys took place with Philibert, in his element, wholeheartedly participating.

Closed in by the winter, they passed the time gaily and magnificently, one ball following another at Geneva, but as soon as the weather lightened, they made preparations for a progress through the duchy. The duke and duchess left on May 1, 1502 for Chambéry in the Rhone valley. On the 15th they arrived in this capital city and spent some time in the ducal palace whose elegant chapel was furnished for the occasion with the Shroud of Turin, a relic belonging to the House of Savoy.

At last on the fifth of August amidst the sounds of bells and the detonations of artillery, Philibert le Beau and Margaret made their joyous entry into Bourg en Bresse. The city was impoverished, but had contracted a loan in order to honor their duke and duchess suitably. The following is Tremayne's account of their reception:

> At last the long-looked-for day came, and the duke and duchess arrived at Bourg on the 5th of August 1502. From early dawn the bells of the monasteries and churches were ringing, guns firing, and a stir of general excitement was in the air. The picturesque wooden houses were hung with coloured tapestries, decorated with five hundred escutcheons bearing the arms of Savoy and Burgundy. Eight platforms had been constructed in different parts of the town on which were to be enacted masques and allegories. At the sound of the trumpet the crowd collected in front of the townhall,

---

142 Christopher Hare, The High and Puissant Princess Marguerite of Austria (London: Harper and Brothers, 1907), p. 88, notes that Louise of Savoy and her children Margaret and Francis attended.

from whence issued the municipal body, preceded by the syndics in red robes, one of them bearing the town keys on a silver salver. The procession marched with trumpets blowing to the marketplace, when soon after a warlike fanfare and the neighing of horses announced the arrival of the ducal cortege, headed by Philibert and Margaret. The sight of the young couple evoked shouts and cheers. Margaret, wearing the ducal crown, was mounted on a palfrey, covered with a rich drapery, embroidered with the arms of Burgundy, and with nodding white plumes on its head. Through a veil of silver tissue her sweet face appeared framed in long tresses of fair hair. A close-fitting dress of crimson velvet stitched with gold, bordered with the embossed arms of Austria and Savoy, set off her graceful figure. With one hand she saluted the crowd, whilst at her right on a fiery charger rode the handsome Philibert, delighted with the enthusiasm which burst forth at the progress of his lovely wife.

The syndics, kneeling on one knee presented the duke and duchess with the keys of the town. John Palluat, head of the municipality, made a lengthy speech according to the fashion of the time, full of whimsical expressions, puns and witticisms, comparing Princess Margaret's qualities with those of the flower that bore her name.

Having entered the town the ducal procession alighted, and two gentlemen--Geoffroy Guillot and Thomas Bergier – advanced towards the princess: the former had been chosen by the council to explain the mysteries, moralities, and allegories; the latter to hold a small canopy over the princess's head. At the market gate on a large platform a huge elephant was seen carrying a tower. This tower, emblem of the town, had four turrets, in each of which was a young girl typifying one of the four attributes of the capital of Bresse. These attributes were goodness, obedience, reason, and justice. After listening to verses sung in her praise by the four attributes, the princess, still preceded by Geoffroy Guillot, arrived at the market-place, where on another platform was represented the invocation of Saint Margaret, virgin and martyr. The saint with a halo, treading an enormous dragon under foot, was smiling at Margaret. She held her right hand over her as a sign of her protection in this world, and with her left pointed to the sky and the eternal throne that God had prepared for her. A group of angels sang a hymn about heaven envying earth the possession of Margaret; whilst the priests of Notre-Dame and the preaching friars enacted the legend of Saint George and the Archangel Michael on the platforms before their church.

Further on, before the Maison de Challes, the exploits of gods and heroes of mythology were shown. Two persons, one wrapped in a lion's skin and carrying on his shoulder an enormous club of cardboard, the other in a helmet and draped in a red tunic, were supposed to represent the departure of Hercules and Jason to conquer the Golden Fleece. At the other end of the theatre Medea, dressed in a silk robe, gave vent to the fury she felt at her adventurous husband's indifference.

Before the fountain of the town the crowd was so dense that the guard and Geoffroy Guillot found it difficult to force a passage for the duchess. There the monks of Scillon had arranged a curious fountain in the shape of a gigantic maiden from whose breasts of tinted metal two jets of wine flowed into a large basin; her body held a puncheon of wine which was cleverly replaced when exhausted. Finally, in front of the entrance to the ducal palace, Margaret witnessed the conquest of the Golden Fleece. Before carrying off this precious spoil Hercules and Jason had to fight a multitude of monsters, dragons and buffaloes, which were disposed of with their club and sword. The crowd having loudly cheered this curious exhibition, the duke and duchess entered the castle situated in the highest part of the city.

The syndics in the name of the town then presented the gift they had prepared for the duchess, a gold medal weighing one hundred and fifty ducats. This medal, struck at Bourg, showed on the obverse the effigy of the duke and duchess on a field strewn with fleurs-de-lys and love-knots, with this inscription:

PHILIBERTUS DUX SABAUDIAE, VIII
MARGARITA MAXI. , AUG. Fl. D. SAB.

On the reverse was a shield with the arms of Savoy and Austria impaled, surmounted by a large love-knot and surrounded with this inscription:

GLORIA IN ALTISSIMIS DEO, ET IN TERRA PAX HOMINIBUS: BURG'US:

This ended the town of Bourg's splendid reception of their young duke and duchess.[143]

Margaret and Philibert continued their tour of the duchy, and in April 1503 they took up their residence at the chateau of Pont d 'Ain. This was a favorite castle of the House of Savoy and especially of the women who married into it.[144] It was a superbly fortified palace which mixed the rudeness of the Middle Ages with the grace of the Renaissance, and mountain simplicity and comfort with gracious living.[145] One of the principal charms of this home was its beautiful placement partway up a mountainside, overlooking the fertile valley of the Ain with its small

---

143 Eleanor E. Tremayne, The First Governess of the Netherlands (New York: G.P. Putnam's Sons; London: Methuen & Company, 1908), pp. 37-40. This account is a condensation by her of the record from the archives at Bourg, and from J. Baux, L'Église de Brou. A bronze copy of this gold medal is in the Kress Collection of the National Gallery of Art in Washington, D.C.; an original in the National Gallery at Paris. Copies also in British Museum and in the Vleeshuis, Antwerp, Belgium.

144 Ibid., p. 49.

145 Elsa Winker. Margarete Von Österreich, Grande Dame der Renaissance \München: Verlag Georg D.W. Callwey, 1966), p. 137. See also Quinsonas, Matériaux…. Vol I. pp. 103-196.

villages, and surrounded by high mountains covered with forests, and filled with game. The chateau is now a home for retired priests, but vestiges of its former grandeur remain, and the foundations for the massive stone walls seem well-nigh indestructible.

Savoy had a policy of neutrality encouraged by the French who paid Savoy to stay neutral. It was one of several lands (along with Burgundy) known as the middle kingdom since Charlemagne's time. Savoian soldiers were used as mercenaries by both the French and the Germans. Though predominantly French in language, politically they leaned toward the German principalities. Savoy had also been ill-served by a series of weak rulers. Philibert himself, though considered a fine soldier and a worthy man, was not interested in government,[146] and his half-brother René, had gradually usurped his powers. He had persuaded Philibert to grant him an act of legitimacy which was affirmed by Maximilian, and to appoint him Lieutenant-General. He was the administrator, and Louis XII conducted French business with him. He had opposition in the person of Blanche de Montferrat, the widow of Charles of Savoy, cousin of Philibert and Louise, and she had gathered strength among the nobles and the people. The presence of these two parties in the duchy caused a great deal of controversy, and the strife at such a small court became unbearable. Margaret, whose sense of justice and rank was offended by René's liberties and power, gradually persuaded Philibert to remove his brother from the government.

In this she was aided by the court preacher, Friar Malet, in convincing the pliable Philibert to banish René. Considering the evenness of her disposition, Margaret showed a surprising vindictiveness in that she saw to it that René's goods were confiscated, and that the act of legitimacy was made null and void.[147] A reason for this may have been that the feudal

---

[146] Ghislaine de Boom, Marguerite d'Autriche-Savoie et la Pré-Renaissance (Bruxelles: La Renaissance du Livre, 1946/1935), pp. 25-26.

[147] Eleanor E. Tremayne, The First Governess of the Netherlands (New York: G.P. Putnam's Sons; London: Methuen & Company, 1908), pp. 41-42; and Elsa Winker, Margarete Von Österreich, Grande Dame Renaissance (München: Verlag Georg D.W. Callwey, 1966), pp. 126-128. See also Quinoas, Matériaux... Vol. III, p. 45.

idea of the legitimacy of the liege lord was still paramount. There was enough evidence to convict Rene of treasonous behavior, but even if he had done no wrong, he still usurped the divine right of Philibert to reign. As a final reason for this coup, there is a good possibility that Margaret had discovered she liked to govern and was good at it.[148]

Winker makes the observation that Margaret became so absorbed in the tasks of government that she soon became as dusty as the documents.[149] Philibert both adored and respected his wife, and let her govern in his place.

The family treated Margaret with warmth. Philibert's stepmother, Claude de Brosse, lived at Chazey-sur-Ain, a few miles away, and they saw each other frequently. Claude de Brosse was a woman of irresistible warmth and humor and called Margaret "ma fille."[150] There were many happy gatherings, with some guests staying over for weeks. It was also a gathering place for men of arts and letters such as Jean Lemaire, and Cornelius Heinrich Agrippa of whom more will be noted later.

A lull in the wars of Europe had cast Philibert into the peacetime amusements of hunting, jousting, tourneys, and feasts which he pursued vigorously and passionately. Margaret often took part in the hunting; they would start at dawn and return only when dusk was falling. One look at the terrain over which they rode so long and hard fills one with admiration for their horsemanship. The hills are steep and thick with woods, the meadows along the river are hummocky and covered with both scrub, tall grass, and stones. One day when they were over in the Piedmont region at Quier (Chieri) just a little south of Turin, Margaret was thrown off her horse. As he reared and plunged, she fell under his feet; her hat flew off, her hair was in disarray, her dress and a heavy gold chain were damaged, but luckily she was unhurt. Margaret was badly shaken, and the company recalled a similar accident from which her mother had not recovered. From

---

148 Paule Henry-Bordeaux, Louise de Savoie, "Roi" de France (Paris: Librairie Académique Perrin, 1971/1954/1943), p. 66, suggests it was a feud between Margaret and Anne Lascaris, wife of René.
149 Elsa Winker, Margarete ... , p. 136.
150 Elsa Winker, Margarete ... , p. 138.

that time on, there are very few allusions to her hunting, leading one to conclude that she had been badly frightened.[151]

Another event in 1503 was Philip's visit to Savoy. Philip, who with Juana, had departed for Castile shortly after Margaret had set out for Savoy, decided to return to the Low Countries, feeling matters there required his attention - and probably also having had his fill of Spanish stiffness and Ferdinand's distrust.[152] Margaret was in her element having together these two men she loved so dearly.

Many events were planned when suddenly Philip and Philibert were seized with some illness and put to bed. They recovered, but in Ghislaine de Boom's phrase, "... death's rough draft would only too soon true."[153] While on this trip, Philip met Louis of France, and managed to earn his distrust also. He appeared unable to apply himself' to governing, and his eye for the ladies continued to cause Margaret consternation. She had some pity for Juana and tried to reason with her willful brother, but to no avail. With some uneasiness, she saw him set off.

In 1504 the summer was hot and dry,[154] but one morning in spite of the suffocating heat, the restless Philibert went hunting while Margaret remained at home. On the trail of a wild boar, Philibert drew far ahead of his company. About midday, he came upon a green and lovely cool grove; overheated and gasping from exhaustion, he drank and drank from the icy cold fountain of St. Vulbas.[155] Others having caught up with him, he ordered their lunch to be served. Not long after, he was seized by a sudden chill and a sharp pain in his side. He mounted a horse which was brought to him for the trip back to the chateau, and then dropped heavily into his bed, perhaps with pleurisy or infectious hepatitis.

---

151 The writer suspects from examining Margaret's portraits before the fall, and those after, that she may have suffered a broken nose.
152 J.N. Hillgarth, The Spanish Kingdoms 1250-1516 (Oxford: Clarendon Press, 1978), Vol. II, p. 588.
153 Ghislaine de Boom, Marguerite d'Autriche-Savoie et la Pré-Renaissance (Bruxelles: La Renaissance du Livre, 1946/1935), p. 27.
154 Jean Molinet, Chroniques ..., p. 544.
155 Spelled also Valbas, and Bulba.

FORTUNE, MISFORTUNE, FORTIFIES ONE

Margaret hurried to his room and summoned the doctors. She handed them her pearls to grind to powder, a favorite remedy; then, distraught, made vows and devout prayers, and sent offerings to distant shrines. Nothing availed. Nine days later on September 10, 1504, Philibert died. He was twenty-four, had ruled but seven years, and he and Margaret had been married only three years. Disoriented, Margaret tried to jump from a window, but was restrained. In wild grief she shut herself up and cut off her hair, almost as would a nun in renouncing the world.[156] When she emerged, she was never quite the same person again.

Philibert's body was embalmed, dressed in his rich ducal robes, and lay in state so that many of his subjects could pay their last respects. He was laid to rest in the Cathedral of Notre Dame;[157] but already an idea was forming in Margaret's mind which was to become a resolve, and then an obsession.

Many years before, Philibert's father had suffered an accident while riding and broken his arm. Perhaps it was a compound fracture, and they weren't able to control the infection. At any rate, he became seriously ill, and his wife Margaret of Bourbon vowed that if he recovered, she would found a monastery of the order of Saint Benedict at Brou. The duke recovered, but the duchess died in 1483 before she could fulfill that vow. Her last wish was for Philibert to take on that duty. His early death prevented carrying out his mother's wishes, and Margaret assumed the task.[158]

Perhaps she sought to propitiate fate, because she began making plans to construct the most magnificent of mausoleums, a convent, a church, and the tombs of Brou. She met with opposition from her council as the cost of such a project would be staggering, and Savoy was not even able to pay her the full amount of 12,000 gold coins due yearly which

---

156 The account of Philibert's hunt and death is taken from Jean Lemaire de Belges, Les Épîtres de L 'Amant Vert (Lille and Genève: 1948, Professor Jean Frappler's notes, p. 46; and Philipp August Becker, Jean Lemaire, Der Erste Humanistische Dichter Frankreichs (Genève: Slatkine Reprints, 1976), p. 51; and Jean Lemaire de Belges, Oeuvres Genève: Slatkine Reprints, 1969), Professor J. Stecher's note on p. 27 following Paradin's Chronique de Savoie, p. 377.
157 Ibid.
158 Eleanor E. Tremayne, The First Governess ... , pp. 45-46.

had been mentioned in the marriage contract as her settlement in case of widowhood. They argued that the new church of Notre Dame was a more imposing resting place, worthy of Philibert's rank, and that she would have the prayers of many as everyone in Bourg attended there daily. They also pointed out to her that Brou was somewhat isolated and would be indefensible in war. But Margaret replied that this was no longer true because of the increased use of artillery. To each of their arguments she had a reply, and, in tears, maintained her determination. She did change the order of monks of St. Benedict to Augustinians from Lombardy under the protection of St. Nicolas de Tolentin, a newly canonized saint for whom Margaret felt great devotion. This saint's day was September 10, the day of Philibert's death, which increased the significance of her choice.

In addition to this she continued to administer the lands of her dowry. Under her energetic leadership, Bourg took on the look of a capital. Schools were founded, hospitals were endowed.[159] She regulated the police, assured food rationing and prescribed the measures of hygiene known at the time to help prevent epidemics. Local barons often operated like thieves using the rugged and inaccessible terrain for escape and hiding, but Margaret saw to it that they were pursued with a vengeance. She was greatly helped in her endeavors by Mercurino di Gattinara, head of her privy council, who served as one of her counselors for years, and later served Charles V as his Grand Chancellor of Castile, afterwards named Cardinal.

Then there was Louis Barangier who had accompanied Margaret to Spain and now acted as her secretary. Later he was to become her Chamberlain in the Low Countries. Second secretary was Jean de Marmix who became the treasurer-general and was instrumental in foreign affairs. He served Margaret until her death. The financial department was handled by Laurent de Gorrevod, and an audit was conducted every three months.[160] Her orderly nature prevailed over everything.

---

[159] Christopher Hare, The High and Puissant Princess Marguerite of Austria (London: Harper and Brothers, 1907, p. 91.
[160] Elsa Winker, Margarete ... , p. 134.

Work gave her life direction and relief from sorrow, and she performed all her tasks with such intensity and capability that her brother-in-law Charles III, who was young and inexperienced, began to feel overwhelmed and his sovereignty encroached upon by this woman. He also was worried about the duchy's finances and was against the project at Brou. Margaret appealed to her father to settle their disputes as he was Charles's suzerain. Finally at a meeting in Strasbourg, with Maximilian present, representatives of both sides met and came to an agreement. Margaret stated that she felt it was incumbent upon Charles to carry out this sacred trust which his father and brother had failed to follow through. Since she had assumed the responsibility, the least he could do was see that she received the revenues due her. On May 5, 1505, in addition to the incomes of Bresse, Faucigny and Vaud, Margaret was granted the county of Villars (which had formerly been René's) and the seignory of Gourdans with all rights of government and the permission to redeem the mortgaged lands of Bresse. Thus with the help of Laurent de Gorrevod, Governor of Bresse, she drew up plans and estimates.

While on this trip to Strasbourg,[161] Margaret journeyed a little north to Haguenau to be with her father and brother, but the war with the Duke of Gelderland forced them to separate. To lessen her worry, Antoine de Lalaing, lord of Montigny, was sent to stay with her.[162] This particular battle must not have lasted long as Molinet relates that soon Philip was at a castle called Rozendaal and Charles d'Egmond, the Duke of Gelderland, was at Arnhem for the pacification of differences.[163] Margaret traveled north to Cologne and then west into the Low Countries.[164]

Several months after the death of Margaret's husband, Queen Isabella of Castile died. Her heir was the high-strung Juana. Co-heir was her

---

161 During this trip to Strasbourg, her parrot, a beloved little pet which had belonged to her mother, was destroyed by a huge dog. To comfort her, Jean Lemaire wrote L'Amant Vert which is a tender, loving and amusing paean to his mistress from the Green Lover.

162 Jean Molinet, Chroniques ..., p. 553.

163 Ibid., p. 555.

164 Jean Lemaire de Belges, Les Épîtres de L'Amant Vert (Lille: Librairie Giard; Genève: Libraire Droz, 1948), see Professor Jean Frappier's note on page 52.

husband, the dashing and shallow Philip the Handsome. Between Philip and Juana's crafty father Ferdinand, there was no love lost. Both of these men wanted that throne, but each needed outside support to strengthen and justify his case.[165] They turned to Henry VII of England who had taken as his motto "Whoever I defend is master."[166] Henry's wife, Elizabeth of York, had died in February 1503 a week after bearing her seventh child.

In the scheming of that day, it seemed to Henry that an alliance with Maximilian and Philip served his purposes best when it came to his relations with France. And with the eligible and rich Margaret, Archduchess of Austria and Burgundy, Dowager Princess of Castile and Dowager Duchess of Savoy, still only twenty-five, healthy and good looking, secretly offered to him as bride, the avaricious Henry must have felt his cup was running over. Two portraits of Margaret[167] (probably by Pieter van Coninxloo), were taken by Philip's ambassador, De Puebla, to England. Catherine, Princess of Wales, who had known Margaret well in Spain, felt they did not do her justice. (One of these showing Margaret in mourning is still at Hampton Court Palace.)[168] De Puebla also related to Henry the arrangements being made for Philip and Juana's second journey to Spain. During their first visit, Juana had given birth to little Ferdinand, and on her return to the Low Countries, she again became pregnant and on September 15, 1505, Mary was born. Eleanor, Charles and Isabel had remained at

---

165   J.N. Hillgarth, The Spanish Kingdoms 1250-1516 (Oxford: Clarendon Press, 1978), Vol. II, pp. 588-597.
166   Eleanor E. Tremayne, The First Governess ... , p. 55.
167   Jane de Iongh, Margaret of Austria: Regent of the Netherlands trans. by M.D. Herter Norton (New York: W.W. Norton & Company, Inc., 1953}, p. 132.
168   Eleanor E. Tremayne, The First Governess ... p. 56. In a "Letter From London" in the December 29, 1980 issue of the New Yorker, Mollie Panter-Downes writes: "The big winter show at the Victoria and Albert Museum, called 'Princely Magnificence,' is an elegantly arranged, scholarly, and stunning exhibition of Renaissance court jewelry, lent by royalties, museums, and private collectors all over Europe ... As a fascinating social-history footnote, there are portraits of monarchs and courtiers wearing similar - or, sometimes the actual - jewels shown here. A portrait from the royal collection at Hampton Court is of Margaret of Austria ... a long-nosed lady looking out of a sort of carapace of rich dress goods stiff with marvelous gems, of which the most riveting to visitors; is certainly the colossal pear-shaped pearl called the Peregrina, which was presented in more recent history to Elizabeth Taylor by Richard Burton..." p. 57.

Malines as Maximilian had refused to give his permission for them to take so arduous a journey. His desire to keep them out of King Ferdinand's power supported his grandfatherly love.[169]

Margaret spent the early part of the summer of 1505 in the Low Countries, and the Fuensalida letters to Ferdinand are helpful in describing some of the court events and Margaret's thoughts concerning them.

In spite of the strong sexual attraction between Juana and Philip, their relationship had deteriorated into arguments and scenes. She attacked with scissors one of her ladies in waiting who had dallied with Philip. Once in order to punish her, he took away her servants, locked her in a room, and departed.

> Her bedroom was above his and when she heard him come in, she began to pound and shout: "My Lord, unlock the door and I'll come and speak to you or you come and talk with me." And he replied: "I am sick (bad foot), tomorrow I will talk to you." She continued to pound with a stone or stick over his bed, and with a cleaver she began to chop a table, and thus no one slept that night.[170]

Ferdinand wrote "that parents feel in their souls over such disconcerts of their children,"[171] and Fuensalida reflected, "She does not have the heart to suffer with patience, she is the cause of her own straits."[172] Women were expected to endure. Maximilian tried to reason with his son, but Philip only commented that his father was "always complaining."[173] And Fuensalida angrily took Philip to task for saying Juana was crazy.[174]

Into this chaos came Margaret to visit. While she was at 's-Hertogenbosch on June 15, Fuensalida approached her to discuss the situation.

---

169 Gutierre Gomez de Fuensalida, Correspondencia ... , p. 214.
170 Gutierre Gomez de Fuensalida, Correspondencia ... , p. 300.
171 Ibid., p. 309.
172 Ibid., p. 351.
173 Ibid., p. 354.
174 Ibid., p. 356.

The Duchess Margaret said: "of me thus they guard as if I were Castillian and wish to give me to understand that everything is fine and there is nothing bad; but for three days I have understood somewhat. First from a paper Don Juan (Manuel) showed me, and I said to him: 'Of such a document, Don Juan, it will not do to show the king, my brother.' He responded to me: 'Why not?' And I replied: 'The reason is that the publishing of it will do no good. Because even if there be truth in such things, good servants cover them up and do not reveal them in order to prevent evil.'"[175]

The document[176] appears to have been damaging to Juana and perhaps useful to Philip in putting her away in order to reign by himself. It had been extorted from a Lope de Cunchillos who had been maltreated in prison according to Fuensalida and who then proceeded to argue with Don Juan Manuel in council over it. Margaret believed that Don Juan and his party had so turned Philip's head that conciliation with Ferdinand was well-nigh impossible. Nevertheless, she offered to mediate between them, but Philip had answered, "No, you are still able to marry and so now is he, and I do not wish a third party between us."[177]

Margaret asked the ambassador to convey to Ferdinand that ...

She will be as obedient a daughter as she was in your kingdom and that she is returning to her own lands now because she is not able to suffer here the things she sees going on ... she feels this is the destruction of her house ... she will be glad to serve him as a daughter... she is not going to speak to the queen because she has not the heart for it (as Don Juan has told her that to speak to the queen is to speak to a stone).

---

175   Ibid., p. 380.
176   This may have been Juana's letter of consent to Ferdinand's regency which was intercepted, and for which Juana was punished by the loss of all her Spanish domestics and confined to an apartment in the palace. See William Robertson, The History of the Reign of the Emperor Charles the Fifth (Philadelphia: J.B. Lippincott Company, 1902-1856), Vol. I, p. 380.
177   Gutierre Gomez de Fuensalida, Correspondencia... , p. 384.

Fuensalida concluded: "All the same, we know Don Pedro, Don Juan and especially Micer (Monsieur) Louis have labored to swing Margaret to their side."[178] According to Martin Hume[179] Monsieur Louis was a servant of Margaret to whom Don Juan Manuel offered, that if he would prevail upon his mistress to follow in all things the wishes of King Philip, her brother, he would get the King to give to Louis from the revenues of Castile an income equal to the highest officer of his household. Louis, he said, knew Castile: let him look about and choose any office or place he liked, and it should be granted to him. Louis succumbed to this temptation; but the Duchess heard of it, and never consented to speak to him again, although he had been her most trusted servant."[180]

On July 15, 1505 Fuensalida wrote from Antwerp that Madame Margaret is detained in an out-of-the-way place in Germany. "The cause of her delay is not known, but it is said that she wished to return to see the Queen in Brussels and the children in Malines … all those places are forbidden to me."[181] Perhaps they were to Margaret also, as she returned to Pont d'Ain in August. In early January 1506, Philip and Juana set sail once again for Spain. They encountered terrible gales and the ships were tossed, driven and dispersed.[182] Martin Hume relates in his Queens of Old Spain[183] that so great was their despair that his attendants dressed him in an inflated leather Jacket on which they had painted "the king, Don Philip." He knelt before a blessed image alternately praying and groaning, while Juana seated herself between his knees saying that she

---

178 Ibid.
179 See Martin Hume's Introduction p. xxviii to Eleanor E. Tremayne's The First Governess … Martin Hume also edited Volume VIII of Calendar of Letters, Despatches and State Papers, relating to the negotiations between England and Spain…
180 Gutierre Gomez de Fuensalida, Correspondencia … , p. 394.
181 Ibid.
182 Molinet, Chroniques … For any who have ever been seasick, Molinet 's description will touch a sympathetic cord: "[this malady] by which the poor and desolated, mortified of rude hope; recovered only enough spirit to yearn towards convalescence, asked only a dram of comfort, an ounce of true hope and a half mark of true understanding, but nevertheless, the torment did not cease, but persisted in its violent train…" p. 564, Vol. II.
183 Martin Hume, Queens of Old Spain, p. 151.

would cling so closely that they would not be separated in death as they had not in life.

Their ship landed at Melcombe Regis, just north of Weymouth on January 16, and on January 31, Henry received Philip a.t Windsor. Ten days later, Juana arrived. She was treated shabbily by Philip which Henry noted, but received by Henry and her sister Catherine of Aragon, widow of Prince Arthur. However, the two sisters were not permitted to see each other alone. We know that each of these women had pride and Spanish temper, and it is surprising that they submitted so docilely - but neither was in a position to resist. In all, Juana had about four days at court, leaving on February 14 to return to the ships.

All the expenses of their stay were defrayed by Henry, but it is Philip who was royally entertained. He had such a merry time and trusted his "father" Henry to such an extent, that the shrewd Henry was able to produce a three-part alliance favorable only to England. Philip, flushed with pride at having just been sworn in to the Order of the Garter, signed with his own hand, as did Henry. They pledged their loyalty on a piece of the true cross.

The first part of the treaty stipulated that the rebel Duke of Suffolk, who had been protected by Margaret of York, who died Nov. 23, 1503, was to be returned to England, though Philip asked that his life be spared. (Henry was faithful to this, but years later Henry VIII had him beheaded.) The second concerned the provisions of the marriage of the Archduchess Margaret to Henry; and the third was a treaty of commerce which was soon known as the "malus intercursus" because it was so detrimental to Flemish business. Then, on March 2, having had a marvelous vacation, Philip left, Henry accompanying him a. short distance, no doubt congratulating themselves and each other over their canny sense of business.[184]

---

184 For an account of Philip's visit, see "A Narrative of the Reception of Philip King of Castile in England in 1506" in Gustav Bergenroth, ed. Calendar of Letters, Despatches and State Papers, relating to the negotiations between England and Spain [London: 1862, vol. I, p. 379. For the treaty, see Vol. I, pp. 382-385.

They reckoned without Margaret. On July 20 Maximilian wrote to Henry from Vienna that he was well pleased that the marriage had been arranged. But only ten days later Jean le Sauvage wrote to him saying that though both he and Maximilian's ambassador had for a month been trying to persuade the Archduchess to consent to the marriage, she had refused. Still they persisted. Two other representatives - Ulrich, Count of Montfort and Claude Carondelet, hurried to Savoy and with the Governor of the Low Countries, Guillaume de Croy, who was already present, urged her very strongly to cooperate in these plans of Maximilian's and Philip's; otherwise the English king would grow cool in his friendship thus spoiling the commercial treaty. They also pointed out that Henry's friendship included his help in keeping the Duke of Gelderland at bay and in securing the Spanish succession – meaning Juana and Philip, and that this was an honorable marriage for her.

The Archduchess replied that "although an obedient daughter, she will never agree to so unreasonable a marriage,"[185] and that "as she has already been three times unfortunate in her marriages, she is much disinclined to make another trial." Besides, she said, "she believed she should have no children, and that she might thereby displease the King of England."[186] Also, she believed that the marriage portion was exorbitant, and she could not have been pleased that "the 30,850 French crowns a year which formed her jointure in Spain and Savoy" was to be paid punctually to Henry.[187] Furthermore,

> With regard to the representations of the Emperor, respecting the necessity for her marriage, she said she was of a different opinion. The Emperor could always easily make peace with the King of France and with the Duke of Gueldres. As far as the King of Arragon is concerned she does not think he intends to exclude the Archduke Philip from the succession in Spain. The King of England

---

185 Gustav Bergenroth, ed. Calendar of Letters... , Vol. I, p. 395.
186 Ibid., Vol. I, p. 446.
187 Ibid., Vol. I, p. 388.

having already concluded a marriage between Prince Charles and the Princess Mary [Henry VII's daughter], he is obliged thereby to be a friend of England.[188]

On September 24, unable to fathom her refusal, Maximilian wrote to Henry that he had not been able to persuade his daughter to marry him, but he would go and visit her in order to plead with her.[189]

Margaret's resistance was sweetly reasonable, polite, tactful, but unyielding, leaving Maximilian's and Philip's advisers paralyzed with frustration, at their wit's end as to what to do next. They thought if only they could discern the convincing argument or compromise, she would agree, but Margaret, though dignified and courteous, was implacable.

The strain of this conflict was resolved suddenly when in September, Philip was taken ill at Burgos. His Flemish doctor was not alarmed at first, attributing the sickness to overindulgence in feasting, playing pelota and dancing. But he grew steadily worse, and died on September 25, 1506. Martin Hume in his Queens of Old Spain gives this version:

> After the feast the King was taken ill of a malignant fever, it was said, caused by indulgence or over exercise, and Philip lay ill for days in raging delirium. Joan, (Juana} dry-eyed and cool, never left his side, saying little, but attending assiduously to the invalid. At one o'clock on the 25th of September 1506 Philip I, King of Castile, breathed his last, in his twenty-eighth year: but yet Joan, without a tear or a tremor, still stayed by his side, deaf to all remonstrance and condolence ...[190]

Although, as was usual, Philip's Italian physician vehemently denied that there were any indications of poison on the remains, there can be but little doubt that Philip was murdered by agents of Ferdinand. The statement to that effect was freely and publicly

---

188 Ibid., Vol. I, p. 446.
189 Ibid., Vol. I, p. 400.
190 Martin Hume, Queens of Old Spain (London: G. Richards, 1906), p. 166.

made at the time, but the authorities were always afraid to prosecute those who made them. There were many persons who attributed Philip's death, not to Ferdinand, but to the Inquisition, which Philip had offended by softening its rigour, and suspending the chief Inquisitors, Deza and Lucero; but this is very improbable.[191] [192]

Juana calmly made arrangements, but it was evident that the shock had overwhelmed her. Philip's body was embalmed and placed in a lead coffin, and she was never willingly far from it. Though Juana survived until 1555, her mind was affected, and though queen, she existed a virtual state prisoner in the palace of Tordesillas with her little daughter Katharine born five months after Philip's death.

Margaret composed this epitaph[193] to honor Philip, but it reveals her own state of mind:
ECCE ITERUM NOVUS DOLOR ACCIDIT
NEC SATIS ERAT INFORTUNATISSIMAE CAESARIS FILIAE
CONJUGEM. AMISISSE DILECTISSIMUM
NISI ETIAM FRATREM UNICUM
MOBS ACERBA SUBRIPERET
DOLEO SUPER TE FRATER MI PHILIPPE
REX OPTIME
NEC EST QUI ME CONSOLETUR
OVOS OMNES QUI TRANSITIS PER VI. AM
ATTENDITE ET VIDETE SI EST DOLOR SICUT DOLOR MEUS
(Behold again new sorrow befalls
Nor was it enough the most unfortunate daughter of Caesar
To have lost a much-beloved husband

---

191 Ibid., Footnote on p. 167. See also Bergenroth's Calendar … Supplement to Vol. I, p. xxxvii.

192 Juana's behavior during Philip's illness is so uncharacteristic, one might even suspect her - especially as she now had Philip all to herself. However, Otto von Habsburg in his Charles V. (New York: Praeger Publishers, 1970), p. 26, maintains that "in fact only the inability of the doctors to make a diagnosis gave rise to these malicious rumours."

193 Christopher Hare, The High and Puissant Princess, p. 107; Eleanor Tremayne, The First Governess…, p. 65.

> But also bitter death steals the only brother
> I grieve over you my brother Philip
> Excellent King
> Nor is there anyone to console me
> O all you who pass this way
> Attend and see if there is any sorrow like my sorrow)

This terrible loss following so many others brought Maximilian and Margaret together, and though Henry wrote again on October 1, commenting that "Madame Margaret makes great difficulties about ratifying the treaty of marriage [and that] it would not be a thing to be wondered at if he were to accept one of the great and honourable matches which are daily offered to him on all sides,"[194] Maximilian did not have the heart to force Margaret into it. She, of course, remained firm in her resolution not to marry again.

In addition to the sorrow of Philip's death, Maximilian had to reassume the regency of the Low Countries. Past experiences had left him bitter in that regard and loathe to take on the burden. Another duty which devolved on him was the guardianship of the four children still remaining in the Low Countries at Malines: Eleanor, Charles, Isabel and Mary. Though he loved his grandchildren and was an indulgent and playful grandfather, he must have known that neither his peripatetic way of living, nor the court at Innsbruck, was a proper life for them. Perhaps also he did not want that responsibility. At any rate, when Maximilian considered these new obligations, in addition to the ones of the Empire, coupled with the worry and intransigence of Margaret; it must have occurred to him that he could resolve several difficulties at once. Therefore, when the States General offered him the regency and guardianship, he turned to his daughter Margaret as the one best able to carry out these duties. He had an admiration, though at times grudging, for her, and had been a witness to her ability in negotiation. He also set great importance on the knowledge of languages and other cultures, and Margaret possessed this ability as

---

194 Gustav Bergenroth, ed. Calendar of Letters... Vol. I, p. 400.

well. Also, the Salic law did not apply in Burgundy, and Margaret was first and foremost Duchess of Burgundy.

Though there is no record of it for this particular period, Margaret probably pleaded with her father for the regency during their visits together. She had asked as early as 1501 before her marriage to Philibert, when she had the support of several strong nobles on the council. Now maturity and the experience of governing in Savoy had strengthened her request. At any rate, Margaret accepted these responsibilities, finding in them the irresistible call of a new work, and a challenge worthy of her rank in life. She left the states of Savoy on October 29, 1506, not without regret, and journeyed to Germany for a short visit with Maximilian.

The memorial at Brou so lovingly and well begun and which would absorb her interest for the remainder of her life, she was never to see again.

Chapter 3

SOVEREIGN OF THE LOW COUNTRIES

By letters of patent on March 18, 1507, at Louvain, at that time capital city of the Duchy of Brabant, the Emperor Maximilian charged his daughter "as the most near after us" to receive the solemn oath that the States of the Low Countries had accorded him as the regent for Philip's heir, the seven-year-old Archduke Charles.[195]

Before installing herself at Malines the following July 7, Margaret made her joyous entries into the principal cities of the Low Countries. These were ceremonial visits in which the contract between the people and the new ruler was revised or renewed. On April 27 she was received solemnly in Brussels, and there "in noble array" she left the Coudenberg Palace which was one of the ducal residences, and went to the City Hall in the Grand' Place where she mounted the great gallery of carved stone decorated in black (mourning for Philip) from where she could have a free view of all the people in the market. Lemaire records that they wept tears of gratitude for their own natural princess. Everywhere she went she was

---

195 Quinsonas, Materiaux ... , Vol. III, pp. 181-196. Powers given by the Emperor 'Maximilian to his daughter Margaret for the regency of the Low Countries, March 28, 1507.

welcomed with enthusiasm by the nobles as well as by the people of the city who waved with great cheers and extreme joy.[196]

Malines, now called Mechelen, lies in the northern Flemish part of Belgium. It is pleasantly situated on the Dijle River about halfway between Brussels and Antwerp. This small city may have been chosen for several reasons as Margaret's place of residence. First of all, it was easily accessible to all the principal cities of the Low Countries and to her dower lands in Savoy. Then too, it had sentimental ties as a city ever loyal to Burgundy and to Maximilian. Also it had been Madame la Grande's home and the children had lived here under her watchful eye all their lives.

Nevertheless, more space was needed for all the people associated with a court, and so Maximilian bought from Jean Laurin, Lord of Watervliet, another house directly opposite which Margaret altered and redecorated to suit her requirements, and to keep her valuable collections of plate, tapestries and books from Spain and Savoy. These palaces, which remain today, were designed in a modest, homelike and private way.

On Sunday and Monday, July 18-19, 1507, a two-day memorial service was held in St. Romboud's at Malines for Philip. Jean Lemaire, an eyewitness, described the scene in infinite detail of which only a synopsis is given below.[197]

A procession, headed by Philip's officers and servants, slowly wound its way through the streets of Malines on its way to the Cathedral. They were followed by priests and chaplains, friars, men of the law and of the guilds, punctuating the parade like modern day advertisements. Poor men bearing torches knelt all the time the service lasted, and there were magnificently dressed ambassadors, bishops and great lords with their arms and mottos. Each contingent, just as in Belgium's resplendent processions today, led by heralds on huge and powerful horses with ornamental cloths and harnesses carrying the banners of Austria, Spain, and all the provinces of Burgundy and the Low Countries. Paintings of these banners are preserved at St.

---

196 Jean Lemaire de Belges, Oeuvres "Chronique Annale," Publiées par J. Stecher, Tome IV (Genève: Slatkine Reprints, 1969), p. 477.

197 Jean Lemaire de Belges, Oeuvres "La pompe funeralle de Phelipes de Castille," Publiées par J. Stecher, Tome IV (Genève: Slatkine Reprints, 1969), p. 243 ff.

Romboud's in the eighth chapel, dedicated to Philip and the Golden Fleece.[198]

There was a sermon by the late King's confessor, John, Bishop of Salubry,[199] who eulogized the virtues, diverse fortunes, great gifts, and deeds of the deceased king. There were many tears, for the handsome, charming and feckless Philip had captured their imaginations and their hearts.

Now they turned to a little boy - frail, slight of build, with a long, projecting lower jaw, but with clear steady eyes and a calm and dignified expression. They removed his cap of mourning and placed in his hands a sword which he grasped by the hilt, and, with the point in the air, advanced to kneel before the high altar. A fitting ceremony for the child who would one day be known as Charles V. In the meantime, there was a lot of growing up to do, and under the able and loving care of his Aunt Margaret, he enjoyed childhood's lessons and pleasures while he was trained to rule.

The States General convened from Tuesday July 20 until August 22, and Margaret, accompanied by her nephew, presided.[200] She ruled as a true heiress of Burgundy, and she governed the Low Countries with a liberty and an authority that no regent after her would ever possess. Margaret was twenty-seven years old and was described as a fair young woman with golden hair, rounded cheeks, a grave mouth, and beautiful clear eyes. Her sister-in-law Louise of Savoy remembered her as having "hair the color

---

198 The Order of the Golden Fleece (la Toison d'Or) founded by Philip the Good of Burgundy in 1430 at Bruges, was one of the secular orders established during the late Middle Ages to defend the Catholic faith and uphold chivalric ideals. During their meetings they settled disputes among themselves and discussed the behavior of their members, sometimes to the point of censure. It is said that even Charles V was subject to this criticism and accepted it in a very positive and reasonable way. The knights had a right to trial by their fellow members which eventually caused Margaret loss of sovereignty. Unlike The Order of the Garter in England which proffered its rights and privileges to female reigning sovereigns such as Elizabeth, The Order of the Golden Fleece did not extend that courtesy to Mary of Burgundy (the Grand Mastership going to her husband Maximilian), nor to her daughter Margaret of Burgundy/ Austria.

199 André J.G. Le Glay, Correspondance de l'Empereur Maximilien I et de Marguerite d'Autriche (Paris, 1839), Vol. I, p. 206 for spellings: Salubre, Salisbury?, Salbrie, Salombrie; Sélivrée (Selivri?). See also Stecher's note p. 262.

200 Jean Lemaire de Belges, Oeuvres, publiées par J. Stecher. Tome IV, p. 311.

of the wheat of the Beauce country, and cheeks the color of the roses of Provins ... dazzling, vivacious and striking as a Spaniard."[201]

Margaret's position was no sinecure. The lands under Burgundian rule were diverse. They did not constitute a kingdom - there were seventeen loosely federated provinces with strong city-states. Some owed allegiance to the Empire; some to the sovereignty of France. The people were characterized by an independence of thought which they guarded so zealously as to preclude helpful cooperation. Different languages and dialects, dissimilar dynastic and geographical backgrounds, distinct cultures, uneven rates of economic progress - all produced varied points of view and animosities, and a provocative array of problems. Their position directly across from England, north of France, and their center as a conglomeration of busy ports on the main north-south river and sea trade routes, along with the manufacturing and the rich cattle and dairy farming, had given economic prosperity and a sense of well-being to the inhabitants. Charles the Bold had tried to unite his scattered possessions, and had succeeded in obtaining a corridor from Franche Comté with Dole and Besançon north to Dijon in Bourgogne, Alsace-Lorraine, to Hainault with Mons and Valenciennes, Namur and the province of Brabant with Brussels, Louvain, Malines, Antwerp and 's-Hertogenbosch (Bois-le-Duc). To the east there was Luxembourg and Limburg, to the west the powerful coastlands and cities of Flanders: Artois arid Picardy with Arras, Lille, Ypres, Ghent and Bruges. Further to the north were the lands of Holland and Zeeland, with Amsterdam, Rotterdam, Den Haag ('s-Gravenhage or The Hague), Leyden, Delft, Veere, Middelburg and Vlissingen. Ecclesiastical lands with their own jurisdiction included Liège, Utrecht and Cambrai, and split the geographical unity of the dominion. Overijssel, Friesland, Groningen, Gelderland and Cleves, though more recently and loosely joined, completed the circle of Burgundy. The court itself with its feudal traditions and chivalric patterns was the unifying factor, and French was the unifying language.

---

201 Paule Henry-Bordeaux, Louise de Savoie; "Roi" de France (Paris: Librairie Académique Perrin, 1954), pp. 25 and 63.

Margaret was no sooner installed than the problems began. France, ever eager to pounce when a vacuum occurred, was warned as early as February 3, 1507 that Margaret "would do her best to defend the estates of Prince Charles," and hoped "that the King of England and King Ferdinand would assist her."[202] However, the Burgundian dukes claimed the highest place in France after the King, thus Mercurino di Gattinara was sent to the Court of France to do homage in Margaret's name. This able legal counselor from the Piedmont region of Italy had come north with Margaret from Savoy. A man of great intelligence, energy and loyalty, he was faithful to her house all his life, acting sometimes as an emissary for Maximilian, and eventually as Charles' Grand Chancellor. He was a proud man. The story is told that he reproached Margaret for losing her temper at him: "These words should be addressed to a stranger and an unknown man, not to me, whom you have known and tried."[203]

When Margaret convoked the States General at Malines July 20, 1507, the first order of business was money to pay the army in Gelderland. This constant and debilitating warfare with Charles of Egmond, Duke of Gelderland (and to a lesser extent Robert de la Marek, Lord of Sedan, called the Wild Boar of the Ardennes, who was a friend of Francis I of France). Starting with Charles the Bold,[204] it absorbed the attention of Maximilian

---

202 Gustav Adolph Bergenroth, ed. Calendar of Letters, Despatches and State Papers (London, 1862), Vol. I, p. 403.

203 Eleanor E. Tremayne, The First Governess of The Netherlands (New York: G.P. Putnam's Sons; London: Methuen & Company, 127 1908), p. 110. Note: Mercurino Arborio was born at Gattinara on June 10, 1465. He studied jurisprudence in his youth and attended the University of Turin. He subsequently developed a large clientele and a name for himself, and was asked to serve on the private council of Philibert of Savoy. He refused this, but in 1501 did accept the office of counselor to Margaret. He remained with her after the death of Philibert, and when she became Regent, he was elevated to the post of president of the parliament of the county of Burgundy. He carried out various missions for her to Louis XII and Ferdinand of Aragon. In 1513 he was created Count of Gattinara. He and Margaret worked hand in glove, and when Charles became King of Spain, he became a counselor to him. Gattinara was instrumental in the election of Charles as King of the Romans in 1519, and later became his Grand Chancellor.

204 Charles the Bold in the 1470's had offered himself as mediator in the conflict between the old Duke of Gelderland and his son Adolph, an intransigent sort whom Charles, with the help of the lords of the Golden Fleece, Jailed for life. The old Duke then sold his rights to Charles. Adolph's children, Charles and Philippa were sent .from Nijmegen to the court of' Margaret of

and Philip, and was a continual thorn in Margaret's side. Molinet said of him: "He persisted always in his quarrel, disturbing the frontiers of the land, deliberately making war and sending defiance to those of the Golden Fleece."[205] The Archduchess's general was Florent of Egmond, a relative of Charles, and this unremitting warfare had something of a blood-feud quality. This feudal lord with his ideal of justice sought to relieve his land from a hated pledge made to Charles the Bold in 1471. He was backed up by his hardy subjects who wanted their independence, and financed by a seemingly bottomless French purse. Margaret was of a mind to end this peacefully, and there was even discussion of a marriage with one of the little nieces. But forces at that time were too strong for her. The French had the persistent and relentless policy of subduing Burgundy and were not above scheming to accomplish it. Maximilian, who hated the French with every fiber of his being, looked on this subornation of his authority as a last stand. If the French were allowed to succeed there, where might they not try next? And so, lost in this international scuffle, the proud natives of Gelderland, led by their beloved duke, continued their successful guerilla war - here a town besieged and citizens massacred, there a castle or a monastery burned or travelers robbed. They were continually on the offense. Though Margaret was sincerely moved to bring these draining skirmishes to an end, and made many appeals to him, the Duke would grant no concessions. In one way, Charles of Egmond was a chivalric leftover, an archaism in more modern times; in another, he presaged the push for independence from outside dominance, either Habsburg or Spanish, coupled with religious differences which led to the bloody wars during the middle and late sixteenth century. War was the sole profession of this gentleman; he had a just cause so he believed, and thus it continued.

York at Malines. Charles of Egmond eventually served under Maximilian, but was captured by the French and that is how the mischief began. He returned to Gelderland in 1491. See Jane de Iongh, Margaret of Austria: Regent of the Netherlands, trans. by M.D. Herter Norton (New York: W.W. Norton & Company, Inc., 1953), p. 149.

205 Jean Molinet, Chroniques de Jean Molinet (Bruxelles: Palais des Académies, 1935), Tome II, p. 535.

In one early matter, Margaret was entirely successful. She declared invalid the hated business treaty between England and the Low Countries known as the Malus Intercursis.[206] Whether Henry VII was eager to be conciliatory in order to win her hand, or to please his own businessmen who were suffering lack of trade, or both; he readily consented and a new agreement remained in force until the end of his life. This was the first of many diplomatic successes, and greatly increased her popularity in her native land. As part of this treaty, her nephew Charles was affianced to Mary Tudor, daughter of Henry VIII.[207]

Personal and family matters also required a great deal of her attention. Henry VII had persisted in his courtship of Margaret (also Juana and Louise of Savoy), once sending six horses and some greyhounds.[208] Maximilian in visits and letters continued to plead saying that she would not only rule the Low Countries, but England, and that she might return for three or four months out of every year to rule her own domains. Margaret remained respectfully adamant, but her intransigence was the gossip in the courts of Italy, France and Spain. Maximilian wrote her September 16, 1507 "…

---

206 The name was given by Francis Bacon because it was not based "on principles that would give the maximum benefit to both sides,[as] it was extorted by Henry out of Philip's weakness, and gave the English merchants in the Netherlands such a privileged position that the nominal benefits were likely to be outweighed by the resentment they caused…in 1507 another agreement confirmed the Magnus Intercursus as the basis for trading relations between the two countries." See Roger Lockyer, Henry VII (London: Harper & Row Publishers, Inc., 1968), p. 70.

207 Jean Lemaire de Belges, "De la nouvelle aliance d'Engleterre," Oeuvres, Publiées par J. Stecher, Tome IV (Genève: Slatkine Reprints, 1969), pp. 267-268.

208 Note: These are the preparations which Henry VII made for Margaret in conjunction with the marriage of the Princess Mary to Charles which was to have taken place at Calais in 1508: Firste, her bedde chambour to be hanged with riche aras. The second chambour also. The iijde of fyne tapestry, a longe trussinge bedde of clothe off golde, and iij (3) cussions of the same. Carpettes about her bedde of wolle, and upon the cubbourd and windowes of velvet…. In the second chambur, a bedde with a sparver and counterpoint of clothe of golde and velvet perpale, courteynes of double sarcenet, with all that belongeth thereto. A cloth of astate of clothe of goulde. A longe carpet on the floure. A chaier covered with crymsyn velvett, and cussions of the same for the saied chaiar and windowes, carpettes for the bourde and windows of velvet or of wolle. Item, a chambour to be hanged and dressed for her chamberlain. Item, to have in store paillet beddes furnished for every chambour where beddes be… My ladie Margaret archduchess [to be lodged] in the tresourer's house. John Gough Nichols, The Chronicle of Calais (London: The Camden Society, 1846), p. 60.

thus you will not feel yourself a prisoner in England ... with a headstrong man... and you will not be left to wander about the world like a person lost and forgotten as you formerly declared to us."[209] The matter was considered before the Privy Council with her father and nephew Charles present. The English ambassador concluded that it was clear that the Emperor had done everything in his power, and could do nothing more. One can't help wondering what inner power enabled Margaret to hold out in the face of such formidable pressure in this day when men had the last word. Coolness, presence of mind and patience she had in prodigious quantities - but that does not suffice to explain. By papal authority, noble women then had to sign an act that they had not been forced into marriage, so she had a little protection there; but this had been circumvented often enough (as perhaps in the case of Anne of Brittany) to be considered of not much account. We can only conclude that she had a very deep revulsion to this particular marriage; that she had an intense and profound fear of any more of the sorrow which had followed her past marriages, and that she wished to retain her autonomy as ruler of the Low Countries. She probably also knew that Maximilian, with all his faults, was too noble and tenderhearted to override her decision in this matter.

Margaret took over the guardianship of Philip and Juana's children with enthusiasm. It was a longing fulfilled. Believing that she would never have children of her own, she lavished all her love on them. The letters she sent to Maximilian were full of her concerns and worries about their care, their education, their health, and what pleasure, amusement and pride she found in them.

There were four who remained at Malines - Eleanor, born November 16, 1498; Charles, February 24, 1500; Isabel (Isabeau), August 15, 1501; and Mary, born September 13, 1505. Two others were in Spain: Ferdinand, born in 1504, and Katharine (Catalina) born in 1507, five months after Philip's death. They lived in the "Keizerhof," Margaret of York's old house opposite Margaret's.

---

[209] Christopher Hare; The High and Puissant Princess Marguerite of Austria (London: Harper and Brothers, 1907), p. 117.

Sir Richard Wingfield,[210] the English ambassador, became close to the family during his years of service in Europe and his reports contain intimate glimpses of family life. He often observed nephew and nieces joyously absorbed in playing outdoors on a summer day, and he reported they danced around a bonfire on Saint John's Eve.[211] For winter they had a sled shaped like a boat which had masts, ropes and flags, and Charles liked to take members of the court for a ride in it. Margaret, and Maximilian on his visits, loved to stand and watch them. They had two wooden horses, and their schoolroom was equipped with "a wonderful school bench decorated with coats of arms in bright colors, and a low table on which to put their ABC books, heavy parchment tomes bound in velvet ... with gold capital letters and gay miniatures."[212] And, of course, there were invitations from grandfather Maximilian to dinner, hunting parties, visits to other cities, choir concerts, acrobats and fireworks to lighten children's hearts. In their nursery days they had been surrounded by "devoted women with melodious names - Philippote, Gilette, Barbe, Josine, Jeanne - supervised by Dona Anna de Beaumont,"[213] who had been a lady-in-waiting to Juana and whom Margaret held in great affection and respect.

As for their education, they were in the hands of many able scholars. Charles's tutor was Adrian of Utrecht who afterwards became pope under the name of Adrian VI.[214] This kindly man of renowned virtue

---

210 There were three Wingfield brothers: Robert, ambassador to the court of Maximilian; Richard, ambassador to the court of Margaret in the Low Countries, also associated with Calais; and Edmund who also served England as a diplomat.

211 St. John the Baptist's Day is June 24; St. John's Eve is thus June 23.

212 Jane de Iongh, Mary of Hungary: "Second Regent of The Netherlands," trans. by M.D. Herter & Company, Inc., 1958, pp. 13-14.

213 Ibid., p . 13. Margaret wrote to Maximilian in March or April 1513 concerning Ferdinand's giving the Order of St. Jacques to Anna de Beaumont: "You will do me great honor and pleasure if you will allow her to accept this honor from the King of Aragon, because my nephew and nieces are well served by her, and this will reward her good services." Le Glay, Vol. II, p. 113. And again on May 1, 1514, she asked that this "lady of honor who has worked so long and hard for the children since their birth be given for the rest of her days one of Charles's houses at Ghent as she has been so badly paid for her grand services." Le Glay, Vol. II, p. 251.

214 The last non-Italian pope until John Paul II.

had been deacon of St. Peter's in Louvain, and was associated with the University there. He was a product of the religious atmosphere derived from the Brothers of the Common Life who believed less in the intercession of saints than in a regulated life as a way of true piety. The children's actual instructors were Robert of Ghent, Adrian Wiele, Juan de Anchiata, Charles de Poupet, Lord of La Chaux who later became a counselor of Charles during his reign, and Luis Vaca who had entered Philip's service rather than Ferdinand's. He was a great favorite of both Margaret and Charles. The best known of course is Juan Luis Vives, the Spanish scholar and educational reformer who later taught the Princess Mary, daughter of Henry VIII and Catherine of Aragon. The subjects included music by Henri Brédeniers, organist of the chapel; art, rhetoric, grammar, history, simple mathematics, science, theology and Latin. Maximilian urged that Charles "learn well the thiois" though there is no evidence that he ever did so.[215] There is a painting of the three eldest children at the clavichord, but Charles, at least, was not a very dedicated student, preferring knightly games with his pages of honor to study, and Margaret may have indulged him due to his frail health. At any rate, he developed a talent for mechanical pursuits and became a superb horseman which filled Maximilian's heart with pride. As Margaret frequently took him with her on her trips, he had first hand tutoring in practical politics.

Many have wondered why the foremost scholar of the day, Erasmus, did not become tutor to Charles. The answer probably lies in his own unwillingness to be tied down; Erasmus wished to be free to travel and write. The royal family thought highly of him, and in the years to come, provided him with a pension.[216] His Education of a Christian Prince was written for Charles, and though published in 1516, may have been

---

215 André J.G. Le Glay, Correspondance de l'Empereur Maximilien I et de Marguerite d'Autriche (Paris, 1839), Vol. II, p. 176. In Vol. II, p. 111 Le Glay explains that "thiois" applies not only to the German language, but also to Nederlands, which is Dutch and Flemish.
216 Allen, P.S.. ed., Opus Epistolarum Des. Erasmi Roterodami (Oxford: 1906), Tome V, p. 312.

composed some time before.[217] The admonitions and ideas it contains reflect the educated thought of this era.

In this treatise, Erasmus advanced the thought that the ruler should be a model for the people, and must not indulge himself. The prince should live prudently and eschew extravagant expenditures and sensual pleasures. He should have an early knowledge of the theory of government, though a good mind is not enough, it must be strengthened with wisdom. The prince should avoid flatterers and choose wise and honorable administrative officials; he should know the characteristics and traits of all peoples as well as his own, which led Erasmus to the conclusion that the prince should be a native of his country. Erasmus held up the ideal of the unity of Christian ethics and ruling authority and maintained that no prince really rules unless over free men. The ruler should govern with equity and justice, mercy, kindness and courtesy; otherwise he is not a king but a tyrant.

As alternatives to the incessant wars of the time which he considered a disgrace to Christianity, he suggested working for the betterment of the lands and not the extensions of the borders. He proposed the encouragement of education for the youth of the country in which they could learn right from wrong; and for the rich, a practical education. He recommended building projects: bridges, churches, canals, aqueducts, road building, sanitary engineering, and scientific experiments in farming. As positive steps toward the welfare of his country, the prince should promote a monetary system that was reliable, and taxation should be made fair. Erasmus felt that corrupt laws were an offence, that they should be checked and corrected, and made known to the people. An interesting sidelight is his contempt for the custom of sending young royal women to "far-away places to marry princes they have never seen, men who differ from them in language, manners and characteristics."[218]

---

217 Lester K. Born, trans. and ed., The Education of a Christian Prince (New York: Columbia University Press, 1936, p. 29. It is said that Charles's brother Ferdinand kept a copy constantly with him.

218 Lester K. Born, trans. and ed., The Education of a Christian Prince (New York: Columbia University Press, 1936), p. 39.

FORTUNE, MISFORTUNE, FORTIFIES ONE

Erasmus concluded that peace, harmony, true religion, education and the prosperity of his people should be the chief aims of the prince and the highest hopes for the Christian world. As Adrian and Erasmus had comparable educational backgrounds and shared similar ideals, we may assume that these thoughts and aims were instilled in the young mind of Charles.[219] Brandi states that "the piety which was Charles's very being had its roots in the teaching of this man,"[220] which can be gleaned from "his pupil's later development."[221]

The nobleman who superintended Charles's education was Guillaume de Croy, Lord of Chièvres. A single-minded man of great intelligence, he nevertheless considered "letters as belonging to gownsmen and that a prince could better bestow his time on manly and chivalrous exercises."[222] He had been appointed governor by Philip during his absence in Spain and continued in that capacity until Margaret became regent. Chièvres's policies leaned toward the French as he belonged to the French branch of the family. This attitude was diametrically opposed to Margaret's. Resentful at being displaced, yet powerful because of his control over the education of Charles, Chièvres was a source of continual conflict within the court. Margaret probably feared his ambition might displace her, as indeed it eventually did.

Charles's youthful lackadaisical attitude toward study was no match for the influence of the chief figures in his life - Chièvres, Adrian and Margaret - who, whatever their personality or political differences, all, shared great intelligence, high ideals, patience and a strong sense of duty.[223] He became like them, and as the years went by remedied the gaps in his learning on his own.

---

219 Karl Brandi, The Emperor Charles V, trans. C.V. Wedgwood (Oxford: Alfred A. Knopf [Alden Press], 1939), p. 47.
220 Ibid.
221 Ibid.
222 William Robertson, The History of the Reign of the Emperor Charles the Fifth (Philadelphia: J.B. Lippincott Company, 1902), William H. Prescott's notes Vol. III, p. 351.
223 Karl Brandi, The Emperor Charles V, trans. C.V. Wedgwood (Oxford: Alfred A. Knopf' [Alden Press], 1939), pp. 47-50.

Having put to rest the question of her marriageability, at least for the time, and having seen to the care and education of the children, Margaret was able to give the closest attention to her plans for this memorial to Philibert and his mother at Brou. On March 1508 she drew up a will creating an endowment to ensure the building of a monastery and church and the three tombs at Brou. She stipulated when religious services were to be held, and when others could use the sanctuary to offer up prayers in conjunction with the monks and priests. Other clauses included the dowering of fifty marriageable young women from Bresse and fifty from Burgundy. There were bequests to the hospital, infirmary and plague house. The Archduchess directed that her body be taken to Bresse and described the manner in which the funeral was to be conducted. But though this project was now in the hands of a committee, and its costs guaranteed, the progress of the work occupied much of her thought and attention all the rest of her life.

Malines is a substantial town of about 65,000 inhabitants today, but at that time, it was much smaller. There were wooden houses, a few of which remain yet, and it had a semi-rural feeling with windmills all around and an outlook of green and neatly-tilled fields with small boats on the river Dijle and its canals, and bridges over them. Within this pastoral setting tapestry making thrived. However, Malines was also noted for its tanneries, and the bell and cannon foundries.

This little private kingdom[224] at Malines of more than 500 people was organized in an orderly and hierarchical way. The chapel was served by a confessor and four chaplains. In the household itself, at the head were

---

224 Margaret of York's palace and Margaret of Austria's palace lie opposite each other on a pleasant thoroughfare between the town square and the railway station. The square contains the city hall and the post office. These and the Busleyden Museum nearby all date from Margaret's time and before. (Jerome de Busleyden, a state counselor and friend of Erasmus, turned his home into a museum. He is also the founder of the College of Three Languages at Louvain.) There is a statue of the Archduchess by Tuerlinckx made about 1885 in the center of the square. Near the palaces is the church of Sts. Peter and Paul built in the baroque style on the site of the former church. These three edifices formed a triangle of activity of which only a whisper remains today. Margaret of York's palace is now a theatre, and Margaret of Austria's was converted to law courts in 1796, but one can still enter the garden courtyard which the Belgians, with their love of flowers, carefully tend. This building, which is called the "Court of Savoy" has two wings which once

the knight of honor and his wife the lady of honor who took charge of the women of the court. Laurent de Gorrevod, who had come up with Margaret from Savoy, was the first knight to hold this position. Under the knight was a steward having under his direction four others which assured the good functioning of the many services.

The department of the chamber was comprised of twenty-seven gentlemen representing the various states, and the doctors, the valets and the ushers of the chamber. The large domestic department was divided into three main services: the office, the kitchen, (cooks, pastrycooks, bakers, cupbearers, carvers) the kitchen, and the library.

The frequent trips called for an equerry who was in charge of all transport, and as Margaret was never poorly accompanied, the logistics of such trips were a heavy and continual duty. This gentleman also had a seat on the Great Council and was in charge of the captain and corps of archers engaged in the protection of the Archduchess.

Permission to see the Archduchess was regulated by the lady of honor, the knight of honor and the steward. There was a strict etiquette for the rules governing the table. For instance, the knives were always placed in

---

housed the service quarters and stables built around the garden. It was remodeled for her, and Italianate detail was added to the plain native Flemish architecture.
The front and newer part Isabel and Albert (1598-1633) had as throne room and council chamber. As one walks through to the older section, the guide indicates an ancient room which still has Margaret's motto, Fortune, Infortune Fort Une, (Fortune, Misfortune, Strengthens a Woman) in the leaded window and dates from her time. That room was also occupied later by Archbishop Granvelle. The walls are perhaps two feet thick and there are five doors which led to passageways under the city as that room was used to keep valuable documents and jewelry. One of the old doors remains, and it takes two keys to open it - one from the inside and one from the outside. The hall leads to a former passageway over a small street to a little chapel where Margaret could go in all kinds of weather whenever she pleased and without fuss. Her bedroom which faces east was not grandly large as might be expected. It was roomy and comfortable, with a large fireplace. Located over the kitchen, it was toasty warm in winter. The room is now a law library and has a door to a small balcony outside which would give a nice breeze in summer. The room faces the inner courtyard and may have been somewhat dark in spite of the many windows. Also, the Sandgate explosion of August 7, 1546, partially destroyed the palace and neither the fireplace nor the ceiling are the originals. Beautiful parquet covers the floors now, but in the sixteenth century, stone and tile were used for flooring to prevent fires. One can only conclude that the Archduchess had no nerves, for there is no evidence that either the noise nor the smells of the kitchen and foundries ever troubled her.

the shape of a Burgundian cross at each place setting. Margaret shared her table only with the lady of honor. Another table was reserved for the steward and the gentlemen present. The maids of honor and others attached to the house all had separate menus, tables or places, but the food was not less in quantity or quality, only different, and since the Flemish-French combination produced the finest dishes, the choicest wines, fish, fowl and game in season, is it unlikely anyone suffered. A saying current today is that the Belgians cook in the French style, but serve Dutch portions.

Margaret herself loved the cordiality of court life.

We read of her attending many feasts, dances, and jousts; and it was seldom she did not have music during her meals, either fife, tambourin, or violin players, or sometimes the choristers of Notre Dame de Sablon (still in existence in Brussels) or Monsieur de Ravestein's singers, who played and sang songs before her. Another day we read of her watching the performance of two large and powerful bears brought by some strolling Hungarian players; or sitting in the vast hall, silent and dreamy, listening to old airs of German ministrelsy.[225]

With all these people an efficient household was needed to control the court, and Margaret's was a model of organization - more orderly than the French, but not as stiff with protocol as the Spanish, and it served as a pattern for other courts. The English with their wonderful traditions of pomp and ceremony owe a great deal to Burgundy.

Around the turn of the twentieth century, the Belgian artist Willem Geets, with a deep love and knowledge of his country's history, painted a series of pictures to be used in tapestry making. The originals are in the City Hall Complex at Malines. They show Margaret enjoying a puppet show with the children; descending the stairs to the garden to serve

---

[225] Eleanor E. Tremayne, The First Governess of The Netherlands (New York: G.P. Putnam's Sons, 1908), p. 111. For more detail concerning Margaret's household, see Max Bruchet, Marguerite d'Autriche, Duchesse de Savoie (Lille: Imprimerie L. Danel, 1934), pp. 71-76. Max Bruchet's life as Archivist at Lille spanned two centuries. He is respected by both the French and the Belgians for the prodigious amount of research carried on in his lifetime. The Archives du Nord are now housed in a very modern building, but there is a framed photo of him on one of the columns in the reading room. See also Quinsonas, Matériaux...

as godmother - which she frequently did for the many babies of court families; watching an archery competition; listening to a choir. The artist has richly caught the spirit and color of the times, and in spite of all the royal trappings, the very real hominess of the court.[226]

In her conduct of state business, Margaret often had to make prolonged trips. Though she would be away at tines for more than half the year, she always returned for Christmas. This lovely residence with the children nearby was home, and it was against this background that she governed the Low Countries.

Margaret always carried herself as the natural princess and rightful heir of the Low Countries, but Maximilian was at first unwilling to grant her full powers, and played an evasive game. But through the efforts of her counselor Mercurino di Gattinara, a steadfastly loyal man and shrewd in his negotiations with Maximilian, she gained more autonomy. When Gattinara declared it was his mistress's wish "to return to the lands of her dowry (Savoy) to live more at her ease," Maximilian caved in. He was probably fearful of having to govern those intransigent Low Countries again. Margaret in turn accepted a council composed of the most eminent men in the Low Countries.

Their letters to each other reveal a close cooperation, and Margaret was scrupulous in informing Maximilian about matters large and small. But sometimes due to the remoteness of the courts, the weather or the delays and slowness of communication, she had to act independently. On occasion he became angry at this, and she was often exasperated with his schemes and pleas for money. Margaret was careful to apprize him of the inconsequential perhaps in order to lull or allay his meddlesome tendencies when it came to more significant concerns. Once, for example, Margaret consulted over whether Charles was to be moved to Malines, or the little sisters moved to him in order to receive the Holy Sacrament of Confirmation and the benediction of the papal legate, Cardinal de Sainte-Croix. Maximilian positively glowed in reply to his "very dear and much

---

226 These pictures can be seen at the Koninklijk Instituut Voor Het Kunstpatrimonium (Institut Royal Patrimoine Artistique).

loved daughter" that he was asking the Prince of Chimay to escort Charles to Malines, and that "... in consulting our wishes in everything, you give us much pleasure."[227]

In a letter of October 1, Maximilian reminded her that he knew the French better than she. Nevertheless, when it was decided to call a meeting at Cambrai with the French, Margaret attending as Regent of the Low Countries, acted as the representative of her father while he stayed behind in Malines to conduct the business of the Empire and the Low Countries in her absence. What is even more significant is that Ferdinand asked her to represent his interests as well. At Maximilian's suggestion,[228] Margaret had engaged half the town for her counselors and company, and the Cardinal of Amboise, representing Pope Julius and Louis XII, had engaged the other half. Chièvres, who accompanied her, with other members of the Council as far as Valenciennes must have been very happy at this rapprochement with France, as he had been angered by her arrangement of Charles's betrothal with Mary of England. Matthaus Lang, Bishop of Gurk (Gorinchem) Maximilian's trusted counselor, and Edmund Wingfield, the English ambassador were present.

The contract, written out by Gattinara, had something in it for everybody.

Historians of that day, and/ more modern times, have credited Margaret for her great skills in negotiating. Jean Lemaire averred that "Madame Margaret has seen and experienced more at her youthful age... than any lady on record, however long her life."[229] Tremayne quotes Du Bos:

> This princess had a man's talent for managing business, in fact she was more capable than most men, for she added to her talents the fascination of her sex; brought up as she had been to hide her own

---

227 André J.G. Le Glay, Correspondance de l'Empereur Maximilien I et de Marguerite d'Autriche (Paris, 1839), Vol. I, p. 92. (Maximilian writing from Schoenhoven, October 8, 1508.)
228 Ibid., Vol. I, p. 100. (Maximilian writing from Breda, October 27, 1508)
229 Eleanor E. Tremayne, The First Governess of The Netherlands (New York: G.P. Putnam's Sons, 1908, p. 91.

FORTUNE, MISFORTUNE, FORTIFIES ONE

feelings, conciliate her opponents, and persuade all parties that she was acting blindly in their interests.[230]

and another contemporary writer:

> This princess received the Cardinal with great honour, captivated him by her courteous, and caressing manners, and was so successful in charming him, that he could refuse her nothing.[231]

Well, not quite. Margaret and the Cardinal of Amboise had many hot arguments and violent discussions. Perhaps it was a tactic, but she wrote to her father that she had decided to leave as the talks were not of service to their house. The Cardinal however, had beseeched her to stay, and, in the end, she gave in.[232] Finally she could conclude that "it often cost us a bad headache, and that my lord the legate (the Cardinal) and I were nearly tearing out each other's hair. However, at the end we were reconciled and became the best of friends possible."[233] Frappier believed that this was Margaret's greatest diplomatic triumph.[234]

With so many sovereigns were involved, the difficulties faced by Margaret were just about insurmountable. However, the conclusions were these: Certain conflicts with France were to be postponed until Charles was of age; Charles of Egmond should have the duchy of Gelderland and the county of Zutphen, giving up all the places he had taken in Holland, and receiving those castles in Gelderland which the Low Countries still held, with the provision that a panel made up of representatives of Maximilian and the King of England on one side and of the Kings of France and Scotland on the other would ultimately make a decision. The second part of the treaty concerned the war with Venice (which was to continue) in which

---

230 Ibid.' pp. 92-93.
231 Ibid.
232 André J.G. Le Glay, Correspondance...., Vol. I, p. 109.
233 André J.G. Le Glay, Maximilien I...et Marguerite..., p. 51.
234 Jean Lemaire de Belges, Les Épîtres de L'Amant Vert (Lille: Librairie Giard; Genève: Librairie Droz, 1948), Frappier's comment on p. xxxvii.

the Pope was to have Faenza, Rimini, Ravenna, and Cervia; Maximilian was to have Padua, Vicenza, and Verona, Friuli and Treviso; the King of France, Cremona, the Ghiradadda, Brescia, Bergamo, and Crema; and the King of Spain, Trani, Brindisi, Otranto and other Neapolitan ports. The Venetian ambassador, who had traveled to Cambrai, learned nothing of the planned partition of his country, because the meeting was conducted with such reserve and dissimulation. He wrote the Doge that it was nothing but an alliance of Louis XII's.[235]

The Treaty of Cambrai was signed on December 10, 1508 and an oath was taken in the Cathedral on the same day. The States General recompensed her work, pain and diligence in having made a "good, sure and honorable peace."[236]

Margaret wrote to Ferdinand's ambassadors in England and was obviously triumphant at the success of her negotiations. Actually the principal object of the treaty was not peace, but the subjugation of Venice; and it looked as though this had been accomplished. The French provoked war on April 16, 1509. Pope Julius followed on April 22.[237] Maximilian was busy trying to subdue Charles of Egmond who, not feeling bound by the treaty, continued his attacks within Brabant and Holland, and his ambushes of Flemish merchants on their way to Germany. The Emperor was also trying to secure money from the Reichstag at Worms, and from the Fuggers of Augsburg, the great banking family of the day. He reluctantly pawned several of the treasures of the Habsburg family of which even he had been careful, and made a list of the Habsburg valuables in a letter to Margaret referring to the safe place which he had told her about "by mouth."[238]

---

235 André J.G. Le Glay, Maximilien I, Empereur d'Allemagne, et Marguerite d'Autriche, sa fille, Gouvernante des Pays-Bas (Paris: Chez Jules Renouard et Cie., 1839), p. 51.
236 L. Ph. C. van den Bergh, Correspondance de Marguerite d'Autriche, Gouvernante des Pays-Bas, avec ses amis (Utrecht: Chez J. de Kruijff, 1849), Vol. I, p. 157.
237 Henry VII died April 21, but news of this did not arrive until May.
238 André J.G. Le Glay, Correspondance de l'Empereur Maximilien I et de Marguerite d'Autriche (Paris, 1839), Vol. 1, pp. 177-178. (August 7, 1509 from Bassano.)

FORTUNE, MISFORTUNE, FORTIFIES ONE

Maximilian wrote to his daughter on May 18, 1509, from Angelberg[239] describing the French victory at Agnadello. Another letter of June 8 from Sterzingen sent good news of his army's success,[240] but it was not until August 18 that he was in the field himself at Padua and again wrote to Margaret about the people and events around him. The siege of Padua continued and in early in October, Maximilian returned to the Tyrol.

It is difficult to understand his withdrawal. In the years before, in a centuries-old claim of the Empire to northern Italy, he had attempted to conquer the Venetian towns though it interrupted the commerce which nourished the Tyrol and Germany. These battles were disastrous,[241] and Maximilian, incensed, took it as a blow to his pride when he had had to submit to a three-year truce. His anger was one of the motivating forces behind the congress which resulted in the League of Cambrai. Furthermore, he went to a great deal of time and trouble to secure money to pay and equip an army of thousands to seek his revenge. And then, with success in his grasp, he left it - his perseverance had run out. He wrote in explanation on October 7, "knowing that some of our soldiers not being strongly inclined to the assault, we have raised the siege."[242] Food for these "thousands" was in short supply. Further, this horde of men, horses and artillery would have turned any encampment to a sea of mud.

Le Glay notes it was the enthusiasm of the Venetians excited anew by the harangues of the old Doge which triumphed.[243] The Venetians under siege had sent word that their town and provinces were released from their allegiance and urged them to provide for themselves. Now the united forces fell apart in their greed at dividing the spoil. Eventually Venice, by taking advantage of this situation, regained part of her territory, and made

---

239 Ibid. Vol. p. 139.
240 Ibid., Vol. I, pp. 150-153.
241 It is another story, but the knowledge that Michelangelo painted the Sistine Chapel between 1509 and 1513 helps to lift us out of the sordid history of these battles.
242 Le Glay, Correspondance de l'Empereur et de Marguerite d'Autriche (Paris, 1839), Vol. I, pp. l-191.
243 Ibid., Vol. I, p. 191.

her peace with Pope Julius and King Ferdinand. But it nearly destroyed Venice, and led to the advance of Spanish power in Italy.

Regardless of the international situation, the correspondence continued. Another feature of these letters between father and daughter is the ease with which they switched from matters of state to the consideration of the children ... almost like turning over a coin. While the preparations were being made to go to Italy, Maximilian wrote that he was thankful the children were recovering from some childhood illness, but warned Margaret not to let a certain doctor and his assistant near Charles as they were Venetian and he was worried about poisoning.[244] In his letter from Sterzingen concerning his army's success, he also related that Ferdinand and his second wife had had a son, but the baby had been born dead.[245] This meant, of course, that Charles was still heir to the Spanish throne. Later Margaret passed on to him a suggestion she had received from the Dowager Queen of Portugal in which that lady suggested a marriage between her grandson Juan III and Eleanor, or possibly Isabel, and perhaps Mary with another grandson. Margaret was sympathetic to these proposals because of the relationship between the two houses. Maximilian's mother had been Eleanor of Portugal, and with the prosperity of Portugal and the small number of princes living at that time, such a marriage would have been most desirable. Eventually an arrangement was made between Juan and Katherine, the daughter born after Philip's death and who remained at the palace of Tordesillas with her mother Juana.[246]

During the siege of Padua, Maximilian informed Margaret that the young Marquis of Brandenburg, who was to enter the service of Charles, was to receive a pension of a thousand livres a year "pour son entretenement." "I hope you will be agreeable to this,"[247] he wrote.

In October Margaret related in great agitation that the nieces had contracted smallpox, and as "this malady is contagious," she decided to

---

244 Le Glay, Vol. I, pp. 129 and 172.
245 Ibid., Vol. I, pp. 150-153.
246 Christopher Hare, The High and Puissant Princess Marguerite of Austria (London: Harper and Brother, 1907), p. 150.
247 Le Glay, Vol. I, p. 188 (Sept. 8).

keep Charles in Brussels and remain with him. Her effort was met with defeat as this frail child caught the disease also, but, miraculously, they all recovered.[248]

During this time Margaret had the seventeen-year-old Duke of Milan, Maximilian Sforza, and perhaps his brother Francesco, staying with her.[249] These young men were the sons of Ludovico Sforza and Beatrice d'Este, and the cousins of her stepmother Bianca. After their father's defeat at Novara, they were entrusted to the care of Maximilian. They apparently were shuttled back and forth between the two courts, being kindly looked after in each. The young Duke was consumed by rank and precedence after the manner of the day, and had a running argument with the Duke of Saxony which Maximilian settled in a practical way, and not without a touch of humor. Taking time out of his busy schedule, he answered that "one enters first today, and the other tomorrow." Margaret was probably more exasperated than amused.

Maximilian had written that Margaret should give the Duke of Milan, a sum of three thousand livres, since his annual sum was sufficient. "Do not fail," he admonished her. Much, much later, Margaret innocently replied that the Duke had been unable to obtain money from the Fuggers because his credit had rim out, and though she would have been glad to advance it herself, she had no funds.

Margaret had bound herself to be security for the penalty of 250,000 crowns should Maximillian and Charles default in any way in the treaty of marriage between Charles and Mary of England.[250] With the expenses of the war with the Duke of Gelderland which never ceased, plus her own personal expenses at Brou, she probably did not have much money at hand. What she had though, she managed well and held for the well-being of the Low Countries. Margaret had written in December 1508 that she had sent an officer to negotiate with the Duke of Gelderland and begged that

---

248 Le Glay, Vol. I, p. 202. (October 29, 1509).
249 Ibid., Vol. I, p. 461. (December 16, 1511.)
250 Gustav Adolph Bergenroth, ed. Calendar of Letters ... (London: 1862), p. 450.

Maximilian would moderate his conditions seeing that the country was suffering so from the continuation of war.

> "Touching the content of the second of your letters making mention of 50,000 florins, it gives me wonder that you write thus, seeing my Lord, that without the assembly nor consent of the estates, I am not able to do this ... and it seems to me, my Lord, that you ought to think well over this, and after you have well thought, demur in your resolution a little, and after you have assembled the estates, propose to them your demands, and ameliorate them a little and it will be all to the better... your very humble and good daughter."[251]

Her treaty with England, including as co-signers the noblemen and towns of Burgundy, Brabant, Flanders and Holland, Maximilian had ratified "without altering a single word."[252] However, as Maximilian himself confessed,[253] the "principal reason which [had] induced him to betroth Prince Charles to Princess Mary [was] to get a good sum of money from the King of England [who had] promised 100,000 crowns."[254] Maximilian, in spite of all Margaret's work, still felt himself free to take advantage of any better arrangement that might be offered. But Margaret herself, always inclined toward England, intended to keep it. Though that part which concerned Charles's marriage was not honored, the alliance was good for the lands under her domain.

There is a very curious letter written from Malines in April 1509 which is thought to have been addressed to Maximilian though disguised to mystify the curious and indiscreet:

> My cousin, Today I have been introduced to your bastard daughter whom you have formerly spoken of to me and whom I have greeted

---
251 L. Ph. C. van den Bergh, Correspondance de Marguerite d'Autriche, Gouvernante des Pays-Bas, avec ses amis (Utrecht: Chez J. de Kruijff, 1849), Vol. I, pp. 153-154.
252 Gustav Adolph Bergenroth, ed. Calendar of Letters. (London, 1862), p. 455. Vol. I
253 Ibid., Vol. I, p. 455.
254 Ibid., Vol. I, p. 461.

very well and treated with the best that I could possibly do for the love of you: and in regard to that which you have said to me by the one who brought her, desiring to rename her as the daughter of my cousin of Utrecht [Frederick of Baden, Bishop of Utrecht]; it seems to me that she would be honored more to be your daughter than of the Bishop. Because you so much desire her well being and advancement, let me have your advice on this. Further as to your affairs, I give to you all the favor and skill in my power as our Lord knows who, my cousin, has you in his saintly guard.[255]

It appeared to Le Glay, who knew her handwriting well, to be an original though it is unsigned. The address (which was put on the outside fold of letters) is to "The Emperor my very honored lord and father."

At this time, the term "bastard" was not always considered a reproach, indeed it sometimes appeared to convey a title of honor as in the "Bastard of Savoy" by which Margaret's brother-in-law René was known. Margaret did not scorn her natural brothers and sisters as evidenced by a letter of February 8, 1519 in which Graff Bal[256] recommended George and Leopold to her. Their reputed father was Guillaume Pigeon. In all, according to Le Glay,[257] there were eight:

1. George, who became Bishop of Brien, Archbishop of Valence, and in 1544, Prince-Bishop of Liégé
2. Leopold, Bishop of Cordova
3. ?, wife of Count of Rochefort
4. ?, wife of Francois de Melun, premier
5. Dorothée, married in 1539 Jean, son of Edzard I Count of East-Friesland
6. Marguerite, wife of the Count of Illi and of Thaure

---

255 L. Ph. C. van den Bergh, Correspondance..., Vol. I, pp. 164-165.
256 M. Le Glay, Maximilien L'Empereur d'Allemagne, et Marguerite d'Autriche, sa fille, Gouvernante des Pays-Bas (Paris: Chez Jules Renouard et Cie., 1839), p. 31.
257 Ibid.

7. ?, wife of the Count of Helfestein who was massacred in 1525 in a revolt of the peasants
8. Anne, wife of Louis de la Marek, lord of Walperg and of Herlemont

There was probably at least one other known as Peter of Ghent (1480-1572):

> Among the dispatch of friars, Franciscan, Dominican and Augustinian to convert the American Indians, teach them in schools and succour them in illness was a spiritual administrator who was an uncle of the Emperor Charles V, Peter of Ghent, a Fleming by birth, and marked by a typically Habsburg face, who served in Mexico for nearly fifty years, and corresponded regularly with his nephew upon Indian welfare.[258]
>
> Arriving in Mexico in 1523, he remained there until his death at an extreme old age without ever revisiting Europe. Famed for his humility and self-effacement, he never took Holy Orders but devoted himself heart and soul to the education of the natives. And in the great school of San Francisco in the Indian quarter of Mexico City, which he directed for over forty years, generations of Indians were taught to read and write, received instruction in various trades, or were trained as painters, sculptors, and silversmiths to adorn the churches arising on every side.[259]

This is Margaret's half-brother, born in the same year as she, but there seems to have been no correspondence between them. Philip the Good of Burgundy had an amazing eighteen bastard children who were recognized and through intermarriage provided most of the nobility with whom his great-granddaughter Margaret had to contend. Ferdinand of Aragon had four, among them an able son, and it must have given him a great deal of

---

258 See Foreword in History Today, October 1974.
259 C.H. Haring, The Spanish Empire in America, A Harbinger Book (New York: Harcourt, Brace & World, Inc., 1963 [1947, 1952]), p. 210.

pain that his child could not succeed him. Charles V would have two, each of them healthy and competent, one of whom, Margaret, would one day rule the Low Countries. In any case, illegitimacy carried little stigma and "members of the blood line generally assumed responsibility for the future welfare of these 'bâstards.'"[260]

As the warfare situations in Northern Italy never ended neatly in decisive victories, skirmishes continued, and Maximilian wrote to keep Margaret abreast of the news there. He also passed on the information that Constantinople had suffered a terrible earthquake and that a third of the wall of the city had tumbled to the ground with more than a thousand people killed.[261] In an era which looked for signs, this surely was the hand of God wreaking vengeance on the infidel. Lastly, he mentioned that Peter of Navarre, admiral of the King of Aragon, had taken the city of Bougie in Africa in hand-to-hand combat.

For Margaret, however, it was a year of frustration. It opened with a letter from Frederick of Egmond, a relative of the Duke of Gelderland, but one who had remained faithful to the houses of Burgundy and Habsburg. This Frederick was also the father of Floris (Florent) who was Margaret's general - obviously a man of power and one to be placated:

> My very redoubted lady and mistress, humbly I recommend myself to your good grace; madame, I understand that you have some treaty or appointment underway between my lord the emperor your father, and his adherents and my lord of Ghelders without consulting me or giving me any notice...Madame the said lord emperor promised to do nothing without my presence; madame you are well aware of the fact that they do not understand our affairs nor those things which touch us. For this reason, my very honored lady, I pray you on my part, that you will please have regard and acknowledge those who are loyal to your father, to you

---

[260] Louise Cuyler, The Emperor Maximilian I and Music (London: Oxford University Press, 1973), p. 67, footnote.
[261] M. Le Glay, Correspondance... (Paris, 1839), Vol. I, p. 234.

and to your predecessors of the house of Burgundy... because we are of the opinion that this will guard our honor the better, and I do not believe that the said lord emperor will abandon us; madame, I pray to our Lord God that he will give you accomplishment of your highest and noble desires.

Your humble servant Frederick of Egmond, Count of Buren, etc. January 1, 1510.[262]

Van den Bergh comments in a note[263] that "Frederick and others were extremely jealous of their rights and believed the government of a woman favored their pretensions." Certainly the letter's arrogance and veiled threat are well covered with scrupulously correct address and phrases. It is a cold letter and must have chilled Margaret.

Nevertheless, even before this, she had taken steps to retain the matter in her own hands. She had charged Louis Maroton, a trusted secretary of Margaret, and emissary of both Maximilian and Margaret, and Guillaume du Guislain Pingeon, one of Maximilian's close personal attendants, with the permission to have a free hand in coming to terms. Their approach was deft and patient in her regard and they wrote that after strong debate on this matter and much thought on the part of the Emperor, they were able to incline "his imperial majesty" to their request, and "he is content that madame his daughter" negotiate an alliance with Gelderland, making no final conclusion without consulting him.[264] Thus began the negotiations for peace, part of which included the betrothal of her niece Isabel born in 1501, to Charles of Egmond, Duke of Gelderland, now in his forty-third year. There was nothing to bind this man to peace, however, and he continued to lay waste to Overijssel. Oppressed once too often by this aggressor and fearful for their future, the towns of Deventer, Kampen and Zwolle agreed to remain loyal to Margaret and provision themselves for

---

262 L. Ph. C. van den Bergh, Correspondance... Vol. I, pp. 175-177.
263 Ibid,, Note, p. 176.
264 L. Ph. C. van den Bergh, Vol. I. pp. 177-178.

defense. Jean, Duke of Cleves asked for help to defend his interests.[265] Matters came to such a pass that Maximilian authorized her to ask for assistance from the Bishop of Utrecht. Her general Floris of Egmond wrote asking for money to pay the troops.[266]

In the midst of this tumult, Maximilian, angry and obstinate in the face of the disintegrating League as the Pope had made an alliance with Venice, vowed to go on alone.[267] Margaret begged him to follow the lead of Aragon and England and pull out as France was only making use of him. He too requested money, but she had to reply that the Low Countries were unwilling to grant money for his affairs in Italy. "My Lord, in all humility I tell you, and it displeases me that there is no way to fulfill your desire,"[268] and she reproached him for his rudeness.

With the deceit commonly practiced within and between the courts of that era, Margaret was fortunate in having many able men stand by her. Jacques (Jacob) Villinger, a relative of Erasmus, and Maximilian's treasurer-general, communicated the information that an ambassador from Floris of Egmond, Lord of Ijsselstein had come to incline the Emperor to the contrary of her wishes, and that the Emperor was very chilly about the proposals she had made, but hoped he would change.[269]

In a letter to Villinger, Margaret complained that she could not negotiate because Maximilian was enflaming the matter by his pretentions, though she added, "your diligence has been irreproachable."[270] Margaret maintained that it was his comportment which was leading to war and not to peace and that he had badly misunderstood two overtures which she had made. Further that there were no problems with Isabel's engagement, though if Charles persisted in his actions he would not have either the cities or the lady. She felt that she had been dealing openly and her father covertly, and that if he did not respond soon to Charles's ambassadors, the

---

265 Ibid., p. 191.
266 Ibid., p. 193.
267 André J.B. Le Glay, Correspondance ... Vol. I, pp. 236-237.
268 Ibid., p. 309.
269 Le Glay, Vol. I, p. 287, note.
270 Van den Bergh, Vol. I, p. 202.

treaty would fall through, the blame being on "the said lord and father for whom we have marvelous regret."[271] He was unwilling to take Margaret's advice and his schemes continued. His distrust of Henry VIII displaced for a while his old suspicions of the French, and the notorious little red book which held a list of France's transgressions he had burned in an outburst of generosity and gratefulness to Louis XII for helping him regain some of his territory in northern Italy. He had put his faith in the Swiss, but they had gone over to the Pope who had early made his peace. The intrigues of the cardinals disgusted him and he scornfully ranted: "Look at them, the fine practicers of the holy mother church!" Though Maximilian was hot with anger at the time, his attitude reflected his own and others' calmer judgments.

The sequence of events, and the machinations and negotiations surrounding the Venetian war and that of the Duke of Gelderland in the north, were impenetrably complex. One thing is certain, nothing was settled for good. In the next generation Charles V and Francis I continued the contest.

Through it all, Margaret acted as clearing house, mediator and advocate with correspondence from Spain, France and England addressed to "Madame." It was Ferdinand's desire that he and Maximilian should act jointly[272] for the sake of their grandchildren, but he acted through Margaret "who is the person who has the greatest influence with her father."[273] Ferdinand was against the betrothal of Isabel and the Duke of Gelderland and leaned toward an already proposed marriage between Isabel and the King of Navarre. Margaret herself was unenthusiastic about the match as being more practical than honorable. She wrote to Henry VIII a most glowing letter,[274] as he too disapproved, saying she hoped for cordial relations between them for the sake of his sister Mary and Charles whose betrothal was being arranged. She also hoped that he might provide

---

271   Ibid., p. 195.
272   L. Ph. C. van den Bergh, Vol. I, p. 222.
273   Bergenroth, Vol. II, p. 27.
274   L. Ph.C. van den Bergh, Vol. I, pp. 247-250.

some help for her against Gelderland. To Van den Bergh, all this pointed to duplicity on the part of Margaret. He commented:

> This letter which has neither date nor address, shows intrigues of House of Austria and clearly proves the bad faith in negotiations with Duke of Gelderland. One sees here that it was she and not he, as she pretended in her official letters, who wanted the war continued until Gelderland was reduced to submission to the emperor. It is by this letter which contrasts so strongly with her public declarations which she drew up herself so that her true intentions would not be known to her subjects. The rest of the letter is also a masterpiece of deception because it was certainly she who had urged the emperor to consent to this alliance, but it was with the intention of breaking it when either his or her affairs took a less menacing aspect. It was for this that she flattered so adroitly the king and his council in order to obtain aid against the Gelderlanders and to make this monarch consent to an alliance between his sister Mary and the young Charles of Austria. The king sent her this year auxiliary troops under the command of Edward Poynings who nevertheless were of no use and returned soon afterwards to England, and he consented to a projected marriage of his sister, but in 1514, he changed his mind and married her to the King of France.[275]

Actually, in the correspondence, we do not have her public declarations, but her letters with her father, their secretaries and emissaries and these give no evidence of double dealing, but rather exasperation with the long-drawn-out affair. The delaying action does not hold water either, as it would have been easier to overcome the Duke while France was occupied in Italy. Furthermore, the marriage between Charles and Mary was not postponed by England which was eager for it and most especially by Catherine of Aragon, Henry's wife and Margaret's sister-in-law, but by Maximilian who hoped to gain either more money or a better marriage somewhere else.

---
275 Van den Bergh, Correspondance ... Vol. I, pp. 247-248. footnote.

Lastly, Edward Poynings' troops were not geared to guerilla warfare, did not know the land, and were sent only for a small term of time. If they were less than successful, it would be due to these reasons. What could be concluded from all this is that the old dynastic traditions could no longer contain or overcome irresistible national feelings and the growth of popular movements, which can be observed in the years to come in their political and religious aspects.

During this year the relationship between Margaret and Maximilian became so strained, that, in a loving attempt to make up, he sent her a precious red stone referred to as a "carbuncle" which her grandfather Frederick had owned, knowing it would please her, and "to make peace between us."[276] On September 9 he wrote, "... concerning the negotiations, you have done well... and now we wish you to conclude the treaty."[277]

At the end of the year the Duke's ambassadors left her court with no peace treaty as Charles of Egmond refused to humiliate himself by swearing allegiance to the Empire. On December 23, 1510 from Malines, Margaret wrote in a panic to her father for aid in fortifying the border against the almost sure raids to come, as there was little assistance to be expected from the States in this regard. She blamed the rupture of the negotiations on Charles's deputies who contended and persisted in changing certain articles of the treaty. This letter has that breathless quality associated with Margaret's moments of stress which is in such contrast to the steadiness of most of her correspondence - fear and despair overwhelmed her:

> ...And in regard to me, my Lord, you know I am a woman and that it is not my place to meddle in war, seeing that there is little assistance from the subjects on this side as in similar cases I have well experienced.
>
> I beseech you, my Lord, to have good advice over all this and to so provide that the lands of this young prince may not be pillaged

---

276 Le Glay, Vol. I, p. 293.
277 Van den Bergh, Vol. I, p. 220.

and destroyed during his minority; for it would be a shame to you and to me a marvelous regret… [278]

Sometimes it has to be conceded that Margaret evoked her nephew Charles's name in order to strengthen her appeal for help and enlist sympathy for her cause; nevertheless, her love for this nephew was boundless and her concern for his future was always uppermost in her mind. When she heard that Ferdinand of Aragon was going to bestow some honors on little Ferdinand who, of course, was his favorite, she wrote to that Spanish grandfather pointing out that those were to be set aside for Charles himself.[279]

Maximilian wrote her in agreement and encouraged her to conclude the treaty with England. At the same time he was persuading Henry to oppose Ferdinand's schemes for Naples, as Maximilian had heard that the King of Aragon wished to place his grandson Ferdinand on the throne there and thus drive Maximilian out of Italy. To aid this effort, Margaret was to give the English ambassador a fine gift.[280] She was also to ask for two thousand archers and the pardon of the Duke of Suffolk. And lastly a favor, "… to give to our fair nephew, the Duke of Wertemberg, two beautiful female dogs and one male."[281] Hunting was one of Maximilian's many delights and he took a childlike pleasure in everything connected with it: the riding, the birds, the beautiful country, his appreciation reads like a rhapsody.[282] He once pointed out to Charles that "the chase gives an opportunity for a prince to be approached by the common man, who can thus bring his complaints in person."[283] As rulers then were not bothered in justifying their diversions, this is a revealing comment. "Charles shot skillfully with the bow and, at ten, took a real pleasure in the chase - a

---

278   Ibid., p. 224.
279   Le Glay, Vol. I, p. 271.
280   Ibid., p. 353.
281   Ibid., p. 355.
282   Ibid., p. 284.
283   Hare, p. 162.

feature which delighted the old Emperor;"[284] for otherwise, "he would be taken for a bastard."[285]

From Freiburg, the last of December in 1510,[286] Maximilian wrote to tell Margaret of the illness and excess of fever of his wife and her stepmother, Bianca Maria Sforza, and asked that there be a consultation of two or three doctors at Louvain to see if there be a remedy for her malady. Though the letter is a model of polite and concerned affection, this is the first time she is mentioned in the correspondence. A woman of little consequence in the affairs of the day or even with her husband and family, it sad nevertheless to consider the life of one so effaceable. Given over for the sake of money and policy, she lived out her young life at the palace at Innsbruck. A year later on January 3, 1512, Maximilian sent the message "with sorrowful grief of heart...his very dear companion" had died on the last day of December, and asked that prayers be said. He directed mourning to be worn by the grandchildren and the "knights of our order" (the Golden Fleece) and some of the principal counselors, and that solemn funeral rites be held "as are customary for such a Princess."[287] And so, unloved, she was correctly, but not warmly, mourned and buried in the ancient church of the Franciscans where her image in bronze is preserved today.

Within this year of 1511, Maximilian was burdened with many matters and Margaret came by some information which she lovingly but diffidently passed on to him, saying in a cover letter in her own handwriting: "I believe, my Lord, that you will find more truths than you wish for and many other things of which perhaps you presently have knowledge."[288]

---

284 Edward Armstrong, The Emperor Charles V (London: MacMillan and Company, Ltd. 1929/1901), Vol. I. p. 9.
285 André J.G. Le Glay, Maximilien I, Empereur d'Allemagne, et Marguerite d'Autriche, sa fille, Gouvernante des Pays-Bas (Paris: Jules Renouard et Cie., 1839), p. 55.
286 Le Glay, Vol. I, p. 367.
287 Le Glay, Vol. I, p. 367.
288 Ibid., p. 386 (March 14, 1511)

Her own hands were full. The state of Utrecht complained that her general Floris of Egmond had attacked the city and done much damage, but they had been "saved" by troops from Gelderland.[289] Margaret replied in Dutch that restitution would be made... "and him [Floris] also I will inform." She wrote to Floris the same day:

> "to cease and repair the said exploits and punish the leaders ... these enterprises are of very dangerous consequence ... it is not permissible for any vassal to conduct such enterprises without the knowledge and express commandment of your sovereign as great evil and inconvenience are bound to ensue."[290]

Floris wrote to Margaret no less than eighteen times in this year about events, conditions, but mostly about the need for money and clothing for his foot soldiers. He warned that they would leave her service and go over to Gelderland. It was difficult to determine which side Utrecht was on, and hard to reconcile Louis's pious and affectionate letters to Margaret with the way he undermined her house by financing Charles of Gelderland. Antoine de Lalaing, one of Margaret's most trusted and beloved nobles, informed her that word had come to him that the Duke of Gelderland had again received money from France.[291] A letter was intercepted in which a "Breton from Liégé" wrote to the Bastard of Gelderland. Margaret had this deciphered by her secretary Marnix and sent on to her father.[292]

Louis wrote to Maximilian that he was displeased to hear about the actions of the Duke of Gelderland and resolved to send a man to put a stop to "these deeds which go against the treaty of Cambrai."[293]

Margaret was so angry at this duplicity she complained to the British ambassador. In due time, she received this letter from Louis:

---

289 Van den Bergh, Vol. I, pp. 231-235.
290 Van den Bergh, Vol. I, pp. 237-238.
291 Ibid., Vol. I, pp. 327-328.
292 Ibid., Vol. I, pp. 342-345.
293 Ibid., Vol. I, p. 250.

It has been reported to me that bad words concerning me and attributed to you have been carried to England ... and I have said to my gentlemen that I know you would not be able to speak such bad and disagreeable words because you are so good, so wise and so virtuous, and that it is nothing but fantasy ... I wish to live with the emperor my brother, and you, in good and cordial fraternity, friendship and alliance.[294]

In spite of his protestations and reminders of their childhood play, Margaret never trusted him. As for Floris of Egmond, she became increasingly aggravated as she suspected him of provoking much of the trouble. From Duisburg, now part of Germany, Charles sent this most polite letter:

... Madame, my subjects are always pillaged and devoured, it is repetition to write you so often, but I do it for the pity which I have of my subjects and also to acquit my conscience. Madame, command me your good pleasure for I will obey as much as possible by the grace of God, to whom I pray, Madame, that he will give you a good and long life ... Your very humble and very obedient servant and cousin, Charles.[295]

Margaret responded in the same spirit that she would do her best for a happy conclusion to all their troubles.

However, when Charles of Egmond's troops attacked Harderwijk, Margaret's courier Hesdin told her that the Duke professed astonishment when he brought up the matter. Charles was also meddling in Amsterdam and making trouble for the Bishop of Utrecht, a cousin of Maximilian who was personally loyal to Margaret in spite of the way some of the people in his city varied.[296] The ubiquitous soldiers of Charles attacked a

---

294 Ibid., Vol. I, pp. 324-325.
295 Van den Bergh, Vol. I, pp. 238-239.
296 Ibid., Vol. I, p. 338.

company of twenty-four merchants from Ghent on their way to Frankfurt. Some were killed, the rest taken prisoner. Ghent had repeatedly through the years refused to give help or money to contain the Duke and now they joined with the other cities of Flanders and Brabant to bring enough pressure to force him back within his own borders. He replied to Louis's letter that he must beg the King to excuse him and hoped that the help he had received would not be withdrawn. When Margaret confronted Louis with a letter in which his aid to Charles was revealed, Louis replied that whoever had written it had lied.[297] Margaret went north to inspect the troops, and with renewed vigor, her army retaliated at last, and captured four hundred outside Tiel and killed or drowned four hundred more.

These hostilities, like the Venetian war, went on interminably. Few of the leaders acted in good faith, only Margaret's strong sense of duty kept her going. She also had a keen sense of justice which caused her to report those who were not living up to their rank such as the magistrate at Brussels who abused his privileges, "and to let him continue would lead to evil consequences."[298] However, Maximilian's desperate and perpetual need for money affected his decisions and often blunted or deflected his daughter's intent, as he excused one after another in return for heavy gratuities. She needed his political and emotional support, and he often failed her. During this year certain vacancies occurred in Charles's household and with the consent of the privy council, she filled them with men who had served her well in the North.[299] This angered Maximilian as he felt that she had encroached on his prerogatives without even consulting him. Though he

---

297 Margaret had sent Maximilian de Hornes, Adrian of Utrecht, the Herald of the Order of the Golden Fleece, and Jacques de Voecht to negotiate. Van den Bergh. Vol. I. p. 315.

298 André J.G. Le Glay, Correspondance de l'Empereur Maximilien I et de Marguerite d'Autriche (Paris, 1839), Vol. I. p. 380. From Malines, January 1511. See Vol. II, p. 106, March 25, 1513, in which Maximilian asks her to "moderate sentences of Jehan de Gilly, Nicolas Marceret and Paris de Vaulx in honor of Good Friday for their part in the matter of the salt at the Saunerie of Salins, and remit to them a gracious sum." And Vol. II, p. 351. August 22, 1517, in which Maximilian asks grace and remission for Chevalier de Loze accused of various crimes.

299 Ibid., Vol. I, p. 498.

often reproached her for her "malgracious" letters, this is his most wrathful in the Correspondance.[300]

Maximilian followed up by appointing men of his own choosing. It was left to Margaret to make apologies and find other places. But mercurial as ever, in another letter he was very agreeable and content when she promoted Floris of Egmond, Lord of Ijsselstein, to lieutenant and co-adjutor governor of Holland.[301]

Margaret's temperament served her well in mediation. Twice during the year of 1511, Margaret had to settle differences. The first was between Henry of Nassau and the Duke of Savoy, her young brother-in-law, and Henry wrote on August 18 to accept her accord of the disagreement and to thank her for the trouble she had undergone.[302] In October Maximilian wrote concerning the conflicting opinions between the Lords of Berghes and Chièvres over the renewal of the laws of Antwerp which had caused a division in the city itself "to our great disadvantage, regret and displeasure." "We ask that you find a way," he wrote, "to reconcile these lords."[303] The result of this was that Chièvres resigned his post as commissioner of Antwerp in favor of Henry of Nassau. There was also discord between Jean le Sauvage and Gerard de Pleine, Lord of La Roche, which counselors from Ghent were trying to resolve. As she told her father, "for the affairs on this side, their differences are not of small importance."[304]

In spite of these grave state affairs, her concern for the children she was rearing never wavered. One of these was the young Claude of Savoy. She requested of Maximilian to attend "to the legitimation of my sister, the 'bastarde' of Savoy about which I have written to Jacques de Bannissiis, your solicitor, as I wish to contract a marriage between

---

300   Ibid., Vol. II, pp. 204-207: "I do not know where you get this bad opinion against me: I believe that you treat me like a Frenchman ... and my little one ... we are tossing your 'disreasonable' letters into the fire; in the future, write me more graciously as I am accustomed to being treated."

301   Van den Bergh, Vol. I, pp. 350-351.

302   Ibid., Vol. I, p. 327. Shortly after this, Henry of Nassau's wife died and he thanked her also for her letter of condolence. p. 341.

303   André J.G. Le Glay, Correspondance ... Vol. I, p. 436.

304   Le Glay, Vol. I, p. 402.

her and the Lord of Epinoi, and if you could please write a good letter to the lady, his mother, in Luxembourg, the affair will be redressed."[305] Margaret never forgot the kindness of those who cared for the children either. There was one "Philippote de la Perrière who with many of her family has served the nieces and their house so well ... she is now going to be married. I ask you to declare to my cousin, the Lord of Chièvres, to make preferment to her future husband."[306] Chièvres had never been willing to do anything Margaret asked, and directions had to come from Maximilian before he acted. Pirenne says he had "sulked" ever since Margaret came.[307]

Margaret managed to juggle all these affairs great and small with aplomb, but the placards against her appearing everywhere on church doors and public places did raise fear in her heart, and she considered them treasonous. Floris of Egmond, in a letter to her dated June 18, 1511, reassured her that the men of the council of Holland had decided to proceed without any delay against those responsible for the placards, but, he continued, "you can see the bad will of Amsterdam where they continue as before..."[308]

The troubles in Italy continued and Margaret wrote Maximilian on July 22, 1511 from. Antwerp to counsel a secret alliance with the Kings of Aragon and England.[309] She had worries enough of her own and less wherewithal and cooperation to deal with them. Her next letter is undated and Le Glay has placed it with the July correspondence from Antwerp,[310]

---

305 Ibid., Vol. I, p. 396. Claude was born in 1495, married Jacques III, Count of Hornes, Knight of the Golden Fleece, in 1514, and died in 1528. The Count was married first to Marguerite de Croy, a special friend of the Archduchess. His third wife was Anne of Burgundy. None of his wives had children. The Count died August 7, 1531.

306 Le Glay, Vol. I, p. 377.

307 Henri Pirenne, Histoire de Belgique (Bruxelles: Henri Lamertin, Libraire-Éditeur, 1907), Vol. III, p. 77.

308 Van den Bergh, Vol. I, pp. 302-303.

309 Le Glay, Vol. I, p. 410.

310 Ibid., Vol. I, p. 423.

but Bruchet places it around August 1 at 's-Hertegenbosch.[311] It reads in part:

> ... My Lord, I am readying myself ... in order to march before our army. The army makes a very good sight, together with the artillery, and be assured that the captains and conductors have deliberated well to make a good campaign ... and seeing that it is necessary for me to come here, I have made arrangements for my nephew and nieces to be conducted to Malines where they shall stay until my return ... I have ordained governors and a guard ... and I tell you this to reassure you.

Margaret spent four months in the northern provinces, going first to Bergen-op-Zoom on July 24, to Breda on July 30, then 's-Hertegenbosch where she remained for some time. On November 18 she traveled to Breda, on the 27th to Hoogstraten, returning to Lier in the southern provinces on November 28, and finally home to Malines on November 30. The trip was not a success. During this time the continuing war with Gelderland enlarged and her army besieged Venlo. Henry VIII sent troops under the command of Edward Poynings for three months which he continued for one extra month. Margaret entreated Maximilian to send money, or the war would be lost for 500 florins. Of her own money she had spent 10,000 francs, and expected to use her money from Spain to pay the men-at-arms.[312] Maximilian made some suggestions about drawing back and building fortifications, but the English commander Poynings and her own general Floris of Egmond were not of this opinion and decided to continue until the end of November[313] the siege which had begun August 28. Charles of Egmond had time on his side, but the English army was there for only a limited period, and winter was approaching. Furthermore, he was not confined to one area and was

---

311 Max Bruchet and E. Lancien, L'Itinéraire de Marguerite d'Autriche (Lille: Imprimerie 1. Danel, 1934).
312 Van den Bergh, Vol. I, p. 349.
313 Ibid., pp. 352-358.

free to roam. In several letters Margaret conveyed these feelings to her father:

> My Lord, it displeases me that I am continually constrained to send you sad and unfortunate news ... I came again in hope to the blockhouse and gave the necessary orders to recover our honor if that were to be possible ... these affairs render me so perplexed that I plainly do not know what to do ... I am here with the States of Brabant ...where I will employ all my power to protect the frontiers, but as you understand through Loys Maraton ...I see all the country in great trouble...[314]
>
> The English acquit themselves very well; and with more artillery, and the reinforcement of men, and with the aid of God in our good and just quarrel, I have hope of a good outcome ... [315]
>
> ...which I desire most in this world to reduce to your obedience the country and subjects of Gelderland caused by the disloyalty of Charles of Egmond ... [316]

Unfortunately, Margaret's forces were defeated, for Charles of Egmond had a loyal following, and he knew this territory like the back of his hand. Maximilian, who came out of the same generation and who considered war his vocation, observed mildly to Margaret "... these are the fortunes of war which we must take as God gives them to us; and it was our advice that our said people would profit nothing before the said Venlo; for we know a little something in these affairs."[317] However, he softened the blow by saying that she had fought "with the courage of a man and not that of a woman."[318]

---

314 Van den Bergh, Vol. I, pp. 342-345.
315 Ibid., Vol. I, pp. 346-348.
316 Ibid., Vol. I, pp. 348-358.
317 Ibid., Vol. I, p. 364.
318 Ghislaine de Boom, Marguerite d'Autriche-Savoie et la Pré-Renaissance (Bruxelles: La Renaissance du Livre, 1946), p. 53.

111

There may have been double dealing here, for the Chronicler of Calais relates this story:

> [The Lord Poynings] continued with his company til after all-halloween tide, and there they were almost betrayed by the Lord Admiral of all the coast, for he went oft into the town of Venlo, and had promised the captain to deceive them all, but the King of England sent for them to come home into England; and then lady Margaret, Duchess of Savoy, aunt to the young Duke of Burgundy, gave to all Englishmen coats of white and green, red and yellow; the white and green for the King of England's livery, the red and yellow for the Duke of Burgundy's livery, and these four colors were melded together ... [319]

It cannot be determined from the text who the Lord Admiral was, but judging from other sources, it may have been Philip of Burgundy. Whether the Archduchess was aware of the deception is not recorded either, but whether or no, she apparently decided to wind up the affair in a fashion guaranteed to keep England's friendship and to show her appreciation for their help.

Now France, not content with its victories on every front, proposed in 1511 a General Council, ostensibly for ecclesiastical reform, but in reality to revenge itself on Pope Julius II. Maximilian fell in with this scheme and directed Margaret to send deputies to Pisa.[320] She, however, had forbidden the clergy of the Low Countries to attend. A realist and a nationalist, she feared the interference of the French church and felt the exchanges and conferences "under the color of religion" were a shield to spies in the service of the French king. So she replied to her father: "My lord, under your great correction, it seems to me you ought not to mix yourself up with this Council which is to be held at Pisa. Leave it to the Pope, to whom the cognizance of such things belongs."

---

319 John Gough Nichols, ed., The Chronicle of Calais ... p. 8. Spelling modernized by SHB.
320 Le Glay, Correspondance ... Vol. I, p. 407.

Touching the sending of deputies to Pisa, of which you have written to me, it seems to me, that as you are the governor of my Lord and nephew, and my Lord and father, it will be sufficient if you send envoys for us both; furthermore, my Lord, to tell the truth, the finances on this side are so short that we will not be able to send one penny for this purpose.[321]

Brewer observed about the two on an earlier difference of opinion of which they had many: "With the tact of a women, Margaret saw through this artifice; but the simple-minded Emperor, in the conceit of his own sagacity, outwitted his daughter to his own disadvantage."[322] The result was that Ferdinand and Julius reproached him for his heresy and Henry "read Maximilian a grave lecture on the sinfulness of setting at defiance the authority of his Holy Father."[323]

Julius, perhaps through anxiety over affairs in Italy was frequently at death's door, and it was about this time that Maximilian began to communicate to others his wish to become pope and thus unite the sacred and the temporal in one person. (It was not so fantastic an idea at the time as it seems to us now. In the middle of the fifteenth century, the reigning Count of Savoy became the reform Pope Felix V and rival to Eugenius IV.) He confided his thoughts to Margaret and excerpts from that letter follow:

Very dear and much loved daughter… we send tomorrow the Lord of Gurk, Bishop to Rome to the Pope to find some way to accord with him to take us as coadjutor, in order that after his death we may be assured of having the papacy and become a priest and after my death, you will be constrained to adore me, of which I shall be very proud.

I send concerning this a post to the King of Aragon in order to ask him to aid us to achieve this which he is as well content, on

---

321 Van den Bergh, Vol. I, p. 357.
322 J.S. Brewer, The Reign of Henry VIII … (London: John Murray, 1884), p. 14.
323 Ibid., p. 17.

condition that I resign the Empire to our common son, Charles. With that as well I am content...

I begin as well to work on the cardinals among whom two or three hundred thousand ducats will give me great service, with the partiality which is already with us.

The king of Aragon told his ambassador that he wishes to command the Spanish cardinals that they favor the papacy for us.

I pray you, keep this matter a complete secret; although in a few days I believe that all the world will know it; for it is not possible to work such a grand matter secretly in which so many people and money are involved ... Written by the hand of your good father Maximilianus, future pope.

P.S. The pope again has a double fever and cannot live long.[324]

Maximilian entered into negotiations with the Fuggers to pawn the treasure of the Empire in order to obtain the money required to assure his election. Julius II, however, recovered and Maximilian abandoned the idea of becoming pope without a backward thought. Pope Julius II, was thus able to get back to his battles. Forces were realigned and the wars continued in Italy. But for Margaret, it meant that while the French were occupied in the South, they were less provocative and meddlesome in the North. However, when Margaret's friend at the French court, the Cardinal of Amboise, who had been a restraining hand in French plots died at Lyons on May 26, 1510, harassment by the Duke of Gelderland with support by Louis XII increased.

By the end of November 1511, Maximilian had concluded that he should return to the northern provinces to command in person. To Margaret, he commented, "As you ordered, you always have the block house at Wageningen (NW of Nijmegen) secured which gives access

---

[324] Christopher Hare, The High and Puissant Princess Marguerite of Austria (London: Harper and Brothers, 1907) Printed in Lettres du Roy Louis XII, Vol. IV, pp. 2-3, September 18, 1512.)

through Nijmegen and the rivers to Cologne by which we can travel to Holland without danger."[325]

Events in 1512 proceeded as before but in a less planned and more desultory fashion. The campaign in the North was on the defensive with little money, resisting here and reacting there, to the Duke's forays. There was backbiting in the court circles as calumnies were spread about Floris of Egmond and Henri of Nassau. Floris protested to Margaret, "I believe that you know me well… I will always be your good and loyal servant."[326] And he was, but with an arrogance that was sometimes hard to take. After the army of Brabant suffered severe losses of 800 soldiers and 500 city and countrymen, Maximilian asked Margaret to send a captain who was familiar with the military operations, and consented to give a safe conduct to deputies of the Duke to negotiate a peace. He also asked her to compose a letter in Latin requesting the Pope to excommunicate Charles of Egmond.[327] After Maximilian threatened the King of France, he agreed to neither help nor hinder the Duke in his wars. André de Burgo, Maximilian's ambassador at the French court at Blois expressed the belief that Louis was sincere in his promise.[328]

In April Margaret wrote to her father, "I try always to conform to your desire and to obey you to the best of my power," but in this affair of Gelderland he did not understand the situation. She continues:

> … Considering the ill will of the people, the murmurings against me saying that I do not demand that the war be ended… and many more evil words that incite the people, and what is worse, Good Friday night they advanced secretly to place some placards on the doors of the church in this city [Malines] … these are all harmful things which your coming will remedy… I do not know where to turn or what more to do, seeing the little assistance that I have

---

325 Van den Bergh, Vol. I, pp. 363-365.
326 Van den Bergh, Vol. II, pp. 9-11.
327 Le Glay, Vol. I, p. 494.
328 Ibid., Vol. II, pp. 27-29.

and the poverty of the finances. And if all is lost for a thousand florins, the treasurer has less to consider. By this, my Lord, you can comprehend the extremity of the said affairs...[329]

Margaret did not take as adamant a stand as her father did. She formulated some articles for negotiation which were forwarded to the Duke. The mediator was Philip of Cleves, Lord of Ravenstein, to whom the Duke wrote from Harderwijk on April 16:

Concerning the several letters written by the very high and powerful princess our very dear cousin Madame Margaret Archduchess of Austria, Dowager of Savoy, Regent and Governor, etc... that deputies of the two parties would meet on the eighth of this month in the city of Vianne... to discuss the proposed articles... it seems strange and against our divine rights and nature to govern my lands as Lieutenant and Governor as we are sole and true heir of the said lands. To abandon and renounce our true and just title is a thing not to be well considered.[330]

In fact he did not think the articles reasonable nor honorable, nor leading to a good and durable peace. He signed the letter with his full title, "Charles, Duke of Gelderland and of Juliers and Count of Zutphen."

Charles of Egmond's letters were always models of politeness, reasonably worded, and as historians before have said, "breathe an air of sincerity and candor which carries through to the present."[331] Why is it then, when Margaret was also reasonable, that they were never able to reach a compromise? There were several factors, but perhaps one outstanding feature; and that is that Charles saw the matter only in black and white. The reason his letters have the ring of sincerity is not that he was always

---

329   Ibid., Vol. II, pp. 31-34.
330   Van den Bergh, Vol. II, pp. 34-37.
331   Van den Bergh, Vol. I, p. 3 citing M. Godefroy and Le Glay.

right, but that he believed he was. Often wrong, frequently cruel,[332] he was never in doubt, never troubled by second thoughts. One might also add that the idea of compromise was an anathema to those holding the knightly code. Justice did not come in gray. When two knights could not agree, it was settled in single combat or on the battlefield - whoever won was right. God made the decision.

This year of 1512 was certainly one of the low points in Margaret's life, for the States refused to cooperate or contribute even when they were being devastated, and the nobles argued among themselves. Maximilian's plans to command the forces in the Low Countries never materialized as his funds were so low due to the long war in Italy.[333] He did make one short trip in June which was really a social and family affair. On June 20, he sent the invitation that "his very dear and loved children come to Brussels to see the park and spend a few days with him."[334] On June 23 Maximilian wrote to Margaret desiring that she and the children come for "souper" suggesting that after midday they could talk for five hours.[335] Once again they found themselves at cross purposes and in a letter of June 29, Maximilian proposed that his solicitor Jacques de Banissiis settle the differences between them.[336] From the letters extant, it would seem that Maximilian was always the one to make peace. He was an affectionate man, perhaps he felt guilty at leaving her in such trouble with so little aid from him. He did send her help in the form of the Duke of Brunswick, well respected by many nations for his ability in the field, but she had regretfully to tell her father that the very able Lord had not been well received 'because the said lands are so obstinant and foul-mouthed in this affair of Gelderland."[337] Her nobles felt Floris of Egmond was more than

---

332 After setting fire to the faubourg of Amsterdam and more than three hundred boats, they engaged in battle on Christmas day with the Lord of Wassenaer, defeated the army, took him prisoner. By order of the Duke, he was placed in an iron cage. He was finally released in 1514. Van den Bergh, Vol. II, p. 61.
333 Van den Bergh, Vol. II, pp. 65-59.
334 Le Glay, Vol. II, p. 13.
335 Ibid., Vol. II, p. 14.
336 Ibid., Vol. II, p. 16.
337 Van den Bergh, Vol. II, pp. 58-59.

sufficient to lead them. Before any more mischief could be done, Margaret was able to persuade her father that his choice of Simon Longin to conduct the finances of Gelderland was not appropriate as

> ...he does not speak thiois[338] which will be required, his age of 60 [is too advanced], and also he doesn't see well and according to my doctor he has an internal malady which prevents hard work and horseback riding.[339]

Instead, she recommended Charles Leclerc.

The situation was bad in the north and the south, and Margaret urged her father to conclude several treaties. Two were drawn to a conclusion at the end of 1512 by the Bishop of Gurk (Gorinchem) at Rome, one between Maximilian and Pope Julius II, and the other between them but including Ferdinand, Henry and the Duke of Milan. Ferdinand censured both treaties according to Le Glay[340] though it is impossible to figure out why. It was his desire that "during his and the Emperor's lifetime, Burgundy and the towns in Picardy, of which France has deprived Prince Charles, should be reconquered," and these treaties were a calculated step in that direction. Nevertheless, Margaret had been working on treaty with England which had been delayed by Maximilian's dilatory ways.[341] She repeatedly wrote:

> To conclude this league between you and England I must have word from you regarding certain points and articles. Let me know as soon as you can; otherwise, if you fail to respond, I can no longer keep the English ambassador here.[342]

---

338 Le Glay, Vol. II, p. 111, Note: Thiois, theotiscus. This word does not apply only to the German language according to Cange, but also to Nederlands spoken in Holland and within a part of Belgium.

339 Le Glay, Vol. II, p. 111.

340 Bergenroth, Vol. II, p. 79.

341 Sometimes in decision making, the Emperor appeared to be immobilized. In the matter of Burgundy, Margaret granted neutrality to the province during a French-Swiss conflict and asked again and again for his confirmation. It was finally forthcoming.

342 Le Glay, Vol. II, p. 64.

...it is time to move in this business as they have been waiting 8 months.[343]

Maximilian replied, "...it seems to me that you are too hasty to make response."[344] He was astonished at the complaints of the English ambassadors. "Henry VIII says well what he wishes of the Emperor, but what does the Emperor receive from all this?"[345] What the Emperor was receiving, of course was a great deal of money. His need was so well known that ambassadors of the time joked about it. Trivulzio commented: "he could dry up a sea of gold."[346]

On the 5th of April, 1513, the Archduchess concluded a treaty between Maximilian and England, but Pope Leo refused to ratify it since it called for the use of papal forces in Province and Dauphine in the southeast of France. The English king was suspected of being somewhat less than eager, and Ferdinand was undercutting the agreement of making his own alliance with France. What makes these dealings so complicated and unfathomable is that they are the products of devious minds which do not readily yield motives five hundred years later. Juana was as good as incarcerated at the palace of Tordesillas so it really did not matter whether her illness was real or ascribed. Ferdinand was regent of Castile in her place until Charles came of age. In the meantime his son-in-law Henry VIII was murmuring that his wife Catherine was heir to Castile. The betrothal of Henry and Catherine's daughter Mary to Charles was a formidable threat to Ferdinand. Furthermore, though he and Maximilian seemed natural allies by virtue of their common grandchildren, Ferdinand looked on Maximilian's power with dread, and viewed any successes of Maximilian in Italy with apprehension.

---

343 Ibid., Vol. II, p. 78.
344 Ibid., Vol. II, p. 82.
345 Ibid., p. 83.
346 Glenn Elwood Waas, The Legendary Character of Kaiser Maximilian New York: AMS Press, Inc., 1966 (1941 Columbia University Press), p. 65.

Even the treaties were a form of combat, and this alliance led to the battle of Guinegate where Maximilian served in the English army at a hundred crowns a day.[347]

Maximilian asked Margaret to join him. In Lille at the time (September 22) she primly replied:

> My Lord, I have received the message that you have been pleased to send me by Marnix, my secretary, about my going to Tournay. As for me, my Lord, if you think that my going there is necessary, and can be of service to you, I am ready in this and in all else that it may please you to command me; but otherwise, it is not fitting for a widow to be trotting about and visiting armies for pleasure ... [348]

Since widowhood did not prevent Margaret from "trotting" everywhere else, we cannot help wondering why she responded so irritably. As the contract for the wedding between Charles and Mary was being drawn up, she may have felt more useful in Lille; and the strain of trying to accomplish this while fearful of her father's capriciousness and wary of her own Council's disapproval, probably manifested itself in this testy reply. At any rate, duty overcame reluctance. She went to Tournai to meet her father and Henry. Later, after the victory at Guinegate, in an outflow of emotion, she gushed, "I am so very joyful that it is not possible to say more."[349]

The plans for this battle had been drawn up in the spring and conveyed to Margaret with the serene assurance she would understand and pass on the directions. King Henry was providing the funds, and Margaret was the one who had to insure the supplies, but Maximilian in sublime egotism wrote to Margaret that though he was serving under the banner

---

347 "The x. of August Maximilian emperowr of Almayne came to kynge Henry of England besyde Teryn (Thérouanne), and there the emperowre had wages of the kynge." Richard Turpyn, The Chronicle of Calais, ed. by John Gough Nichols (London: The Camden Society, M. DCCC. IX. VI), p. 14.
348 Le Glay, Vol. II, p. 203.
349 Le Glay, Vol. II, p. 211.

of England, he was actually at the head of the whole campaign because of his experience. When Maximilian arrived on August 10, he appeared suddenly on foot among Henry's German mercenaries and spoke to them in their language. He was recognized with joy which transmitted itself to the other regiments. This great knight, this character of epic proportions, had charisma. On that trait of' the Emperor there seems to be no dispute.

Though the battles were absorbing and costly in men and materiel, it sometimes seems as though they were conducted as a part-time activity. They provided time for state visits, ceremonies, treaty arrangements, jousts and tourneys, and banquets. Marriages were arranged and love affairs carried on. Henry had three marriages in mind: Mary and Charles, the first part of this ceremony had already taken place in England in 1508; the Archduchess Margaret and Charles Brandon, the Viscount Lisle; and Maximilian with his sister Margaret, recently widowed by the death of James IV of Scotland at the battle of Flodden. "Henry reasoned that the thrice-pledged Emperor would find it difficult to desert him even if he desired to do so."[350] So it might be said that Henry set the stage for what followed. From the Chronicle of Calais comes the following account of these intriguing pursuits:

> Monday, the 11th day of October, the King received the Prince of Castile, the Lady Margaret, and diverse other nobles of their countries, outside the town, and brought them into Tournai with great triumph. The noise went that the Lord Lisle made request of marriage to the Lady Margaret, Duchess of Savoy, and daughter to the emperor Maximilian, who had departed before that time with many rich gifts and money borrowed from the King; but, whether he proffered marriage or not, she favored him highly. There the Prince and Duchess sojourned with great solace for the space of 10 days. During which time, the 18th day of October, began the jousts; the King and the Lord Lisle answered all comers; upon the King attended 24 knights on foot, in coats of purple velvet and cloth

---

350 Walter C. Richardson, Mary Tudor: The White Queen (London: Peter Owen, 1970), p. 71.

of gold. A tent of cloth of gold was set in the place for the contests; the King had a suit and armor of purple velvet set full of sterling silver of fine bullion, and the Lord Lisle the same. There were many spears broken, and many a good buffet given; the strangers, as the Lord Walon and Lord Emery, and others, did right well. When the jousts were done, the King and all the others unhelmed themselves, and rode about the tilt and did great reverence to the ladies, and then the heralds cryed, To lodging.

This night the King made a sumptuous banquet of a hundred dishes to the Prince of Castile and the Lady Margaret, and to all other lords and ladies, and after the banquet the ladies danced; and then came in the King with eleven in a mask, all richly appareled with bonnets of gold, and when they had passed the time at their pleasure, the garments of the mask were cast off amongst the ladies, take who could take.

The 20th day of October the Prince of Castile and the Lady Margaret, with many great gifts to them given, returned to Lille with all their train.[351]

[In the month of May following when at home in England] the King and the new Duke of Suffolk [Lord Lisle elevated February 1. 1514] were defenders at the tilt against all comers [attired as white and black hermits. On their black staves was written with white lettering, "Who can hold that will away:" This motto was judged to be made for the Duke of Suffolk and the Duchess of Savoy.

The gossips on both sides of the Channel had a field day. King Ferdinand wrote to his ambassador in England, Luis Caroz de Villaragut, asking if it were true that Madame Margaret was to marry Lord Lisle.[352]

---

351 John Gough Nichols, ed. Richard Turpyn's The Chronicle of Calais. (London: The Camden Society by J.B. Nichols and Son, 1840), Vol. XXXV, pp. 69-70. The Prince of Castile is Margaret's nephew Charles, one of his many titles. SHB rendered Hall's account into modern spelling and changed a few French terms into English, but otherwise kept the flavor of the old passage.
352 Tremayne, p. 129 from Calendar of Spanish State Papers. Vol. II.

Even Erasmus commented in a letter to William Gonnell, "rumor is that Margaret, daughter of Maximilian will marry the Duke..."[353]

Deeply embarrassed by these stories, and taken to task by her Council, Margaret tried to find the source in order to put an end to their circulation. As a good client should, Margaret confessed all (or almost all) to her advocate Sir Richard Wingfield. All that exists today are the copies in which he translated her French into English, or that we must assume, as they are in his handwriting.

(Sheet marked A.)

My Lord the ambassador--
Since I see that I may not have tidings from the emperor soon, it seems to me that I should do well to tarry no longer to dispatch this gentleman. As for my letters to the king and the duke, I dare not venture to write on to them so at length of this because I fear my letters to be evil kept, I determine to write to you at length to the end that of all you may the better advertise to them of my intent.

You may know, my lord the ambassador, that after some days having been at Tournai, knowing from day to day the great love and trust that the king bore and had to the personage [Brandon] which is no need to name; also with the virtue and grace of his person, the which seemed to me that I have not much seen gentleman to approach it; also considering the desire the which he always showed me that he had to do me service; all these things considered by me, I have always forced me to do unto him all honor and pleasure, the which seemed to me to be well agreeable to the king his good master; who, as I may imagine, seeing the good cheer and will which I bore him [Brandon], with the love which he bore unto him, by many tines he spoke of unto me, for to know if this good will

---

353 P.S. Allen, ed. Opus Epistolarum Des. Erasmi Roterodami (Oxford: 1906), Tome I, p. 550, letter no. 287 dated February 14, 1514.

which I bore to the said personage it might stretch on to some effect of promise of marriage, seeing that it was the fashion of the ladies of England, and that it was not there holden for evil; whereunto many times I answered the most graciously as possible, knowing this thing to proceed from the love which he [Henry], bore him, the several reasons why it was not possible, unless I should fall in the evil grace of my father and of all this country. Also that it was not here the custom, and that I should be dishonored, and holden for a fool and light. But all my reasons might not help me, that without rest he spoke thereof to me. Seeing that he had it so much at heart, in order not to anger him, I found one other reason saying to him, that if now I had well the will to do so, I would not durst think, seeing his return to be so nigh, and that it should be too much great displeasure to lose such good company; of the which he contented himself somewhat better, and passed the thing unto his departing, and then began to say to me that the departing drew nigh, and that he knew well that the ladies should forget them; and that he knew well I should be pressed to marry, and that I was yet too young to abide thus; and that the ladies of his country did remarry at fifty and three-score years.[354]

(Second Sheet)

Whereupon I answered that I had never had will so to do, and that I was too much unhappy in husbands; but he would not believe me. And after, by two times, in presence of the personage that you know, he returned to say the same words, saying more, "I know well, madame, and am sure that my fellow [Brandon] shall be to you a true servant, and that he is altogether yours, but we fear that you shall not do in likewise, for one shall force you to be again married; and that you shall not be found in this country at my return." That I promised him I should not do; and for that he

---

354 Nichols, The Chronicle of Calais ... pp. 71-72.

desired greatly thereof to be more assured, he made me promise in his hand that howsoever I should be pressed of my father, or otherwise, I should not make alliance of marriage with prince of the world, at least not until his return, or the end of the year. The which I did willingly, for I think not to again ever to put myself where I have had so much of unhappiness and misfortune. And afterwards [the king] made his fellow to do the same, who, as I believe and seem to me, said of the venture, as his master showed me again, that he should never do a thing, were it of marriage, or to take a lady or mistress, without my commandment, but would continue all his life my right humble servant … And these words were said at Tournai in my chamber one night after supper, well late. The other time was at Lille, the day before their departure, that he [Henry] spoke to me long at the head of a cupboard, he and his fellow, of the departing, which was not without displeasure well great of all persons. And again, after many devices and regrets, he made me reconfirm in his hand, and the same of his fellow, the like promise aforesaid. And the said personage in my hand, without that I required him, made me the same, and that for always he should be to me a true and humble servant; and I to him promised to be to him such mistress all my life as to him who desired to do me most of service. And upon this there were no more words of this affair, nor have not been since, except some gracious letters, the which I know have been evil kept.[355]

> Further as to the words.

(Third Sheet)

And I promise you, my lord the ambassador that this is the truth, and I know not other thing. I cannot tell if the king, who was interpreter, because of the love which he bears him [Brandon],

---

355 Nichols, The Chronicle of Calais …, pp. 72-73.

might have taken it more forward for to interpret more his desire, but the thing is such, and truth. My lord the ambassador, because it has been said unto me that he might have showed a diamond ring of mine, which I cannot believe, for I esteem him much a man of virtue and wise, but always I will well show you the truth, to the end to answer to all. I take none in this affair to witness but the king and him; and himself first; it is that one night at Tournai, being at the banquet ... he [Brandon] put himself upon his knees before me, and in speaking and playing, he drew from my finger the ring, and put in upon his, and then showed it to me, and I took to laugh, and said to him that he was a thief, and that I knew not that the king had led thieves with him out of his country. This word <u>laron</u> he could not understand; wherefore I was constrained to ask how one said in Flemish <u>laron</u>. And afterwards I said to him in Flemish <u>dief</u>, and I prayed him many times to give it to me again, for that it was too much known. But he understood me not well, and kept it on to the next day when I spoke to the king, requiring him to make him give it to me, because it was too much known. I promising him one of my bracelets which I wear, the which I gave him. And then he gave me the said ring, the which one other time at Lille, being set nigh to my lady of Hornes, and he before upon his knees, took it again from my finger. I spoke to the king to have it again, but it was not possible, for he said that he would give me others better, and that I should leave him that. I said unto him that it was not for the value, but because it was too much known. He would not understand it, and departed from me.

The morrow after, he brought me one fair point of diamond, and one table of ruby, and showed me that it was for the other ring; wherefore I durst no more speak of it, except to beseech him that it should not be shown to any person; the which has not been done. (Thus, my lord the ambassador, see all of this affair, and in order to know my advice upon all, I shall give it to you more at length, which is this.)

(Sheet D)

That if the thing had not been so published, which I find the most strange of the world, knowing ... at the least on my part I could never speak thereof, for that which I had said and done was in order not to annoy the king, for I knew well that it came to him of great love for to speak so far forth as of marriage. And of none other prince would I have taken it so well as of him, for I hold him all good, and that he doesn't think evil, wherefore I have not willed to displease him. And in this business I have found myself more contrained to know what touched the king than what touched me.

By one note I shall put to you in writing all the inconveniences which may happen of this thing. Also what seems to me the remedy; but, for that I have no leisure, I shall make an end, praying you to do with this what the bearer shall say to you, and no more. I trust that you know this hand.[356]

(thus signed, M.)

The second writing.

My lord the ambassador, you may have seen how the things have been, and you know the unhappy rumor which has run not only here but in all parts, as well in Germany as in all countries. Whereof I have found myself so much abashed that I cannot imagine why this thing is said so openly as in the hands of merchant strangers. And to tell you the truth, I have been constrained as well by the advice of my council such as the lord of Berghes and others, to make inquiry whereof it came, and by information and writings as well I have always found that it proceeded from England. Whereof I have had a marvelous sorrow. And I have letters of the self hand

---

356 Nichols, The Chronicle of Calais ..., pp. 73-74.

of an English merchant who has been the first to make the wagers, as Bresylle[357] knows well.

Now, my lord the ambassador, the king, at the request of Bresylle, and the personage also, have done many things to remedy this situation for which I am beholden to them, but yet I see that the rumor is so imprinted in the fantasy of people, and fear if that should continue long, that all which is done is not enough, for I continue always in fear. And also I know that I may not show the good will and honor toward that personage which I desire to do as before.

(Sheet E)

Now I dare not write unto him when I have anything to do towards the king, nor do I dare even speak of him. And I am constrained to entreat him in all things like a stranger, at least before folks, which causes me so much displeasure that I cannot write it, seeing that I take him so much for my good friend and servant; and that I am constrained so to do, and also I see that when this gentleman is here I dare not speak or look at him. Nothing could displease me more. He himself perceives this well ...

And as to the return visit of the king, it shall behoove me to speak as soberly as I can, there is nothing I desire as much as his coming. And the same of my lady Mary, as God knows. My heart breaks within me when it behooves me to dissemble, not only in this matter but in many others. And it seems to me that this fear will prevent me from serving the king as well as before; so that when the king lands, I shall be always in this pain, and I feel I shall not dare speak nor show a good presence to the said personage;

---

357 Spelled variously Bresille, Bersselle, Breselle, Borsele, and by Richardson (the most modern version) Bregilles, p. 157. This was Philip, Lord of Bregilles, who served as steward and messenger for the Archduchess. See also Van den Bergh, Vol. II, p. 51 – he was obviously a most trustworthy servant, but perhaps lacking somewhat in polish - at least in the written word, as his spelling is worse than the usual middle French disregard for such matters.

whereas I would make to him much honor and good cheer, I shall not dare behold him with a good eye which will bring displeasure to him and to me. And I know no remedy[358] but the same that Bresylle shall tell you. I would not constrain him to it against his will [Brandon's marriage to the lady Lisle], when he desired ever that I do him honor or pleasure, yet it is necessary that it be so, not because I have not good will towards him such as ever I have had, but because for my honor I am constrained to do so.

I pray you well to take much pain in order that the king and this personage will understand, to the end that I may do him better service, and to his fellow graciousness. I pray you to do of this as of the other.

(likewise signed, M.)

(Indorsed, Secret matters of the duke of Suffolk.)[359]

Perhaps on those few nights at Tournai "well late in her chamber" after Henry had retired and the ladies-in-waiting nodded sleepily and discreetly in the outer chamber, they turned to each other and made love. It would explain her rapturous note to her father "I am so very joyful that it is not possible to say more,"[360] and her excess of agitation as the gossip swirled around her, and her apprehension about how much more was to be revealed. In their public behavior, there could not have been anything unseemly in a flirtation carried on among so many people - some holding of hands, a kiss or two, the meeting of eyes over a glass of wine.

What sort of man was Charles Brandon? He has been described as a "handsome giant of solid stupidity."[361] But as the son of a standard bearer to Henry VII, raised with Henry VIII and his lifelong friend, he must

---

358 In the margin is written, "Bresylle said there was no way to avoid the bruit but that my lord should marry the lady Lisle, as more at length I have written on to my said lord."
359 Nichols, The Chronicle of Calais ... , p. 76.
360 Le Glay; Vol. II, p. 211.
361 Encyclopedia Britannica (GRE), Duke of Suffolk 1484-1545, Vol. 21, 1972.

have had more ability than history generally credits him. Richardson says he had a graceful figure and engaging personality, that he was a good commander of men, and that the people on his lands in England thought well of him. What he saw in Margaret was "a most unusual woman - gay, sophisticated, charming and discreet..."

> Despite being in her early thirties, the "Blooming Duchess," with the light brown eyes and wavy golden hair much admired by Continentals, captivated Brandon as she had others with her animated face and brilliant conversation; indeed, he may have felt suitably overwhelmed by this intrepid lady whose citadel had been unsuccessfully stormed by far better men than he: two kings, Henry VII and Louis XII, and the second Duke of Norfolk.[362]

Margaret had been led into this compromising situation because of her own desire that the treaty with England be secured and that Mary and her nephew Charles be married. Having been led to feel safe enough to flirt for the good of the cause, and, loving attention, Margaret's natural diplomatic reserve was swept away by the wooing of this most attractive man who seemed to combine all the dashing qualities she admired. Charles Brandon may or may not have been sincere; perhaps he too was playing a role for England and then found himself in love. Though their promises to each other were not a formal betrothal, according to Richardson they "amounted to some degree of understanding."[363] Discretion was called for and Margaret trusted in their honor; but their boasting caused her a "marvelous sorrow" and ended the romance.

Meanwhile, at Brandon's request, the Archduchess had taken into her care Brandon's eight-year-old adopted daughter. This little child was Magdalen Rochester, the daughter of an Englishman living at Calais.

---

[362] Walter C. Richardson, Mary Tudor: The White Queen (London: Peter Owen, 1970), p. 158.
[363] Richardson, The White Queen, p. 160.

FORTUNE, MISFORTUNE, FORTIFIES ONE

Brandon had rescued her from drowning "and had become so attached to her that he wished to provide for her future."[364] He asked Margaret to take her as well his daughter Anne. However, Margaret had at least eighteen young women being educated at her court, from Spain, France and England. One daughter of Thomas Boleyn was also there - many have thought Anne, but it was probably his older daughter Mary.[365]

In spite of all this, Margaret continued to support Henry, and he wrote a letter of apology to her and Maximilian on March 4, 1514 in which he reveals that he had come to grips with the untenable situation:

> Because it has come to our knowledge that a strong-running common rumor in various places that a marriage has been made between you and our very dear and loyal cousin and counselor the Duke of Suffolk, we are trying in every way possible to know and understand from where this rumor comes and proceeds; and if we discover that it proceeds from this side, we will make such grievous punishment that all other inventors and sowers of lies will take example.[366]

Whatever Margaret's private feelings were, state and family matters went on as usual. She had succeeded in July 1513 in making a four-year peace treaty with the Duke of Gelderland which, unfortunately, did not entirely stop his forays (or his trips in disguise to France[367]), as Arnhem was "surprised" in March 1514.[368] The truce, coupled with a more strongly fortified frontier, however, did reduce the number and force of the attacks.

---

364 Ibid., p. 162.
365 Le Glay, Maximilien I, Empereur d 'Allemagne, et Marguerite d'Autriche sa fille, Gouvernante des Pays-Bas (Paris: Chez Jules Renouard et Cie., 1839), p. 461.
Note: Probable birth dates for these young girls: Mary Boleyn 1503; her sister Anne, 1507; and for Anne the Duke's daughter, 1502; for Magdalen Rochester, 1505. See also Francis Hackett, Henry the Eighth (New York; Horace Liveright, Inc., 1929), pp. 154-159.
366 Le Glay, Maximilien I, Empereur d'Allemagne, et Marguerite d'Autriche, sa fille, Gouvernante des Pays-Bas Paris: Chez Jules Renouard et Cie. 1839), p. 54.
367 Van den Bergh, Vol. II, pp. 94-95.
368 Van den Bergh, Vol. II, p. 85, note.

Earlier in 1513, Danish ambassadors had arrived in May, and this news had been included in a sad letter in which Margaret related that Charles had been involved in an unfortunate hunting accident and that he had killed a working man of Wure, a "drunkard and ill-conditioned man," nevertheless causing much regret to all concerned.[369] And there is a charming and familial letter from Margaret to her father to let him know a box of jellies made by that "good apothecary," Margaret of Croy, the Countess of Hornes, was on its way to him.[370] The Countess was a close friend of Margaret and had been by her side at Lille and Tournai during the romantic interlude. It was not long after this, however, that she died. Another loss was the death of Madame Halewijn (Jeanne de Comines April 11, 1512) who had been tutor and lady-in-waiting to her mother, and her own tutor when she returned from France. The absence of this sensible woman with her indomitable will and peppery tongue left a great hollow in her life.

The year of 1514 brought separation to the family. Little Mary, only nine years old, was sent to Vienna to be betrothed to Louis, the eight-year-old son of Wladislav II, King of Hungary and Bohemia and his French wife Anne de Candolle. 'This was one-half of a two-part agreement made by Maximilian. The other called for the uniting of his grandson Ferdinand with Anne of Hungary, sister of Louis. While Margaret knew that these marriages were politically necessary, she spared no effort to insure the comfort of the young girls in her charge. Margaret's anxiety is betrayed by the many actions she took regarding Mary's future. She sent an equerry to the Hungarian court to ascertain the conditions there and make a report to her; she named a suitable knight and lady of honor; she requested Mary's governess and her assistant to accompany and remain with her; she selected the tapestries and furniture which should go with Mary; and most importantly she took steps to secure her safe-conduct to Vienna because there was still fear of the Duke of Gelderland. Even after the company was well on its way, Margaret besieged the lord in charge of the undertaking, her general Floris of Egmond, for frequent news.

---

369   Ibid., Vol. II, p. 80.
370   Le Glay, Vol. II, p. 187.

A pert and hardy youngster, independent, open-minded and self-assured, Mary was a cheerful and robust tomboy. In later years, she outshot and outran men in her company, and when Margaret died, Mary was a worthy successor to her energetic aunt as regent of the Low Countries. She left May 2, 1514, and made the journey without incident, but the marriage to Louis of Hungary did not take place until seven years later.[371]

The next child to leave was Isabel who had been born in 1501. The Danish ambassadors, who had arrived in May 1513, had come to make arrangements for a marriage between Isabel and Christian II, King of Denmark. At his request, the marriage by proxy ceremony was to be held on Trinity Sunday, June 11, 1514, the anniversary of his coronation. However, the ambassador had not put this request until Saturday June 10. Margaret wrote her father:

> My lord, it was very difficult to arrange such a solemn function in so short a time, for it could not be as honorably held as I should have wished, but, anxious to please them and gratify their desires, I agreed that the said ceremony should be held… and I did my best to have everything arranged and put in order. The parties assembled on the said day between ten and eleven o'clock, with as much state and honor on our side as was possible, owing to the short notice, in front of the great hall of this house… and it certainly did one good to look at Madame Isabel, my niece …
>
> Charles showed himself such a good brother, and carried out everything, even to the dances in which he accompanied the said lady, his sister, to perfection … and a little more perhaps than his constitution could bear, for the day after the said espousals he was attacked by fever.[372]

---

371 For a warm and scholarly account of Mary's life, see Jane de Iongh, Mary of Hungary: Second Regent of the Netherlands (New York: W.W. Norton and Company, 1958).
372 Le Glay, Vol. II, pp. 256-259.

These royal marriages were of a two-part nature, the first being a covenant of betrothal and marriage to follow called per verba de futuro; the second part followed by consummation was known as per verba de praesenti. As Isabel was only thirteen, it was agreed that she should remain at home for another year. Margaret, and Mary after her, postponed the consummations as long as possible. When the "real" marriage took place in August 1515, it led only to unhappiness, for Isabel, gentle and sweet, did not have the strength of mind and character of her sister Mary. Isabel wrote on August 7, 1515, to her "Aunt and kind Mother" in Malines:

> Madame, if I could choose for myself I would now be with you. For to be parted from you is the greatest sorrow which can happen to me, especially as I do not know when I may hope to see you again.[373]

Margaret's feelings about these alliances are alluded to in Maximilian's letter about the middle of March 1516:

> ...you write that your nieces and daughters, Isabel and Mary, are badly served in their marriages giving us great astonishment in a view of the fact that we strongly advanced these two marriages with Hungary and Denmark... I would like to know where my error lies.[374]

Early in the year of 1514 on January 9, Anne of Brittany, wife of Louis XII of France, and widow of Charles VIII, died after a long illness. An imperious woman, nevertheless, she and Margaret had transcended politics and past bitterness and maintained an amiable[375] correspondence, often

---

[373] Jane de Iongh, Mary of Hungary: Second Regent of the Netherlands (New York: W.W. Norton and Company, 1958), p. 35.

[374] André J.G. Le Glay, Correspondance de l'Empereur Maximilien I et de Marguerite d'Autriche (Paris: 1839), Vol. II, p. 320.

[375] Eleanor E. Tremayne, The First Governess..., pp. 133-134. See also Christopher Hare, The High and Puissant Princess. pp. 212-213; Godefroy's Lettres du roy Louis XII.'

having news of one another through the artists such as Jean Lemaire, who served at the two courts. Anne's dearest wish had been that her daughter Claude should marry Charles, and this agreement had been made while the Archduke Philip was still alive in October 1501. It was in effect until 1507 when negotiations were made for Mary of England and Charles. However, soon after Anne's death, since Louis had no son, he married his daughter Claude to Francis, the heir to the throne. Louis adored his daughters, and for personal and dynastic reasons, this marriage seemed more sensible to him. At least it kept Claude in France near him and secured Brittany to the French crown.

But still Louis had flirted with the Claude-Charles proposal, and suggested his daughter Renee for young Ferdinand (already thought of for Anne of Hungary) and King Ferdinand of Aragon suggested that Louis marry either Margaret[376] or her niece Eleanor. It was settled that Eleanor should be the one since Margaret probably could not bear children. Though agreed to by Ferdinand, Maximilian and Louis, Maximilian was negotiating with the King of Poland for the hand of Eleanor.[377] When the Archduchess heard of this, she delivered several vigorous objections. Ferdinand was astonished that Madame Margaret opposed his plans as he is doing nothing except following the counsel of the Emperor her father."[378] Ferdinand directed his ambassador Juan de Lanuza to respond:

---

376 Gustave Adolph Bergenroth, ed., Calendar of Letters, Despatches and State Papers (London, 1862), Vol. II, pp. lxxxi-lxxxiii, editorial comment: "A lady who had great influence in the councils of Europe had given up the resolution to which she had adhered during so many years not to marry a third husband. There is no occasion for us to enter into conjectures as to the reasons which induced the Archduchess Margaret to offer herself in marriage to the King of France. She did so, and thereby placed herself in open opposition with King Ferdinand ... when she had been obliged to give up all hope of marrying King Louis, she was not deterred by her bad success. If she could not be Queen of France, she desired to marry the Duke Maximilian Sforza, and to be Duchess of Bergenroth is a respected source, nevertheless I can find no evidence to support his assertions; on the contrary, they seem to stem exclusively from King Ferdinand's directions to his ambassador. It may be however, that Margaret, like Elizabeth of England a generation later, used marriage negotiations as a diplomatic weapon, but I do not believe she would ever willingly have abdicated her regency for marriage.
377 André J.G. Le Glay, Correspondance ... Vol. II, p. 319.
378 Gustav Adolph Bergenroth, ed., Calendar of Letters, Despatches and State Papers (London, 1862), Vol. II, pp. 204-205.

... that since Madame Margaret ... is persuaded that the Prince Charles ought to remain faithful to his engagement to the sister of the King of England, he will do what she thinks right.

Nevertheless, he felt that she had not weighed the advantages of the overall plan which included the rights to Naples, Milan, Genoa and Venice.

It is true that the King of France has not fulfilled his former promises concerning the affairs of Guelders. The reason, however, is that he had concluded the treaty with the Prince Charles alone. As, this time, the King of France is to conclude the treaty with the Emperor, him (King Ferdinand) and the Prince, he will not dare to break it. Moreover, the marriage of the King of France with Madame Eleanor ... would be additional security for the good faith of the King of France.

Madame Margaret dwells on the great difference of age between the King of France and Madame Eleanor. He is to tell her that in marriages of great kings differences of age is never taken into account ... a son of Eleanor's would be heir to the throne of France...Madame Margaret is mistaken if she thinks it a disadvantage that Madame Eleanor is so thin. Thin women generally become sooner pregnant, and bear more children than stout ones.[379]

Ferdinand directed his ambassador to speak to Margaret's confessor to remind her of her Christian duty since she is "a very pious and virtuous lady."

Ferdinand also wrote an affectionate letter to Margaret, "his beloved Daughter," in which he thanked her for all the great services she had rendered to him and to the Emperor, their grandson Charles, and to the King of England. He described her as "the most important person in

---

379 Gustav Adolph Bergenroth, ed., *Calendar of Letters* ..., (London: 1862), Vol. II, pp. 204-205.

Christendom, since she acts as mediator in almost all the negotiations between the princes of Christendom."[380] In a private letter to Lanuza he admitted to being worried that Margaret would oppose the truce with France and added "Madame Margaret is the person on whom, more than on any one else on earth, peace or war depends."[381]

While they were absorbed in these plans, King Henry VIII became uneasy about this proposed alliance. He had become more and more displeased with Maximilian's constant monetary requests and with his indecision on the marriage date for Charles and Mary. Margaret tried to warn her father saying that these "fair offers" were only put forward by France and Spain for their own ends. She felt that if Henry became suspicious, he could make his own arrangements with France, which had no need of them, and that France would accept such an alliance with open arms.

> My lord, if as to prevent it, you in person and in finances, without any trickery. I assure you that there is no double dealing in him … and for that reason he ought to be treated in the same manner, and any promises made to him should be kept.[382]

This good advice Maximilian did not follow. Much to his surprise arid sorrow, Cardinal Wolsey engineered a treaty with France in which it was agreed that Mary, repudiating her betrothal to Charles, should marry Louis. The plans were carried out so secretly and swiftly in late winter that Margaret could not believe the news, attributing it to gossip. But on August 13 the proxy ceremony was held in England, on October 9, Mary

---

380 Ibid., Vol. II, p. 214.
381 A revealing sidelight of this time is given in a letter from Mercurino di Gattinara dated February 12, 1514, telling Margaret that on the tenth of the month he had seen three suns and three moons and asking her to consult Louis Marlien and Peter Picot in the medical service of Charles and Margaret and who apparently also interpreted signs. See: Andre J .G. Le Glay, Correspondance… (Paris, 1839), Note, Vol. I, p. 437.
382 Le Glay, Vol. II, p. 225, February 24, 1514.

and Louis were married, and on November 5 Mary was crowned at St. Denis.[383]

A sick man, Louis altered all his healthful habits to suit his new queen, and historians down through the years have found great fun in contemplating Louis's last wonderful but debilitating months. He died the first of January 1515, leaving no son, only daughters, and his heir, Francis, son of Louise of Savoy, was now King of France.

Charles Brandon, Duke of Suffolk, headed the embassy to bring the young Queen Mary back to England. He was in love with her, and so apparently was Francis, though it could be truly said of each that they loved power and position more. Historical gossip tells us that the astute Louise warned her son away, reminding him that he could beget Louis's heir and thus do himself out of the kingdom. With Francis's blessing, Charles Brandon married the young widow who kept her title and dowry. Cardinal Wolsey had the disagreeable task of reconciling Henry to this fait accompli. Everything that Margaret had achieved by patient diplomacy was swept away by the inconsistency and errors of her father's politics. "The penance," she complained, "is greater than our offense towards England." In March, Margaret coldly informed her father about the embassy to France and added "...I will not be able to do anything more for now I do not meddle in any affairs."[384]

As for her feelings about the marriage of Mary to Charles Brandon, she commented, "I cannot clearly get it into my head as there is neither reason nor any appearance of good [concerning it]."[385] A coolness developed between the two and their letters became much less frequent.

There were two new rulers that year. In France excited crowds had rushed into Francis's chamber and hailed him King of France. He was young, only twenty-one, good looking and charming - a dashing figure,

---
383 Numbered among her attendants was Mademoiselle Boleyn, but this was probably Mary and not Anne as several historians have suggested. John Gough Nichols, ed., The Chronicles of Calais, p. 77.
384 Le Glay, Vol. II, p. 285.
385 Jane de Iongh, Margaret of Austria: Regent of the Netherlands (New York: W.W. Norton & Company, Inc., 1953), p. 203.

and utterly spoiled. His wife Claude, daughter of Louis and Anne of Brittany, was "very small and extra-ordinarily fat, but her graceful way of talking makes amends for her lack of beauty" - this according to Mercurino di Gattinara in a letter to the Archduchess.[386]

To the north, the Archduke Charles came of age and was declared in charge of the government of the Low Countries by Maximilian. Though Charles was fifteen, and according to the old agreements now entitled to rule, Maximilian acted short-sightedly in response to the States General who in December 1514 had called for the government of their natural prince. They proposed that Maximilian revoke the rights of the Regent Margaret for payment of 140,000 florins and a pension of 50,000 pounds.[387] Secret negotiations were carried out between the Emperor and Guillaume de Croy, Lord of Chièvres, governor of the Archduke Charles. This gentleman and Margaret had frequently differed politically, sometimes acrimoniously. He advocated closer union with France no doubt because of his own holdings in that land. At age 57, the Lord of Chièvres finally realized his ambition, and his personal authority was substituted for the powers of the Regent.

In vain, Margaret attempted to regain ground by proposing to her father a transfer of the regency to a council of representatives of the Emperor, of Ferdinand of Aragon, and Henry VIII of England, which she would head. This would have amounted to a coalition against France which should have pleased Maximilian, but as always, he was in straightened circumstances and preparing for another campaign in Italy. He who had once tried to pawn the Holy Roman Empire to the highest bidder[388] obviously had no qualms about accepting the offer of money made by the States General even if it meant undermining his daughter's government. This widened the conflict between the old Governor and the Regent and led to her downfall as he swayed Charles to his point of view. Behind the proposal of the States General in 1514 lies a story full of hate, double-dealing and intrigue

---

386 Eleanor E. Tremayne, The First Governess of the Netherlands (New York: G.P. Putnam's Sons; Longon: Methuen & Company, 1908), p. 141.
387 Quinsonas, Matériaux ... Vol III, pp. 237-240.
388 J.S. Brewer, The Reign of Henry VII...(London: John Murray, 1884), Vol. I, p. 75.

going back to the year 1495, involving the Lord of Belmonte, Don Juan Manuel of Castile. It was during this time that Don Juan Manuel was one of Ferdinand and Isabella's emissaries to Maximilian in the arrangement of their children's marriages. In the bargaining, he attempted to set a lower price on Margaret as "used merchandise," since she had been married before. These marriage negotiations generally involved hard-headed and canny financial dealing, and no doubt Don Juan Manuel was set to the task by King Ferdinand. Nevertheless, there were no secrets in the courts of those days, and when Margaret learned of this it must have rankled.

Some years earlier in the summer of 1505 when Margaret, recently widowed, made a trip to the Low Countries, Don Juan then tried in various ways to enlist her in his schemes. He attempted to buy her servant Louis and sought to win her to her brother Philip's side and against King Ferdinand, when what she desired was cooperation. Margaret said to her brother that she thought Don Juan might serve well if he were held more accountable for his actions. She felt that he was full of deceptions and said to Fuensalida that he looked from one to the other, and "if he didn't receive here, he would seek there."[389] Even as early as 1500 when she had returned home to Flanders following her Spanish marriage, she observed the intrigues of the courtesans, and especially Don Juan Manuel.[390] Margaret must have known someone so brilliant and unscrupulous would bear watching when the government was put into her hands. Perhaps she thought it would be easier to do this if he were in her employ as Fuensalida, writing from London in March 1508 implies: "Don Juan was with the Princess Margaret in Flanders and from there came here… well I know he is a rogue."[391] And later,

> …Now I know for sure that Madame Margaret provides the money which sustains him, and I believe that Don Juan Manuel is plotting something because the king [Henry] has said that he knows that

---

[389] Gomez de Fuensalida, p. xlviii.
[390] Ibid., p. xxvii.
[391] Ibid., p. 416.

he is in Germany and that even there he will do something else galling...[392]

In 1511, he surfaced again in the enigmatic postscript of a letter from Margaret to Maximilian:

> My lord, as for Don Juan Manuel, he offers himself to do whatever will please you, concerning money; but the treasurer doesn't know where to catch him ...

It is in 1513, however, that we read in the Spanish State Papers[393] of Ferdinand's request to Margaret for the arrest of Don Juan Manuel and the directions for carrying out the plan. The Ambassador Juan de Lanuza was instructed to tell Madame:

> ...that Don Juan has not only rendered bad services to him (King Ferdinand), but also speaks so ill of her that for this alone he deserves punishment. [He is sending] Artieta, who is the bearer of this dispatch, with a ship, which ostensibly sails with merchandise, but which, in fact, is sent for no other purpose than to convey Don Juan as a prisoner to the place of which Artieta is informed. If Madame has not changed her mind, he is, with the greatest dexterity, and in such a manner that nobody may be aware of it, to transport Don Juan on board ship, and to deliver him to Artieta. To carry away Don Juan Manuel seems to be a small thing, but in fact, it is very important. If it were done, his relations with the Emperor and with the Prince (Charles) would at once be much improved. Is willing to pay the desired pensions to the four persons he has named in case Don Juan be delivered to him.[394]

---

392 Ibid., p. 423.
393 Bergenroth, Calendar of Letters, Despatches and State Papers (London: 1862), Vol. II, pp. 138-139. 199-200.
394 Bergenroth, Calendar of Letters, Despatches and State Papers (London: 1862), Vol. II, pp. 138-139.

However, the wily Don Juan would not have survived this long without his own network of informers and accomplices. He was able to engage a Spanish merchant of Antwerp, Juan Adursa, to aid him, by promising him a high office in Charles's court. A close relative of this merchant was a lady-in-waiting to Henry's wife Catherine, and thus he was able to poison two courts with his conspiracies.

Margaret had not changed her mind; she did have Manuel and several other Castilians arrested and put in prison in Vilvoorde.[395] Unfortunately for the Archduchess, Manuel was a member of the Order of the Golden Fleece which enjoyed certain unique privileges, one of which being their right to correct, try, judge and protect one another, and they voted to censure Margaret to protest her conduct. They reminded her that she had given up all her rights when she married the Duke of Savoy, and she replied that her mother's will was the stronger document, but out of regard for her father, nephew and nieces, would hold those rights only during her lifetime. In another item of business she requested the collar for the Count of Montrevel for his long and faithful services.[396] He was qualified but they tabled it, obviously unwilling to show her any measure of respect or submission.

Later Philip of Burgundy and Don Diego petitioned Margaret for the release of Don Juan claiming he was the victim of envy of his enemies. A few days following, a letter to Maximilian went out over the signatures of Charles, Henri de Witthem, Guillaume and Michel de Croy, Floris of Egmond, Ferry de Croy and Henri de Nassau, protesting the irregularity of his arrest. There was no answer, and so, on March 29, 1514, more than a month later, they wrote again.[397] Meanwhile Margaret had had a reply on January 10 to her own private letter in which Maximilian cautioned "If Don Juan has committed a crime which is punishable by law, he may be

---

395 Vilvoorde would later have a place in history as the town where John Tyndale was taken and put to death.
396 Le Baron de Reiffenberg, Histoire de L'Ordre de la Toison D'Or (Brussels: Fonderie et Imprimerie Normales, 1830), pp. 278-293.
397 Le Baron de Reiffenberg, Histoire de L'Ordre de la Toison D'Or (Brussels: Fonderie et Imprimerie Normales, 1839), pp. 278-293.

arrested, if not, it will be sufficient to banish him from the court."[398] In April Margaret communicated to them a letter from Maximilian directing that Don Juan be released from prison. When they asked her to conform to the letter, she responded that she would obey the Emperor, but that he would be conveyed by an armed officer out of the Low Countries. She delayed until the end of April at which time he left the chateau at Vilvoorde for Brussels, Louvain, Cologne and Vienna, to the court of Maximilian who as the head of the Order, claimed the contested prisoner. Juan Manuel later became an ambassador to Rome. He also served Charles and is considered influential in the elevation of Adrian to the papacy.[399]

Margaret had to wage a constant battle to safeguard her authority within the country. When the knights first met to censure her, they sent a delegation "headed by the young archduke, who was opposed to his aunt, partly on principle as Knight of the Golden Fleece, and partly from personal motives."[400] She was so enraged by this treachery on the part of the men who had served her and in whom she had placed her trust, and so infuriated by her nephew's adolescent arrogance that she replied with force: "If I were as much a man as I am a woman, I would make you sing your statutes!"[401]

All this took place following the wedding of Louis and Mary, his death, and the accession of Francis. It was the time Ferdinand was proposing all sorts of marriages, the time of the break with England, and Maximilian's preparations for another campaign in Italy. Margaret was aware that her power was slowly being eroded by the Lord of Chièvres. Nevertheless it still came as a shock when the States General called for a new government to be headed by Charles. Her father had readily complied in order to improve his own treasury.[402]

---

398 Bergenroth, Calendar of Letters, Despatches and State Papers (London: 1862), Vol. II, pp. 199-200.
399 Van den Bergh, Vol. I, p. 345.
400 Otto von Habsburg, Charles V (New York: Prager Publishers, 1970), p. 33.
401 Ghislaine de Boom, Marguerite d'Autriche-Savoie... (Brussels: La Renaissance du Livre, 1946), pp. 49-50.
402 Ghislaine de Boom, Marguerite d'Autriche-Savoie... p. 33.

It was with a numbness that she listened to Charles's address in Brussels on January 8, 1515:

> Very dear and well beloved, It has pleased the emperor my lord and grandfather to emancipate us and free us from his guardianship and regency, placing the government of our country and lordships on this side in our hands, and consenting that we be received and sworn to the principality and lordship of the same. Therefore it is fit and reasonable that all things which concern our rights, greatness, lordship, and even the doing of justice and our other affairs, should be drawn up and dispatched under our name and title, placing at the end of the letters: Given under the seal which the emperor, my lord and grandfather, and we have used during the time of our minority...[403]

There was no reference to his aunt. Though she had always consulted others, Margaret had ruled the Low Countries with liberty and authority as their natural princess for eight years. What resentment, shame and grief must have boiled up in her at the dishonorable way she had been removed. Excluded from the Council of State, she was no longer even consulted.[404] Maximilian's letters were withheld from her and she lost touch with Charles except for ceremonial meetings. She also was accused of personal avarice and of having ruled unsuccessfully; so, added to the thoughtless and disloyal treatment by her father, she had to endure the ingratitude of her nephew. The Lord of Chièvres had become the master of Charles's spirit and completely changed the direction of all the policies she had labored so long to effect.[405]

---

[403] Van den Bergh, Vol. II pp. 113-114. "par deca" (on this side, or over here) was the term commonly used to indicate the Low Countries. It probably meant this side of the Empire or this side of the Rhine.

[404] Ghislaine de Boom, Marguerite d'Autriche-Savoie..., p. 34.

[405] It can be shown that in later life, Charles regretted the conduct of this whole affair. Armstrong records: "Charles in after years would speak openly of the discredit which his subordination to Chièvres had brought upon his youth." Edward Armstrong, The Emperor Charles V (London: MacMillan and Company, Ltd., 1929), p. 145. And when his daughter Juana was

Trying to put a good face on it, Margaret appeared with Charles before the assembled States in Brussels where Charles made this short address:

> Gentlemen, I thank you for the honor and great affection you bear me. Be good and loyal subjects, and I will be your good prince.[406]

She accompanied Charles on his joyous entries[407] into the principal cities of the Low Countries where, after taking the oath of fealty, he hardly stopped for the parades, games, banquets and other events held in his honor. However, Margaret, more experienced and politically wiser, took part in everything and pretended to be happy being free of the duties of governing. The Venetian ambassador, Pietro Pasqualigo, reported she was looking "more beautiful and fresher than ever."[408] Such a painful period was nothing new in Margaret's life and she endured this as she had the others. But in close quarters before the trusted English ambassador, Sir Richard Wingfield, she spoke with tears in her eyes of the utter desolation and the cruel humiliation of this great loss of her honor.[409]

---

serving as regent of Spain in Philip II's place, he reminded her "how important it was for members of the same family to maintain an affectionate intercourse with one another." William Robertson, The History of the Reign of the Emperor Charles the Fifth with an account of the Emperor's life after his abdication by William H. Prescott (Philadelphia: J.B. Lippincott Company, 1902), Vol. III, p. 400. And finally, there is this warm passage from a letter on February 9, 1526 in which Charles in continuing to keep Margaret informed about negotiations for peace, concludes that "it is not only as nephew to aunt, but also as a good son to a true and good mother." Karl Lanz, Correspondenz des Kaisers Karl V, p. 191.

406 Eleanor E. Tremayne, The First Governess of The Netherlands (New York: G.P. Putnam's Sons; London: Methuen & Company, 1908, p. 146.

407 Joyous entries were a remnant of Roman days when the conqueror or ruler made a grand entry into a city. Renaissance artists and craftsmen had a passionate interest in these old ceremonies and the engineering and architectural ornamentations which remain are considered works of art. (French: Joyeux entrée; Flemish: blijde inkomst. Many a Belgian street still carries these words as names.)

408 Henri Pirenne, Histoire de Belgique (Brussels: Henri Lamertin, Libraire-Éditeur, 1907), Vol. III, p. 79. Also, Ghislaine de Boom, Marguerite d'Autriche-Savoie et la Pré-Renaissance (Brussels: Maurice Lamertin, Libraire-Éditeur, 1935, p. 34.

409 Ghislaine de Boom, Marguerite d'Autriche-Savoie..., p. 34.

Ferdinand, not fully grasping the situation, thought that Charles had been named one of the governors with which he was very pleased, and commended both Maximilian and Margaret. But, he added, "It would be a good thing if Monsieur de Chiévres could be removed from his place."[410]

Maximilian, who had considered it his right to meddle in the policies of the Low Countries was now shut out of the government. He began to perceive he had committed a great tactical error in letting the government be removed from the hands of a daughter so able, dedicated and conciliatory. To rectify this he wrote to Charles:

> ...We make no doubt, because of the honor and love you owe to our very dear daughter, your aunt, that you communicate your chief and most arduous business to her, and that you take and use her good advice and counsel, from which, for natural reasons, you will always find more comfort, help, and support than from anyone else. In which, as a royal father, we exhort you always to continue, begging you affectionately to remember the way she labored during your minority in the administration of your country ... and also that you are her whole heart, hope, and heir, that you will give her a good allowance, such as she has had until now ... for she has well deserved it from you.[411]

In a covering letter to Margaret, Maximilian enclosed a copy of this graceful letter. But it was too late, the letter had no effect. In regard to two requests from her father, Margaret made these sharp replies:

> ... With regard to the secret matter, my lord, ... and concerning the last letters that you have written on the said affair, [you should submit the request to Charles's chancellor (Jean le Sauvage)]. As

---

410 Bergenroth, Calendar of Letters, Despatches and State Papers (London: 1862), Vol. II, pp. 250-251.

411 This shortened version in English is found in Eleanor E. Tremayne's The First Governess of The Netherlands, pp. 147-148. The original version in French may be found in Van den Bergh, Vol. II, pp. 133-136.

my letters will have no effect for better or worse, I desire that you comply with his wishes.[412]

And from Brussels on December 21, 1515:

… My lord, I will not be writing more about this matter, nor do I have a desire to talk any more about it. At all events, my lord, I will in no wise trouble myself, nor have I a wish to meddle in other intentions of yours, nor aid your service, nor follow your desires. Furthermore, I will no longer constrain the people by advocating what is not to their pleasure, because I will respond less to you. For this cause, my lord, and since I have written to you all my thoughts in this, let us make an end to it, and praying our Lord, my very revered lord and father, give you a good and long life.[413]

Following this time, as has been noted, the correspondence falls off. Kinder letters did ensue, but of those which remain, Maximilian wrote about five to Margaret's one. On August 20, 1515, Margaret submitted to Charles before the assembled council, her defense of her reign. This quite lengthy memorandum in which she explained the political events and her conduct of them, includes as proof an inventory of the gifts she made, the money received from the States, and her own savings during her administration. She had not spent any of Charles's money, but had used her own dowry instead. After Charles had listened, he declared that "Madame is held fully discharged from all things," and the others concurred. Perhaps they remembered that blood is thicker than water, or perhaps they felt guilty, or merely wished to mollify this vexatious woman. For Margaret had learned many things over the past eight years concerning culture, people, government and diplomacy, but the most important lesson, of a private nature, was that she stood alone. There was no one to defend her. No longer did she turn breathlessly to others for help. After the tears

---

412   Le Glay, Vol. II, p. 284.
413   Ibid., Vol. II, p. 314.

and depression passed, righteous anger and a sense of her own ability took over, and she arose to become her own advocate.

Those who were present signed: Charles the Count Palatine, the Lord of Ravenstein, the Prince of Chimay, the Lords of Chiévres, of Saint Py, the Chancellor, the Count of Montreval, the Governor of Bresse (Mercurino di Gattinara), the deputies of Louvain and Cambray, the auditor for the whole group. Their signatures can be found on the back of the document, indicating their assent, and thus the matter was closed.

Chapter 4

MARGARET'S INVOLVEMENT IN THE ARTS AND HUMANITIES

While this sudden alteration in government in January 1515 removed Margaret from the administration and control of affairs, she still remained the Archduchess of the Low Countries and as such took part in all the ceremonial activities required of her rank; for example, the obsequies of King Ferdinand on March 13, 1516. For another, the festivals with their games always called her out. Archery was very popular, and Margaret did not hesitate to mingle with the exuberant crowds. She took part in the crossbow competition where a target consisting of a wooden parrot on a pole, called the popinjay, is moved back and forth, and won. These affairs were sometimes fixed; however, Margaret was considered to be a good marksman, and happily paid the "penalty" of 22 pounds to the Confraternity of Saint Sebastian because "we are Queen of the Popinjay."[414]

And just as her indomitable old grandmother, the Dowager Duchess of Burgundy, had made her court a haven for the Yorkists, so Margaret made hers a home for the English faction. She still had her able and loyal counselors,

---

414 Jean Lemaire de Belges, Les Épîtres de l'Amant Vert (Lille: Librairie Giard; Genève: Librairie Droz, 1948), Professor Frappier's notes on p. 77.

and her information network of confidential agents, thus correspondence was maintained. Among the letters is one dated July 12, 1516 from Charles's former tutor Adrian who was now acting as his emissary in Spain. Foreign ambassadors even yet paid homage and were made welcome. Thus in a subtle way, she continued to influence policy. Once Margaret perceived this and began to recover from the shame and hurt of this palace coup, the relief from the daily burden of government routine freed her to follow those artistic pursuits which because of duty had always been relegated to second place. This too lifted her despair. Forbush writes that Margaret's "real involvement in art began in the middle of the second decade of the century..." which places us at this juncture of her life. "From this time onward she began to award her commissions to those artists who would form the forefront of Italianism in the Southern Netherlands..." Before this time her patronage of art had been passive. Now she was able to make a real commitment to Italian classicism. What the government lost during that time is more than made up to posterity by the forces she set in motion in the art world with her "interest in creations inspired by antique and Italian models."[415]

Margaret had been taught to paint while a child in France. De Boom reasoned that she might have been instructed by Jean Perréal,[416] but there was another Jean of Paris, Jean Hey, thought to be the Master of Moulins, who painted Margaret at least twice, and was well liked in her small court."[417] As an adult she had a small silver box containing five paint brushes decorated with silver,[418] but her interest in art as a young

---

415 Frances Lawhon Forbush, "The Patronage of Margaret of Austria: Taste in Transition" (unpublished M.A. thesis, University of Virginia, May 1977), p. 54. The author was able to reconstruct her artistic life year by year from 1497 in Spain until her death in 1530.
416 Ghislaine de Boom, Marguerite d'Autriche-Savoie et la Pré-Renaissance (Bruxelles: La Renaissance du Livre, 1946 [1935]), p. 101.
417 Yvonne Labande-Mailfert, Charles VIII et Son Milieu (1470- 1498) (Paris: Librairie C. Klincksieck, 1975), p. 495.
418 Eleanor E. Tremayne, The First Governess of The Netherlands (New York: G.P. Putnam's Sons; London: Methuen & Company, 1908), includes in an appendix, the 1524 Inventory, Item number 106, p. 312. states "... to paint serves as a pastime for Madame." See also André J. G. Le Glay, Correspondance de 1 'Empereur Maximilien I et de Marguerite d'Autriche (Paris: Chez Jules Renouard et Cie., 1839).

girl was very probably conventional. Though she was surrounded by beautiful objects from birth, Margaret's own first real appreciation may have been aroused with her exposure to Spain. According to Molinet, she, accompanied by her grandmother, a goodly number of ladies "richly dressed" and gentlemen of the Order of the Golden Fleece, traveled to Antwerp to meet her new sister-in-law Juana of Spain when she arrived in 1495.

> Margaret went forward to the place where Juana was lodged and after waiting outside for a little, went in and found her sister-in-law lying sick on a pallet. The chamber was furnished so beautifully with cloth of gold, vessels of gold...she had never seen such richness or such stateliness or such treasure. These same preparations had been made for Margaret also by the Queen of Castille along with beautiful robes and chains without equal in this world - rich stones of inestimable value.[419]

When Margaret arrived in Spain in February 1497, she learned that many Flemish artists had found their way to that land, and it may be, thrust into such a stern and alien society, that only this one aspect of its culture was familiar and comfortable. After the tragic double loss of Juan's death and the death of her baby, Margaret turned to art to assuage her grief, establishing a pattern which was to last throughout her life. She contributed her revenues from Spain to the building of a tomb for Juan at St. Thomas de Avila by the master Domenico of Florence[420] and began to buy and commission paintings. When Margaret was finally permitted to leave Spain in the autumn of 1499, her wedding and departure gifts of jewelry, plate, tapestries and paintings, and her own acquisitions established the nucleus of a fine collection.

---

419 Jean Molinet, Chroniques de Jean Molinet (Bruxelles: Palais des Académies, 1935), Tome II, p. 429.
420 Eleanor E. Tremayne, The First Governess of The Netherlands (New York: G. P. Putnam's Sons; London: Methuen & Company, 1908) p. 29.

In 1501, with her marriage to Philibert of Savoy, a whole new world opened up to her in the art of the Italian Renaissance. The love she felt for her husband, and the lively court they established, so in contrast to Spain, gave her leave to abandon the conservative demeanor she had adopted, and allowed her naturally buoyant temperament to re-emerge. When he too died, Margaret nearly lost her reason. But once again art pulled her back into life. She became committed to a memorial for him and his mother which bordered on obsession. She commissioned Renaissance sculptors and artisans to carry out the task of building a memorial to this beloved husband - something that would express the rapture and exaltation which their life together had given her. In 1506, Margaret laid the first stone of the church of Brou, famous within the history of the arts, and a national treasure of France today.

In 1509 Jean Perréal, probably through the efforts of Jean Lemaire, brought his designs to the task of supervising this endeavor. Years later, however, swamped in the morass of government burdens and crises, she became annoyed with Jean Perréal's temperament - his inability to cooperate, his feuds with other artists and craftsmen. His lack of respect is patent in his letters,[421] and finally her patience was exhausted. Stecher is of the opinion that "Margaret became fatigued with these incessant recriminations."[422] She then called Louis van Boghem to this great architectural undertaking. It is said that he traveled from Brou to Malines twice a year to consult with the Archduchess. Artistic, yet reliable, he perhaps lent a restraining hand to temperaments and artistic fancy as well. In 1516 Margaret requested Jan van Roome to submit plans for the tombs. All work on these had stopped in 1512 when Lemaire and Perreal had departed. Van Roome was a Gothic and conservative artist. The genial Michel Colombe and his three nephews, in signing their contract in 1511 with Margaret, had agreed to supply a scale model of the project so that she could follow both the plans and the progress. A pleasant and very human

---

[421] Jean Lemaire de Belges, Oeuvres, publiées par J. Stecher (Genève: Slatkine Reprints, 1969/Louvain, 1882-1885). See under "Lettres" pp. 379-380.
[422] Ibid., Stecher's Introduction, p. lxxiii.

picture of Margaret comes forth - of her stealing time from duties to gaze, to touch, to contemplate the work - her inventive mind bringing up images of details to make the whole perfect, because through all the travails, the lack of money, the sluggishness of its progress, Margaret remained in charge. Margaret gave visibility to her own essentially moderate nature in the creation of Brou, a church whose flamboyant Gothic is permeated with the art of the Renaissance.

The actual carving of the tombs was not begun until 1526 when the sculptor Conrad Meyt was engaged. Long a favorite of Margaret, and well thought of by Dürer and other artists, he had come to Malines from Germany before 1514. He had done numerous small works in wood and marble, and there is a small work of his which can be seen in Sts. Michael's and Gudule's in Brussels – a life-size bust of the Madonna and Child for which Margaret was a model. Conrad Meyt was a more naturalistic artist than others of his time who tended to idealize their subjects. It is due to this Madonna and the effigies on the tombs that we have a true impression of what Margaret actually looked like. Further in this regard, the Bayerisches National Museum in Munich has a bust of the Archduchess sculpted in pearwood by Conrad Meyt c. 1518. Hannelore Sachs relates that Margaret asked to be pictured as a simple burgher's wife in a plain costume.[423] The expression is so pleasant, the eyes have a soft, benign look, and her lips are breaking into a smile – certainly a very successful study, and one of Munich's treasures.

When Margaret returned to take over the reigns of government in 1507, she again found safety in the old Flemish style of art. It may have been the more conservative art atmosphere of the Low Countries then, or the unsettled conditions, or the arduous work and worry which was her daily life, or her own chronic depression which influenced her. Pieter van Coninxloo was among the court painters at Malines. Philip had commissioned him to paint Margaret's portrait for Henry VII when he was courting Margaret. Van Coninxloo also painted the four children:

---

423 Hannelore Sachs, The Renaissance Woman, trans. by Marianne Herzfeld (New York: McGraw-Hill Book Company, 1971), p. 86.

Eleanor, Charles, Isabel and Mary. Lucas Cranach visited Malines in 1509 and painted a portrait of Charles. The record of payment is preserved at Lille, but the portrait itself is lost. Jan van Battel was another. He painted the decoration on a chariot for the children and executed portraits.[424] Painting at that time was considered more of a craft, and most artists were skilled in such dissimilar materials as walls, canvasses, parchment, wood and varied objects. Another versatile artist was Paul Tubach who decorated the apartments for the children of Christian II of Denmark and Isabel. There were also several local artists attached to the court whom Margaret, with her keen eye for the good, had discovered.

Two of these artists attached to the court but more loosely connected and much better known were Quentin Massys and Lucas van Leyden. The former came from Louvain and painted for the Cathedral of Antwerp. Between 1508 and 1511, by order of the Carpenters' Guild, he created The Lamentation for Christ. Lucas van Leyden is noteworthy for many reasons, but in regard to the life of the Archduchess, he has left us at least three compositions in which Margaret is shown at a game of cards. The one is an indoor scene with eight figures in which kibitzers and players are amusingly depicted in various expressions of concentration.[425] A second portrays three figures in an outdoor setting, two of which are unmistakable, Margaret and her nephew Charles; of the third, various explanations are offered - it could be Cardinal Wolsey or the Bishop of Liege, Erard de la Marck.[426] Van Leyden was one of the first artists to show gambling, which is a more seventeenth century theme, but it is interesting to note that this was a form of leisure for the court and that Margaret could become totally absorbed in it.

During this radical change in her life, she was blessed with a visit by Michael Sittow known as "Master Michel le Flamand," but who was

---

424   Frances Lawhon Forbush, "The Patronage of Margaret of Austria: Taste in Transition" (unpublished M.A. thesis, University of Virginia, May 1977), p. 27.
425   Lucas van Leyden (1494-1533) The Card Players, Samuel H. Kress Collection, National Gallery of Art, Washington, D.C.
426   Lucas van Leyden (1494-1533) The Card Players, from the collection of Baron Thyssen-Bornemisza which toured the United States in 1980.

not really Flemish as he came from Reval (Talinn) in Estonia. He was, nevertheless, associated with the form of art practiced in the Low Countries, and had also spent many years in Spain where Margaret came to know him. He is the one who had done her favorite little Madonna and Child which she described as "saying her hours, and the little God sleeping," and which she used to caress and call it her "mignonne" (darling).[427]

Gerard Horenbout of Ghent, a miniaturist, came to Margaret's court in 1516 and served until 1522. He is thought to have done the sixteen miniatures inserted in the Sforza Hours which had been damaged.[428] Either he or Simon Benning of Bruges, also a miniaturist, may have executed the celebrated volume Hortulus Animae as a gift for her father and now in the Library of Vienna.[429]

Adrian van den Haute was employed by the Archduchess from 1509 to 1521 in various capacities. To his old style Flemish art, he brought classical elements. He was a designer of windows, medallions, coats of arms, and executed the reverse drawings by which tapestries are devised. The tapestries ordered from Pieter van Aelst are thought to be his designs. Besides bringing beauty to a room, they helped to keep it warm. The making of tapestries contributed to the prospering economy of the Low Countries; several thousand being employed in this ancient art. The vivid colors and exquisite detail utilizing silk threads, as well as silver and gold, made the weaving process slow and painstaking. These artistic productions were valued throughout Europe, were frequently commissioned by kings and popes, and often presented as gifts. Today, they are museum pieces.[430]

---

427 Ghislaine de Boom, Marguerite d'Autriche-Savoie et la Pré-Renaissance (Bruxelles: La Renaissance de Livre, 1496 [1935], p. 90.

428 Frances Lawhon Forbush, "The Patronage of Margaret of Austria: Taste in Transition" (unpublished M.A. thesis, University of Virginia, May 1977), p. 28.

429 Ghislaine de Boom, Marguerite d'Autriche-Savoie et la Pré-Renaissance (Bruxelles: La Renaissance de Livre, (1496) [1935], p. 83.

430 Jan Cornelisz Vermeyen from Holland painted a series of family portraits and later served Margaret's niece and successor Mary of Hungary and also Charles V. Vermeyen accompanied the Emperor Charles V to the siege of Tunis in 1535 where Charles defeated Barbarossa and retook Tunis. He memorialized the episodes in twelve cartoons, later interpreted by Guillaume de Pannemaker in tapestry. (See de Boom, p. 87.) This historical tapestry was in the Museum of Madrid until after World War II when it was purchased for 800,000 Belgian Francs. Repair work

Jan Mostaert from Haarlem came to the court at the young age of 18 and served the Archduchess from 1517 to 1526. He also combined Renaissance elements such as architectural details in conventional Flemish compositions. He is perhaps best known for a bizarre "West Indian landscape with many nude figures, a curious cliff, and exotic houses and huts."[431]

Testifying to the interest in the newly discovered Western World, the picture points to the court of the Regent, where there was far more concern and information about the deeds of the Spanish conquerors than elsewhere in the Netherlands. Charles V had presented his aunt with marvelous objects from the 'Indies.' Among the Spanish and Portuguese merchants residing in Antwerp there must, of course, also have been a lively interest in the new discoveries. [It is believed] that the conquest of Mexico by Cortes provided the occasion for this scene, commissioned by Margaret in 1523.[432]

One of the Archduchess's favorite artists was Jacopo de'Barberi who had served her father as well. Her tender regard for this elderly Venetian is indicated not only by her pension to him, but by the fact that he occupied a studio within the palace itself. Several of his works became part of her collection. De'Barberi was admired and respected in his own time, and exerted tremendous influence, acting as the catalyst between Flemish and Italian art. De'Barberi's works, based on mythological themes, served as models for such artists in the Low Countries as Jan Gossaert and Conrad Meyt. It was mainly through these models and the Raphael drawings, which arrived in Brussels in 1517, that Flemish and Dutch artists developed their own form of Renaissance art with its attention to detail, its simple

---
cost 200,000 BF. It now hangs in the city hall at Mechelen/Malines. Protected by a curtain from dust and sun, it is shown if the tour group is very small.
431 Max J. Friedlander, Lucas van Leyden and Other Dutch Masters of His Time, trans. Heinz Norden (Brussels and Leyden, 1973), p. 13.
432 Ibid.

intensity and deep religious themes, all executed with a technique so fine that they in turn became the teachers of Europe, and left to future generations works of unparalleled appeal.

Bernard (Barent) van Orley, who painted several portraits of the Regent, came to Margaret's court in 1515. A many sided talent, he was equally at home in designs for stained glass and tapestries and large altarpieces. In 1516 he superintended the weaving of the Raphael tapestries. In addition to executing paintings of her nieces and nephew, van Orley painted several religious works revealing the Italian influence. One of these is The Ordeal and Patience of Job triptych now at the Royal Museum in Brussels. The theme of Job's suffering was very close to Margaret's heart, and she had composed a poem about it. Her poem may have been the inspiration for the work. One of the items in Margaret's will mentions that she gave the triptych to Antoine de Lalaing, Lord of Hoogstraten, to decorate the mantelpiece of the chamber that she customarily occupied during her visits to his residence.[433] Van Orley was known in his own time as the Flemish Raphael because of his exquisite Italianate Madonnas. Forbush concludes:

> What places van Orley in the front rank of Flemish painters of the time was his ability to present these themes in the newly-introduced Romanist style, and this aspect of his work was evidently appreciated and encouraged by Margaret.

There is a copy of his portrait of Margaret in the museum at Brou. It depicts her in the simple black widow's gown with a beautifully pleated wimple and a sheer white headband. Her hands are in a graceful position, and there is a delicacy of expression in the face.

One of the most familiar names to us today is Jan Gossaert van Mabuse mentioned above in connection with de'Barberi. His chief patrons were members of the Burgundian court, such as Adolph of Burgundy, Lord of Beveren (Beveland) Veere and Middleburg, who was married to Anne of

---

[433] Le Comte Emmanuel de Quinsonas, Matériaux pour servir à l'histoire de Marguerite d'Autriche (Paris: Chez Delaroque Frères, 1860), Vol. III, p. 402.

Berghes, and Philip of Burgundy, Bishop of Utrecht. For that reason he was seldom at Malines. Another reason may be gleaned from an early art historian Carel van Mander (1548-1606) who in his Schilderboeck relates that Mabuse "led a very irregular life and often visited inns to drink and fight..."[434] His art mirrored his life and he painted in a lively and zestful style, though sometimes over-done and complex. He had great technical dexterity, and took on the delicate task of restoring several old paintings in the palace collection as well as painting several family portraits. Gossaert was very skillful in reproducing physical traits, and since the likenesses were flattering, he was very popular. He also built a Renaissance-style mausoleum for Isabel, one of Margaret's nieces, after her death in 1526.[435]

Of all the artists of this time, perhaps the best known to us today is Albrecht Dürer (1471-1528) the German engraver and painter - a great favorite of Maximilian. Dürer toured the Low Countries on a working journey with his wife Agnes during the years 1520-1521. Along with household items, they packed engravings, woodcuts and prints to be sold as they traveled, to pay their way. His journal of their experiences brings that era to life. Cortes's Aztec treasures were on display, and what images they must have summoned! Another time he described a parade in Antwerp:

> The whole city was there, all the guilds and trades, each man dressed according to his rank and most richly ... The procession also included a large troop of widows, who keep themselves by the work of their hands and live by a special rule. They were dressed in white linen from head to foot - a moving thing to see. Among those women I saw some of very high estate.[436]

---

[434] Elka Schrijver, "The Life of Jan Van Scorel," In History Today (London: February, 1978), p. 122.

[435] This can be seen at St. Peter's in Ghent.

[436] From Tagebuch der Reise in die Niederlands, quoted in Not in God's Image: Women in History from the Greeks to the Victorians, edited by Julia O'Faolain and Lauro Martines. Colophon Books. (New York: Harper and Row, 1973), p. 157.

Dürer's interest in all kinds of animal life was well known. He noted in his journal the price of a cage he bought for a parrot which had been a gift to him. Then, hearing of a lion in Ghent, he made the trip over from Brussels to see it, becoming the first artist in history to draw a lion. Later, he was told there was a beached whale in Zeeland, and went off immediately to see for himself.

Dürer found congenial friendships with other artists such as Quentin Massys and Lucas van Leyden. He painted a portrait of the handsome Bernard van Orley and twice he painted Erasmus the famous one of him in his scholar's cap with the earflaps is now in the Louvre. During the festivities following Charles's coronation at Aachen October 13, 1520, he was able to win from Charles a yearly annuity in continuation of the one which Maximilian had always granted. He was obviously a man of great warmth and eager curiosity, and a keen observer. Dürer recorded in his Sketchbook:

> Dame Margaret showed me all her beautiful things, among which I saw about forty small panels painted in oil colors, the like of which, for the quality and fineness of their painting I have not seen before.[437]

But he was stunned and hurt when she refused to buy one of his portraits of Maximilian, saying she did not think it was a good likeness of her father. Dürer had cooperated in a painting with de'Barberi in Venice. When he asked if he might have de'Barberi's "little Book" the Archduchess replied that she had already promised it to van Orley.

From this account, it appears not to have been a very cordial meeting, and yet Margaret did appreciate his work. His masterpiece The Assumption of the Virgin she had incorporated into the design for the stained glass windows at Brou which depict her and Philibert praying to their patron saints. She also owned several of his engravings.

---

[437] Frances Lawhon Forbush, "The Patronage of Margaret of Austria: Taste in Transition" (unpublished M.A. thesis, University of Virginia, May 1977), p. 65.

The forty panels which Dürer admired were portions of an altarpiece called the Oratoriurn of Isabella which Juan de Flandes had painted while Margaret was in Spain,[438] though two had been painted by Michael Sittow. (By the 1524 inventory, only 22 remained.) These were purchased by Diego Flores for Margaret after the death of Isabella of Spain on November 26, 1504, only two months after Philibert's death. According to Isabella's wishes, her possessions were to be sold to raise funds for a memorial, and Margaret, having spent two years at the Spanish court, knew exactly what to buy. She may even have watched the progress of this painting and been early captivated by it. Juan de Flandes was another favorite of Maximilian who had sent him to the Spanish court for portraits of the royal children before the double betrothal of his children to Juan and Juana of Spain.

Another famous painting among the Burgundian treasures is known as the Arnolfini Wedding by Jan van Eyck (1370? - 1440) now in the National Gallery in London. But most of the paintings were portraits of the family and other royal and noble families. They were confined to a few of her rooms, and the library and chapel, and judging from their numbers, must have been hung vertically and horizontally, "frame to frame" as Forbush puts it.[439]

As any woman might during one of life's lulls, Margaret decided to make some changes in her home. This was not the first time. Between 1501 and 1504, when she was married to Duke Philibert, she had redesigned furniture so that it would be much lighter in weight. The young couple was constantly on the move, and as much of their furniture went with them, especially the beds, it occurred to her that the trips could be accomplished far more easily with pieces that were plainer and of lighter weight. Then she relied on her decorating skills to arrange art objects on the simplified cabinets in such a way that these changes were not evident.[440]

---

438 Two of these had been painted by Michael Sittow. By the 1524 inventory, only 22 remained.
439 Frances Lawhon Forbush, "The Patronage of Margaret of Austria: Taste in Transition" (unpublished M.A. Thesis, University of Virginia, May 1977), pp. 17-18.
440 Elsa Winker, Margarete Von Österreich, Grande Dame der Renaissance (München: Verlag Georg D.W. Callwey, 1966), p. 136.

However, in 1517 and 1518, her decision to remodel the palace presented a larger challenge. According to tradition, she engaged Rombaut Keldermans, though later scholarship is crediting the design to Guyot de Beaugrand.[441] Anyone visiting Mechelen/Malines and looking for a palace-like structure will be disappointed. What he will see is a roomy and unpretentious Gothic city mansion such as any wealthy merchant of the time possessed. Its many windows, so necessary in Belgium's dark winters, face into an interior courtyard and onto the street outside. The stately Renaissance front is thought to have been done at this time.[442] Way ahead of its time architecturally, it is conceded to be the first Renaissance structure in northern Europe.[443]

In 1523, Margaret commissioned Bernard van Orley to design stained glass windows for St. Gudule's (now Sts. Michael and Gudule). A family tribute, they include Maximilian and Mary of Burgundy, Philip and his wife Juana, Margaret and Philibert and the nephews Charles and Fredinand. A window was commissioned for St. Romboud's in Mechelen/Malines designed by Jan van Roome (Mentioned earlier in connection with the tombs of Brou) giving the genealogy of Charles V.[444]

In addition to the above, Tremayne found that during Margaret's regency, "architecture made great progress, and many beautiful buildings were designed and executed."

> The belfry at Bruges, the cloisters of the Convent of the Annunciation near the same town, and the Tower of St. Rombaut [Romboud] at Malines, the Hotel de Ville at Ghent, besides several churches which were restored and embellished, such as the churches of St.

---

441 Frances Lawhon Forbush, "The Patronage of Margaret of Austria: Taste in Transition" (unpublished M.A. thesis, University of Virginia, May 1977), p. 45.
442 The edifice now affords the law and justice departments' quietly elegant office space.
443 J.R. Hale, Renaissance Europe 1480-1520 (London: Fortuna/Collins, 1977), p. 274.
444 Unfortunately, that has been destroyed, but the drawing can still be seen in the Archepiscopal Museum at Malines.

Peter and St. Stephen at Lille, the spire of Antwerp Cathedral and St. Gudule [St. Michael] at Brussels.[445]

Margaret's life was busy but she did find the leisure to read, and her private rooms contained many handsome books. De Boom offers this glimpse of these rooms:

> ... ornamented with family portraits, art objects of high taste and also strange accoutrements of feathers coming from the Indies... volumes of books placed flat on tables or carefully enclosed in a metal cabinet, because in this era the book was still an object of art and luxury, often offering the triple splendor of admirable calligraphy, magnificent illustrations and sumptuous bindings. While the new printing industry was multiplying books and at the same time vulgarizing them, Margaret possessed many fine specimens of first editions which could compete with manuscripts [in beauty].[446]

The library was a joy to her and she took good care of it. There was a very old and precious section which her ancestors Philip the Bold and Margaret of Flanders had begun. According to Hughes:

> ... the Burgundian library reached an impressive size through the efforts of Philip the Good, whose love of books, as of all else in the realm of art, made it one of the most remarkable collections of the fifteenth century. To the interests and influence of the dukes in the expansion of the library were added those of the duchesses... and in the cases of Isabel of Portugal and Margaret of York, were

---

445 Eleanor E. Tremayne, The First Governess of The Netherlands (New York: G.P. Putnam's Sons; London: Methuen & Company, 1908), p. 279.
446 Ghislaine de Boom, Marguerite d'Autriche-Savoie et la Pré-Renaissance (Bruxelles: La Renaissance du Livre, 1946/1935), p. 80.

equally responsible for new developments in the trends in making, gathering and reading of books.[447]

This Burgundian library contained well over 200 manuscripts, including ten Bibles, twenty-five books of hours, thirteen books of prayers, and five books of music. Four large volumes on civil law included the second part of Justinian's Digest and the first part of his Civil Law. Other juridical books were Honoree Bonet's Arbre des batailles, 1386, which were rules for international and military law; also a volume by Paleologus translated into French. There was a book on astronomy, two treatises on medicine, and on King Arthur, Lancelot, Merlin, The Holy Grail, and many fabliaux. Aristotle's Ethics and Politics are included as well as a volume entitled Government of Kings and Princes which scholars of that time attributed to him. There is Boethius' Consolations and a volume by Cassiodorus, the sixth-century Roman statesman and educator who emphasized the sevenfold grouping of knowledge known as the quadrivium and trivium, and "gave it sanctity by connecting it with the text: 'Wisdom hath built her house, she hath hewn out her seven pillars.'"[448]

There were Chronicles of Flanders and France, and tales of travels to the Holy Land, Constantinople and Mongolia, and the discovery of the Canary Islands 1402-1404. The Duke and Duchess were loyal patrons of Christine de Pisan, and her Cent Ballades, a book of poetry, is included in this collection. Hughes quotes Professor M. Meiss's remarks about Giovanni Boccaccio's Nobles femmes renominées:

> This treatise on women - the first ever written - appeared in French (1404) in the years when Christine de Pisan was attempting to improve the traditional low estimation of the weaker sex.[449]

---
447 Muriel J. Hughes, "The Library of Philip the Bold and Margaret of Flanders, First Valois Duke and Duchess of Burgundy" in the Journal of Medieval History (4, No. 2, North-Holland Publishing Company, June 1978), p. 145.
448 William Boyd, The History of Western Education (New York: Barnes & Noble, 1966), p. 103. The quadrivium included geometry (with geographical facts), arithmetic, music and astronomy; the trivium, grammar, rhetoric and logic.
449 Muriel J. Hughes, "The Library of Philip the Bold and Margaret of Flanders, First Valois Duke and Duchess of Burgundy" in the Journal of Medieval History (4, No. 2, North-Holland Publishing Company, June 1978), p. 181.

Among the bookbinders and craftsmen in the employ of the first duke was a Colette of Paris who, in 1387, supplied silk and ornamentation for a book of hours.[450]

Margaret's own library of 148 volumes was inventoried first in 1516 and later in 1523.[451] It includes several items from Margaret of York, her step-grandmother and godmother, one of which is Benois seront les miséricordieux (Blessed are the merciful), which had been a gift to the old archduchess. The margins are drawn with fruits, flowers and animals in a glorious triumph of coloring and phantasy.

Another section is part of her dowry from Savoy.[452]

Both sides of Margaret's family found music enriching and inspiring, and she continued the tradition. One volume known under the name Album de Marguerite d'Autriche is a choir book containing sixty-one musical compositions by Alexander Agricola, Loyset Compere, Josquin des Prés,[453] Pierre de la Rue, Orto, Mathieu Pipelare, Jean Prioris, Antoine Brumel, and other musicians of the Low Countries. The words are in Flemish, French or Latin, and many are attributed to Margaret. De Boom describes the first page as a rich frame sewn with precious gems, fruits and flowers, above all marguerites, surrounding a curious portrait of Margaret which shows the

---

450 Ibid., p. 167.
451 La Bibliothèque de Marguerite d'Autriche (Bruxelles: Ministère de l'Instruction Publique, Bibliothèque Royale de Belgique, Mai-juillet 1940).
452 This ancient library of the Royal House of Savoy, housed at Turin University, as well as 400 Greek codices, and 1,200 manuscripts written in Latin, was completely destroyed by fire in January 1904. The manuscripts included palimpsests (parchments used one or more times after earlier writing has been erased or scraped) of Cicero and two volumes of Pliny's Natural History. Francesco Basso's celebrated map of the world, executed in steel studded with gold, which dates from 1670 was also destroyed. While the fire was at its height, the chief librarian was seen rushing about in a frantic condition, weeping bitterly. See International Herald-Tribune "75 Years Ago" (Paris: Saturday-Sunday, January 27-28, 1979).
453 According to Henry W. Littlefield, History of Europe 1500-1848, Barnes & Noble Books (5th ed. New York: Harper & Row, 1939), p. 29, Josquin des Prés (c. 1450-1521) was the first of the great modern composers. He was "known as the 'Prince of Music' and showed a finished mastery that justifies regarding him as the father of modern composition."
In regard to the music, many of the pieces from the time and the court of the Archduchess Margaret were performed at Mechelen/Malines in September 1980 in commemoration of her 500th birthday. Brussels intends to have an exhibition and celebration during 1983.

princess kneeling peacefully and contemplatively at her prie-dieu wearing a magnificent gown of gold and ermine, but remaining faithful to her white hood and widow's wimpel.[454] Another is a choir book containing six masses by Pierre de la Rue and one by Henry Isaac who was a musician at Maximilian's court, and this quite large volume was a gift from the Emperor to his daughter.

The Recueil de "basses danses" is of black parchment with the music and writing traced in silver and gold. It contains a series of diagrams of dances which de Boom judges to date from the era of Margaret of York and Marie of Burgundy.[455]

Margaret's court became a center for the humanists and writers of the Renaissance as well as artists and musicians since she supported them all. Molinet, an eloquent writer and the uncle of Jean Lemaire, wrote of Margaret on the occasion of her final return to the Low Countries:

> Virtue surrounds you,
> It grows and flourishes
> In you and over the Empire.
> Dignified it is to have the throne,
> Royal scepter and crown,
> of a glorious Empire.[456]

Later on Jean Lemaire wrote Les Chansons de Namur to celebrate the triumph of a small group of peasants over a large French army in the

---

454 Ghislaine de Boom, Marguerite d'Autriche-Savoie et la Pré-Renaissance (Bruxelles: La Renaissance du Livre, 1946/1935), p. 85.

455 Ibid., p. 85. This volume was shown to me and is in very poor condition. These books are so rare and valuable and fragile, that they are almost never shown, as the library has been unable to devise a way to display them that will not hasten their destruction. But fortunately we do have some pictures, and we do have access to the archivist Ghislaine de Boom's meticulous descriptions. Those with a deeper interest should turn to her works for knowledge which this short review cannot provide.

456 Ghislaine de Boom, Marguerite d'Autriche-Savoie at la Pré-Renaissance (Bruxelles: La Renaissance du Livre, 1946/1935), p. 75.

battles waged from October 17, 1506 to June 1507.[457] The Archduchess appreciated this so much she forwarded it to Maximilian to have translated into Latin, as the University of Vienna had an excellent faculty of Latin poetry and literature.

Of all the humanists who thronged to the court, Erasmus was the most illustrious. Traveling throughout Europe and England, he found a home in many places. He was associated with the University of Louvain for several years, and also lived for a time in a religious house in Anderlecht.[458]

Of his many works, the two which apply to this study are his Institutio principis Christiani and one part of his Colloquia. The first was a treatise on the education of a Christian prince published in 1516, but thought to have been composed earlier.[459] The fine principles and aims he set forth, though written with the prince in mind, were meant to apply to any ruler; and certainly Margaret espoused these ideals, not only in theory, but in practice. His feeling against the barbarism of sending royal young women abroad to be married[460] must have touched a sympathetic chord in the soul of the Archduchess.

Adrian of Utrecht, and not Erasmus, had been chosen as tutor to Charles. Perhaps just as well, as Erasmus was against instruction being imposed without the participation of the student, and Charles was not eagerly disposed to learning in his youth.[461] Nevertheless, Erasmus was held in high regard by both Charles and Margaret. Later in 1523, Charles learned that Erasmus was irregularly paid by his own officials, and suggested that Aunt Margaret was the one most capable of insuring that he be favorably treated because of

---

457 Jean Lemaire de Belges, Oeuvres, publiées par J. Stecher, Tome IV, pp. 293-317.

458 Anderlecht is now a suburb of Brussels which is not far from Mechelen/Malines. The house is well maintained. Situated on a busy corner, it nevertheless preserves that serenity which Erasmus so appreciated. It has a quiet, enclosed garden. Inside, the polished floors, the books and desk placed by the window give one a pleasing sense of the order this scholar required.

459 Lester K. Born, trans. and e., The Education of a Christian Prince (New York: Columbia University Press, 1936), p. 29. See earlier in this work, Chapter II, on the education of Charles.

460 Ibid., p. 39.

461 Karl Brandi, The Emperor Charles V, trans. by C.V. Wedgwood (Oxford: Alfred A. Knopf [Alden Press], 1939), p. 48.

his "great doctrines and writings."[462] And in turn, in the laudatory manner of the time, he referred to her as the "most accomplished princess of our times." Though he was a product of a time and culture which believed women were weaker in both mind and body, he frequently rose above this, and his intelligent sympathy for women is expressed in the Colloquia for which either Margaret or her niece Mary was the inspiration.[463]

The second most highly regarded humanist of the Low Countries was Jean Everardi known as Jean Second or Janus (Johannes) Secundus. "In pure and grave verse, he sang of the glory and the virtues of the illustrious Margaret."[464] His time occurs somewhat later in Margaret's life, as he celebrated the Ladies' Peace at Cambrai and composed Margaret's epitaph. The portrait of him by Jan Van Scorel shows a very handsome young man.[465] Another humanist of the time whose name comes down to us for his sympathetic words about women is Cornelius Agrippa of Antwerp. Though a native of Germany, he was a former professor at the University of Dole, then in Savoy, and Margaret must have met him during the years of her marriage to Philibert. A man of his time, he was a curious mixture of intelligence, erudition in ancient and modern languages and writers, and in contrast to most humanistic thought, an, earnest student of the occult. Though he had many quarrels with the Inquisition, he always found protection under Margaret, and at her death, he gave the funeral oration. His De nobilitate et praecellential foeminei sexus declamatio and other treatises give us insight into what a modern man of that period thought about women. He observed that:

> ... only masculine tyranny and lack of education prevented women from playing a role in the world equal to man's...physically, women were finished off more neatly than men.[466]

---

462 P.S. Allen, ed., Opus Epistolarum Des. Erasmi Roterodami (Oxford: 1906), Tome V, p. 312, letter 1380.

463 Ghislaine de Boom, Marguerite d'Autriche-Savoie et al Pré-Renaissance (Bruxelles: La Renaissance du Livre, 1946/1935), p. 78.

464 Ibid., p. 78.

465 Elka Schrijver, "The Life of Jan Van Scorel" In History Today (London: February, 1978), p. 122.

466 J.R. Hale, Renaissance Europe 1480-1520 (London: Fontana/Collins, 1977), p. 128.

The only difference between man and woman is physical... In everything else they are the same. Woman does not have a soul of a different sex from that which animates man. Both received a soul which is absolutely the same and of an equal condition. Women and men were equally endowed with the gifts of spirit, reason, and the use of words; they were created for the same end, and the sexual difference between them will not confer a different destiny...[467]

Wishing to take on human nature in its lowest and most abject state, so as the more effectively by this humiliation to expiate the first man's pride of sinning, Jesus Christ chose the male sex as the more despicable, not the female, who is nobler and more regenerate than the male. Moreover, because the human species was driven to evildoing more by the sin of man that of woman, God wanted the sin to be expiated in the sex that had sinned, whereas he wanted the sex which had been taken by surprise and tricked to bring forth Him in whom the sin was to be revenged.[468]

It is no wonder that he was a great favorite of the Archduchess.

Sir Thomas More wrote his Utopia in Antwerp and served at various times as an ambassador from England, but he was not involved in the court life of the Low Countries except to the extent that his ideas on many subjects were introduced. For those who considered political systems at the time, there were various shades of opinion. Erasmus in his Institutio principis Christiani held that if the ruler were a good Christian and followed the principles of Jesus, all would be well in his kingdom. He still believed in the sovereign as God's viceroy. This very idealistic view was even then often regarded as impractical. Cornelius Agrippa, though he was a royalist as far as the Archduchess Margaret was concerned, believed that any system could be good if those in charge had ability and integrity.

---

467 Julia O'Faolain and Lauro Martines, ed. Not In God's Image: Women in History from the Greeks to the Victorians. Colophon Books. (New York: Harper & Row Publishers, 1973), pp. 183-184.
468 Ibid.

No matter what the shade of thought, what can be distilled from this is the humanistic belief in man: that the events on earth were not planned, executed and solved by God exclusively, but were often the result of man's actions, and were subject to man's solutions.

Three other men close to the Archduchess should be included in this study for the variety of thought they brought to this circle. Nicolas Perrenot de Granvelle is known as the father of the famous cardinal of the next generation, and is somewhat overshadowed in history because of this. Among his admirable gifts were a keen intellect, great tact, and a nature so trustworthy that Margaret employed him as her emissary in matters of great secrecy. The Archduchess had an acute sense of the duties of her rank, and in this she had the able legal counsel of Viglius ab Aytta de Zuichem. In matters of state, she relied upon the advice of Jerome de Busleyden, a man so interested in education that he turned his home into a library and museum,[469] and founded the famous College of Three Languages at Louvain.

There are others who were illustrious men of letters and science: the classical philologists Langius, Barthélemy Latomus, Clénard, Martin Dorpius, the syriacisant Masius, the botanists Rembert Dodoens and De l'Escluse, and the geographer Gerhard Kremer who gave us the "mercator projection" in maps.[470]

This was an astonishing array of artistic, literary, musical, educational, philosophical and legal talent with which Margaret associated. The court circle was, however, not just an exclusive intellectual club. Informally by word of mouth, formally by sermons and printed treatises, their ideas spread out into the community. In this climate of free thinking, reason, simple religion and commercial success, religious and municipal schools, it is revealing to listen to a comment by the Italian humanist Guicciardini:

---

469 This exists today in Mechelen/Malines.
470 Henry Pirenne, Histoire de Belgique (Bruxelles: Henri Lamertin, 1907), Vol. III, p. 301. Pirenne also includes in his list Andre Vesalius (1515-1564) the great anatomist, but his birth date appears to be too late for him to be included among the savants at Margaret's court, though he may perhaps have been in Queen Mary's, her successor.

The education of the people was highly developed especially among the wealthy Netherlanders with their bourgeois policy, and often even the peasants were no longer illiterate. The women were commended by their contemporaries for their beauty and chastity and because they were keen on reading and writing, liked to quote from the Holy Scriptures, and could argue about dogma as well as the learned scholars. This certainly furthered the spread of the Reformation.[471]

This period, beginning in 1515 when life was at a very low ebb for Margaret, brought her cultural and artistic enrichment and depth of a kind which she might not have attained in any other way. For her personally, it was salvation.

---

471 Hannelore Sachs, The Renaissance Woman, trans. from the German by Marianne Herzfeld (New York: McGraw-Hill, 1971), p. 17.
For those doing basic research, the writer suggests A. Pinchart, Archives des arts, lettres et sciences. Documents inédits (Ghent: 1860-1881), 3 volumes containing extracts from the archives concerning the role of Margaret of Austria in these fields. For musical activity at the court of Margaret of Austria, see E. Van der Straeten, La Musique aux Pays-Bas avant le XIXe siècle (Bruxelles: 1867-1880), Tomes VI and VII.
Lastly, the writer had the great good fortune to be placed back to back in the upper "sale" (or "zaal") of the Bibliothèque Royale at Brussels with Ed Caraco. The conversations were mutually enriching. His work on "Archaisms in Early Netherlandish Art" may be available from the University of Virginia in 1981.

Chapter 5

THE TUMULTUOUS YEARS OF THE REFORMATION

While Margaret was in semi-retirement, events continued to occur which would eventually involve her, and for which she would have to find solutions.

One must go back to 1515 for the background of these developments. When Francis I assumed the throne of France, he found his country prepared for war in Italy. Young and eager for glory, he entered with enthusiasm into all the preparations with Venice. His foes were the Emperor, the King of Aragon, and the Swiss; the easy-going Pope Leo decided to make a compromise. The French forces crossed the Alps in August, and in September after several minor engagements, took up a strong and well-fortified position southeast of Milan at a place called Marignano (now known as Melegnano). On September 12, 1515, the Swiss, numbering about 20,000 attacked the French. The battle recommenced at dawn the next morning. There were about 3,000 dead on each side. While at first it appeared that the Swiss had triumphed, in the end, the French won a great victory.

Maximilian wrote to Margaret on October 7 giving her this report and adding that he was gathering a great number of men and intended to go himself. However, the news was much worse than Maximilian realized. The result of this battle was a brilliant and complete victory for the French. The young Maximilian Sforza, Duke of Milan, was deposed and sent to France where he lived as a pensioner until his death in 1530. His younger brother Francesco assumed the title, but fled to the Tyrol where, under Maximilian's protection, he waited for a better day. Before the end of the year another league was formed against the French by Maximilian, Ferdinand and Henry. Peace between France and Switzerland was confirmed by the Treaty of Geneva on November 7, 1515.

But dynastic matters were never far from Maximilian's mind, and his thoughts turned to Eleanor, his first grandchild and the only one not betrothed. It occurred to him that the widowed King of Poland, Sigismund I, though older, might make an honorable and happy match. He sent this description to Margaret with the request that she discuss the matter with Eleanor:

> ...The said King of Poland is a handsome person, somewhat plump, anyhow he will never be any fatter; a white face and body and his hands very white, the height of M. de Berges at twenty years of age, a face more handsome; for his face is open and honest ...He is, as he told me by his own mouth, which is beautiful and red, of the age of forty-six years ... his hair is already a little gray ...[472]

Margaret replied:

> ...If you desire to carry through this intention to marry Eleanor with the King of Poland, I will speak with her and tell her of his virtues, handsomeness, the grandeur of his realm, and anything else you wish...[473]

---

[472] André J.G. Le Glay, Correspondance ... Vol. II, p. 319.
[473] Ibid.

She did speak to Eleanor who "listened willingly and sweetly, though with a little fear," but in spite of many words on my part, I was not able to draw her out.[474] Ferdinand suggested another match and Maximilian asked her for her opinion on that, as privately Margaret was not in favor of the marriage with Sigismund. By all accounts he was as fine as Maximilian judged, but he was not for Eleanor. He chose instead Bona, the daughter of Galeazzo Sforza, former Duke of Milan, and Isabella of Aragon.[475]

Apart from this, Eleanor and Frederick, the Count Palatine and closest friend of Charles her brother, had fallen in love. Charles seemed unaware until the Lord of Chiévres informed him. One morning, on the pretext of greeting his sister, he grabbed a lovenote in a playful scuffle, and with this incriminating evidence, put an end to the affair. To Charles's credit, and their own sense of duty to sovereign, all three continued to maintain a friendly relationship. Though he was banished from the court, the Count Palatine remained one of his worthiest and loyal nobles, and Eleanor was his favorite sister.[476]

On January 23, 1516, Ferdinand of Aragon died leaving Charles heir to all his estates, as was considered just at that time. It was a deathbed change, as he really desired to leave Aragon to his favorite grandson Ferdinand who had been raised in Spain under his care. Until Charles should arrive, Cardinal Ximenes was named regent in Castile, and the Archbishop of Saragossa, the King's natural son, regent in Aragon. Juana was still living in the castle at Tordesillas with the little Katherine and remained Queen of Castile, but in name only.

The Archduke, now Charles I of Spain continued with deliberation his progress through the Low Countries in spite of entreaties by both Ximenes and Maximilian. The latter, however, had been engaged in campaigns in Italy during this spring; but due to mutiny and lack of funds, or perhaps a dream he had which he found upsetting, he had pulled out. Charles

---

474 Ibid.
475 Thirty years later after her husband's death in 1548 and over the entreaties of her children, Bona retired to sunny Italy where she died in 1558 at age 65.
476 Eleanor married first King Emanuel of Portugal, her Aunt Isabella's and Aunt Maria's widower; secondly, King Francis I of France.

may have been slow to act, but he was not stupid, and he had been well trained. He reflected on the serious problems confronting him in Spain, the continuing campaigns in Italy, and the advances of the Turks. He sent Adrian of Utrecht to Spain to oversee his interests there, and, under the counsel of the Lord of Chièvres, he concluded the Treaty of Noyon on August 13, 1516 with Francis. By the terms of this treaty the French retained Milan, but gave up Naples. Maximilian was to return Brescia and Verona to Venice in return for a payment of money. Another provision of the treaty was that Charles should marry Francis's daughter Louise. The most significant feature surrounding this treaty is that Charles did not consult his grandfather Maximilian. Nevertheless Maximilian ratified it even though it was against his better judgment. He wrote Margaret that no good would come of it since he felt that the French could not be trusted. Still the desire of his heart was for universal peace, so that they could unite against the infidel Turks. But then, typically, he switched from such weighty matters to ask her advice about the painting of a port of honor which he hoped would be so beautifully executed that it would remain forever for their perpetual glory. "He who during his life provides no remembrance for himself, has no remembrance after his death and the same person is forgotten with the tolling of the bell."[477] The dream he had had in Italy was strong enough to cause him to return home, though he never complained about the rigors of army life for an aging man. On March 2, 1517, twenty days before his fifty-eighth birthday, he wrote:

> My good daughter, thinking day and night about the affairs of my heirs, I have decided, principally for the good and honor of my son King Charles to write to my deputies who are with him, certain things concerning their welfare and that of their subjects. Knowing that you will be required by my said son to accomplish an honorable charge, we desire and we require that you comply with it; in doing which you will do a thing very agreeable and

---

[477] Glenn Elwood Waas, The Legendary Character of Kaiser Maximilian (New York: ANS Press, Inc., 1966) [Columbia University Press, 1941]), p. 97 quoted from Der Weisskunig.

honorable to yourself, as you will more plainly understand from our deputies, Messieurs André de Burgo and Nycasy. And to God.

Written on the second day of March by the hand of your good and loyal father, Maxi.[478]

As for Adrian, this well-meaning but rigid man did not get along with Cardinal Ximenes who was very jealous of his authority, and who resented what appeared to him as a takeover by the Burgundian delegation. Adrian wrote a pitiful letter to Margaret from Madrid dated July 12, 1516:[479]

Madame… I thank you very humbly that it has pleased you to bear me in mind touching my promotion to the bishopric of Dervise [Tortosa in Catalonia]; I pray God that He may give me grace and power to do you agreeable service, for which I shall never want either will or diligence.

Madame I should often have wished to write to you, had it not been that there are some who look upon all I do with evil eyes; I hope that God will sometimes reveal whether I have done good or ill. Madame, I pray to God that He may give you the entire accomplishment of your very noble desires …

Your very humble servant, Adrian d'Utrecht

These years are marked for the Archduchess by a greatly enriched personal life and a considerable number of journeys. E. Lancien listed in her itinerary:[480]

1515 -	February	Brussels
		Malines
		Antwerp

---

478 André J.G. Le Glay, Correspondance … Vol. II, p. 345.
479 Van den Bergh, Vol. II, p. 136.
480 Max Bruchet and E. Laneien, L'Itinéraire de Marguerite d'Autriche (Lille: Imprimerie L. Danel, 1934), p. 162 ff.

	Ghent
April	Bruges
May	Middelburg
	Bergen-op-Zoom
	Oudenbosch
June	The Hague
	Haarlem
	Rijnsburg
	The Hague
July	Malines
	Brussels
August	Louvain
	Heverle
	Brussels
November	Mons
	Jodoigne
	Louvain
December	Malines

Maximilian visited in January. Her travel schedule during the year 1516 was even heavier, with Douai, Arras, Lille and Aardenburg added to her schedule.

Little by little, the task of government began to devolve once again on Margaret, and Charles appointed a council to assist her. She, in the meantime, had become reconciled with her adversary, the Lord of Chiévres, perhaps because she realized the peace with France would provide funds Charles badly needed for his trip to Spain.[481] Chiévres became less provincial and more international in his attitudes, and this too helped effect a rapprochement. On September 8, 1517, Charles set sail from Vlissingen for Spain with his sister Eleanor, the Lord of Chiévres, and a large and

---

481 J.S. Brewer, The Reign of Henry VIII ... (London: John Murray, 1884), Vol. I, p. 166-Note: Tunstal wrote to Wolsey that the treaty of Noyon was beneficial to her lands. (Cuthbert Tunstal from Mechelen, February 13, 1517.)

glittering company of nobles with their servants. This voyage too was harrowing. One would think that with the peace with France concluded, they would have taken the overland route. Nevertheless, they landed only eleven days later on September 19, on the Asturian coast in northern Spain. Then the company, unmet, wandered for six weeks through the wild mountain area, never entering any town.[482] Finally, on the last day of October, the Constable of Castile and others of the nobility met Charles and his retinue. They were less than impressed with this gangling youth,[483] their new ruler. He did not seem to have a mind of his own, and he could not speak the language. The first thing Charles did, with Eleanor, was to visit their mother.[484] Poor Juana could not believe that such grown-up children belonged to her. If the children through the years had entertained feelings of suspicion or hope about their mother's condition, those were now dashed forever. This haggard and unkempt woman in perpetual mourning, both harried and neglected by her keepers, presented so great a contrast to their Aunt Margaret that they were moved to pity. They tried to do what they could in removing their little sister Katherine from these unwholesome surroundings, but her absence made Juana inconsolable, and this brave and kind child was returned. Gifts and letters for Katherine, and comfortable apartments of her own, now made her life more bearable. She adored Charles and he was charmed by her.

Cardinal Ximenes died at the age of eighty-three on November 8, 1517. He had preserved Castile for Charles, but Charles's counselors had estranged them. Though the triumphal entry into Valladolid, the capital

---

482 Historians are perplexed over the reason for this. Could such a company wander or camp unnoticed? Was Charles trying to see his mother at Tordesillas before taking on the reins of government? Were the different parts of the company trying to reunite? Were Charles and his council marking time until the aging and ailing Ximenes should die? Did an illness of Charles slow their progress? We do know that years before Margaret's and Philip's companies had been received warmly and promptly, though their landing times and places were expected.

483 Gustav Adolph Bergenroth, ed., Calendar of Letters... Vol. II, pp. 281-283.

484 Karl Brandi, The Emperor Charles V, trans. from the German by C. V. Wedgwood (Oxford: Alfred A. Knopf, 1939), p. 81. "The historian Vital accompanied Charles to the threshold of the Queen's room, but when driven by curiosity, he tried to bring a light into the room itself, Charles barred his way... We shall never know what he found."

of Castile, on November 18, was on the surface joyful and full of pomp; there were undercurrents of discontent as it was learned that all high posts were being given to the gentlemen from the Low Countries. This alienated the nobility and the clergy who retaliated by refusing to quarter the royal party.

There were angry debates following the opening of the Cortes of Castile on February 2, 1518. The oath of allegiance was given to Juana and Charles, in that order, and her name was ordered to be placed first on all acts. Though a subsidy was granted since Charles had had no money, he was petitioned to marry at once; to keep Ferdinand his brother in Spain; to ameliorate the Inquisition; and to learn Spanish.

Charles had no better success in Aragon with their Cortes which behaved in a hostile and arrogant manner. They would have preferred to have offered the crown to Ferdinand, their favorite, but that young man was on his way north to meet, for the first time, his Aunt Margaret.

The Bishop of Badajoz made this assessment:

> The Prince [Charles] has good parts, but he has been kept too much isolated from the world, and in particular, he knows too little of Spaniards. He does not understand a single word of Spanish. He obeys his councilors implicitly; but, as he has entered the seventeenth year of his age, it would be well if he took part in the discussions of his Council.
>
> Monsieur de Chiévres is the most influential person in the court of the Prince. He is prudent and gentle, but avaricious. The same may be said of the Chancellor of Burgundy [Jean le Sauvage]. On the whole, love of money is the besetting sin of the Flemings. They buy and sell the government offices, and it is to be feared that they will introduce the same customs into Spain.
>
> Some of the Spaniards who are in Flanders speak badly of the Inquisition, telling horrible things of it, and pretending that it ruins the country...

> Monsieur de Chiévres is a Frenchman by birth, and keeps the Prince very much under subjection to the King of France. The Prince signs his letters to the King of France "Your humble servant and vassal." As the Prince and the King of France are the two greatest monarchs of Christendom, it is desirable that they should live in peace with one another. Thinks it, however, impossible. The French have already intercepted the couriers who travel between Spain and Flanders… The Prince has not answered the French with as much firmness as could be wished, whilst the ambassador of the Emperor is treated as though he were a servant of the bedchamber of the Prince.
>
> …The Duke of Gueldres is much feared, as he is favoured by the French. He is very overbearing.
>
> …An alliance with the English can be trusted most of all. The English love the house of Austria and abhor the French. The Prince cannot go through France from one of his dominions to another, and going by sea, he may occasionally be forced to enter into an English harbour. On such occasions the friendship of the King of England would be of the greatest value to him…[485]

Margaret and Maximilian, like two anxious parents, could only follow these events from afar through letters and couriers.

Another important event of that year was the marriage of Eleanor to King Emanuel of Portugal. He had first been married to Isabella, then Maria, daughters of Ferdinand and Isabella. Emanuel's daughters Isabella and Beatrice were, therefore, her cousins. It was quite a family occasion, and her new stepdaughters and cousins greeted Eleanor warmly. She had motherly qualities and in the years to come, was to prove a good stepmother to Francis's children.

---

485 Gustav Adolph Bergenroth, ed., Calendar of Letters … Vol. II, pp. 281-283. Written from Brussels March 8, 1516, to the Cardinal Fray Francisco Ximenes de Cisneros, Governor of Spain.

Aunt and grandfather could not have had many regrets over this wedding since Portugal at that time was a leading country in exploration, shipping, and commerce.

Of significance in international terms was the appointment of Mercurino di Gattinara as Chancellor on the death of Jean le Sauvage June 7, 1518 during an epidemic. He immediately set sail for Spain, and arrived October 8. This decision indicates very clearly the continued influence of the Archduchess in the affairs of her nephew, as this man had been her favorite counselor since her years in Savoy.

Charles, over his adolescent rebellion and with his hands full in Spain, became aware of how much he needed his aunt, and that it was not possible for her to function effectively without the power to make decisions. Accordingly on July 24, 1518 at Saragossa, Charles issued the following edict with its graceful preamble:

> …We make known the great and singular love, affection, and confidence that we have and bear to the person of our very dear lady and aunt, the Archduchess Dowager of Savoy… and knowing by true experience the great care and solicitude which she has taken and daily takes for the management and conduct of our affairs in our Low Countries, as much during the time of our minority and youth as since, and even since we have been absent from our said country, without having spared her person or her own goods; we to this same lady our aunt, moved by these causes and others, also that she may be so much the more esteemed and authorized, and have better courage and occasion to continue the care of our said affairs as she has done hitherto…[486]

And alluding to the powers given here, the following authorization was presented to the council at Malines October 3, 1518, "so that no one can pretend ignorance."[487]

---

[486] Christopher Hare; The High and Puissant Princess Marguerite of Austria (London: Harper and Brothers, 1907, pp. 249-250.
[487] Van den Bergh, Correspondance… Vol. II, pp. 140-141.

By our letters-patent given in our town of Saragossa on the 24th day of July, and for the things contained therein, we have ordained that our very dear lady and aunt, the Lady Margaret, Archduchess of Austria, Dowager of Savoy, etc., shall sign from henceforth all letters, acts, and documents with her own hand, which are issued for us, and for our business on this side, which ought to be signed with our seal... Placing in the signature these words: By the King. Marguerite; that she will have charge of the seal of our finances, and she alone will provide and dispose of the offices of our country over here ...[488]

Maximilian, both relieved and delighted, wrote from Wels on December 12, 1518:

Very dear and very loved daughter, we have received your letters of the 25th of October, and by them understand the honor and authority which our good son the Catholic King has recently bestowed on you, of which we are very joyful, and have good hope that you will so acquit yourself to the welfare, the guidance and the conduct of his affairs that we will have cause to be not only content, but also increase your authority more and more, as your good nephew. In which doing, nothing could be more agreeable to us. So God knows, and me He, very dear and loved daughter, guard you.
 Your good father, Maxi.[489]

This letter was written one month before his death, and though ailing, not one word of complaint or discouragement is given, and Maximilian had plenty of cause for both. In July he had presided at the Diet of Augsburg wherein we mark one of the beginnings of the Reformation.[490] Night and

---

488 Van den Bergh, Correspondance... Vol. II, pp. 140-141; Christopher Hare, The High and Puissant Princess Marguerite of Austria (London: Harper and Brothers, 1907), pp. 249-250.
489 Eleanor E. Tremayne, The First Governess of The Netherlands (New York: G.P. Putnam's Sons; London: Methuen & Company, 1908), p. 162.
490 Christopher Hare, The High and Puissant Princess ... p. 251.

day had been busy as he strove to accomplish two objectives close to his heart: 1) the securing of the succession of the Holy Roman Empire to his grandson Charles and 2) the financing of an army to defeat the Turks. The electors, however, had more immediate concerns. They sought help in dealing with the religious unrest which had crystallized since Martin Luther, an Augustinian monk, had nailed his ninety-five theses to the church door in Wittenberg on October 31, 1517.

Nevertheless, Maximilian obtained the promises of the electors of Mainz, Cologne, the Palatinate, Brandenburg, and Bohemia with pledges of money so large that Charles was alarmed. In an allegorical letter, Margaret wrote:

> The Lord King, my nephew, has written to us that the horse on which he wishes to come and see us is very dear. We know well that it is dear; but as matters stand, if he does not wish to have it, there is a buyer ready to take it, and, since he has broken it in, it seems a pity that he should give it up, whatever it costs him.[491]

The other buyer was France. Margaret was above all a realist. In the end, it would be much of her collateral and that of Flanders-Brabant, held as security by the Fuggers, which would ensure Charles the imperial crown. Other decisions reached at this famous Diet concerned taxes. It was decreed that a tax of one-tenth was to be levied on the clergy, and a tax of one-twentieth on the laity. And for the crusade, every fifty households were to supply one armed man to fight the infidel. Further, in preparation for this assembly, Maximilian had written to Pope Leo and asked him to mediate in the burgeoning religious controversy through his representative the cardinal-legate. Martin Luther had also been requested to appear before the Diet and was issued a safe conduct by the Emperor.

---

491   Eleanor E. Tremayne, The First Governess of The Netherlands (New York: G.P. Putnam's Sons; London: Methuen & Company, 1908), p. 163. Taken from: M. Gachard's Rapport sur différentes séries de documents qui sont conservés dans l'ancienne Chambre des Comptes à Lille, Bruxelles, 1841, which contains extracts and documents concerning the intervention of Margaret in the imperial election of Charles V.

Luther arrived too late to meet Maximilian who had gone on to Innsbruck. The assembly was over, but still the cardinal-legate kept him waiting. When the meeting finally took place, it was in the overwhelming richness of the Fugger palace. He was treated with contempt and intimidated in subtle and overt ways. There was no real discussion, for Luther was simply told to recant or depart. He chose to depart and the safe conduct was honored. He returned to Wittenberg to write an account of the meeting which was widely read, and further inflamed the hearts and minds of the dissidents.[492]

Maximilian had warned the Pope to be cautious in dealing with Luther as he feared with the growing restlessness, this confrontation would be more divisive than healing. Waas comments that in Maximilian's relations with the Church, he "dealt with careful audacity."[493] Luther's feelings toward Maximilian were warm, humorous and yet respectful.[494] Maximilian had no personal vanity, his manner was conciliatory, and he was a very broad-minded thinker, especially on religious issues.[495]

---

492 Eleanor E. Tremayne, The First Governess ... p. 164.
493 Glenn Elwood Waas, The Legendary Character of Kaiser Maximilian (New York: AMS Press, Inc., 1966), p. 170.
494 Ibid.
495 Ibid., Note: pp. 100-101. "Maximilian was not prevented by superstition or traditional inhibitions from criticizing the popes nor from asking questions concerning religion, such as those which he handed the Abbot Trithemius in 1508."
  1. Why does God want rather to be believed by mortals than recognized?
  2. Can they, who by no fault of their own know nothing of the Christian religion, become blessed although without baptism and Christian belief, if they are faithful to the religion which they know?
  3. Why are prophets of false religions also able to do wonders?
  4. Why are the Holy Scriptures neither so clear nor so complete as they really ought to be? Why do they conceal so much and hide it in riddles? Why does one not find in them much which is also required for perfect belief?
  5. How does it happen that magicians have power over evil spirits?
  6. How can the doctrine of the righteousness of God be reconciled with the allowance of so much evil, often to the damage of good and pious people?
  7. Is the special providence over the actions and destinies of men, and in general over everything that happens on earth, demonstrable from reason and documents?
Cf, Karl Klüpfel; Kaiser Maximilian I (neue Ausg.; Berlin, 1870), pp, 179f.

The Emperor had stayed in Augsburg until the end of September, working all day and, then in the evening, taking part in the dancing, banqueting and masquerades of which he was so fond. It was an act of will and courage. What had once been sheer joy to this exuberant figure now became an arduous task to an ailing man. Since hunting had always restored his spirits, he and his company set out for Innsbruck, but they were unable to remain there as the Court was so deeply in debt. Instead, they went on toward Wels, his favorite hunting retreat in Upper Austria. During this part of the journey, Maximilian was reduced to traveling by litter and by boat, but his cheerful nature never deserted him. At Wels he bravely attended to business, forced himself to hunt, and to eat, hoping his health would be restored in the clean country air. But finally, his condition was aggravated by too much exercise and "an imprudent indulgence in melons."[496] He developed "inflammation of the entrails,"[497] and just before dawn on January 12, 1519, he passed away, two months short of his sixtieth birthday.

It would be hard to express what his death meant to Margaret. He had always been sincerely affectionate and a doting parent. Though he had often exasperated her with his wild schemes and extravagant ways, had been thoughtless to the point of disloyalty, was interfering and vacillating in decisions; his good qualities far out-weighed these defects. He was rarely too busy to write. From his different cities, and battlegrounds, the letters continued to come. He had a keen mind, and a kind and generous heart. Maximilian was a brilliant military adviser. He was supportive of her in many ways and exerted a calming influence. They shared a love of arts and music, both choral and instrumental. They both supported men of letters, not from duty but from admiration. All in all, in spite of his failures, Maximilian had left the house of the Hapsburg and its dominions in better shape than when he received them.

Margaret composed a long poem in French in memory of her father entitled "Complainte que fait la fille unique de Maximilien empereur,

---

[496] André J.G. Le Glay, Correspondance … Vol. II, p. 412.
[497] Ibid., (dysentery).

depuis son doloreaux trépas." She sadly recalls it in her successive encounters with death's cruel hand. The lovely translation which follows is found in Christopher Hare's work on Margaret.[498]

This is the complaint of the only daughter of Maximilian after his sad death:

> If it were possible, Celestial King,
> For me to blame Thy deeds and sinless be,
> My mouth is ready and my grief consents,
> As his sole daughter and his only child.
> But none may dare to murmur against Thee
> Till he have lost alike all hope and faith,
> From which God guard me and His patience give,
> As from my childhood He was ever wont.
> O Atropos! From thee is no defence,
> With thy fell dart to ashes hast consumed
> The four great Princes whom I loved the best,
> Yea, thou hast murdered them before mine eyes.
> Two noble husbands were the first to pass,
> Whom mighty nations mourned with sorrowing heart.
> The Prince of Spain, the Duke of fair Savoy,
> Than whom the world has seen no goodlier man.
> Still that the outrage might more deadly be,
> Both Princes in the flower of their age
> Were taken from me – one was scarce nineteen
> When death remorseless pierced her youthful heart.
> Then Savoy's duke thou didst conspire to slay,
> At three-and-twenty all his days were told.
> My only brother was the third to die,

---

[498] Christopher Hare, The High and Puissant Princess Marguerite of Austria (London: Harper and Brothers, 1907), pp. 256-258. For original in French, see E. Gachet's, Albums et oeuvres poétiques de Marguerite d'Autriche (Mons: Société des Bibliophiles, 1849); or M. Francon's Albums poétiques de Marguerite d'Autriche (Paris: Droz, 1934). Original in the manuscript room of the Bibliothèque Royale (Koninklijke Bibliotheek Albert I) at Brussels.

King of the Spanish realms and Naples' Lord.
Alas! To smite him with so cruel a blow;
Thou sparest neither Prince nor Duke nor King.
While for the fourth, O most outrageous Death!
Thou hast put out the flower of chivalry
And vanquished him who first had conquered all,
Great Maximilian, Emperor most high,
To whom, in goodness none may be compared.
Caesar! my father and my only lord;
But thou hast left him in too sad estate,
Entombed within his Castle Nieustadt.
O sacred majesty, imperial lord!
If in me there be any filial love,
Why doth my heart not break and rend in twain
No more to suffer pain and evil fate!
Did ever lady on this earth of ours
Of such misfortunes meet the fierce onslaught
As I have borne, ah me! unfortunate.
Too heavy for endurance is my fate.
Of every creature, Thou Creator, Lord,
I pray Thee guard my noble house and race
And me forlorn, who thus laments to Thee;
For I no longer can the burden bear
If Thy great clemency and goodness infinite
Preserve me not the rest of all my life!
I pray Thee from the bottom of my heart,
My God and my Redeemer, that the soul
Of him who was imperial here below
May find a place near Thy celestial throne;
And that his fair fame never more grow dim
Nor be extinguished, nor by ought made less,
But after death in high renown may life,
And his great virtues in his children shine.

Leisure is rarely granted in times of grief. At age thirty-nine, Margaret found herself the elder statesman[499] of western Europe with a great many tasks still to accomplish. Fortunately she was blessed with skill, experience and energy, and as passionate an interest in the glory of the house of Habsburg as Maximilian's. Now she took up the campaign to ensure Charles's election to the Emperor's throne. The electors whom Maximilian had bribed did not remain bought. Spanish nobles became angry because Charles was making preparation to leave for Germany, his appointment of Adrian of Utrecht, his former tutor and present Bishop of Tortosa, as regent in his absence, was also resented. The proud and xenophobic Spanish hated the thought of a Netherlander in that high position and considered him a person of low birth and little ability. Full of discontent and misery, they felt themselves abandoned. In addition to this, Francis with winning ways and a willingness to spend three million gold coins had succeeded in persuading the electors that he was a likely candidate.

Margaret despaired, and on hearing that Ferdinand might be more acceptable to the electors and the Pope, she proposed to Charles that he step aside and let Ferdinand carry on his interests in Germany.[500] In this she had the support of her council. Pope Leo also preferred someone with less power than Charles or Francis. Charles, however, reacted with strong indignation. He reminded her that he was the elder son and that it was his grandfather's wish that he should succeed to that throne. He had many plans to carry out and to do otherwise would be divisive. This is a far cry from the timid letter of the year before in which Charles, an eighteen year old, had protested the large sums of money promised in order to win for him the imperial crown. Maximilian had somehow transmitted his dreams of family and imperial glory to the youthful ruler.

The Archduchess set about writing letters which were paragons of diplomacy. She bestowed gifts on those servants, friends, relatives or clergy who had influence on the electors, and raised still more money for the large

---

499 Henry VIII of England was 28; Francis I of France, 25; and Charles, 19 years of age.
500 Edward Armstrong, The Emperor Charles V (London: MacMillan and Company, Ltd., 1929/1901), Vol. I, p. 45.

amounts needed for the principals themselves.[501] Margaret drew from her own revenues received from the Fuggers, the great banking family of that era, a loan guaranteed by the merchants of Antwerp.[502] The Germans most certainly were anxious that the port of Antwerp would be kept open for their own countrymen.

Ultimately, Charles was elected at Frankfurt on June 28, 1519, at a cost of 850,000 florins. Margaret immediately proclaimed the news and ordered celebrations of thanksgiving to be held by "processions, sermons, pious prayers and orisons... and to have fireworks, rejoicing, and other suitable festivities."[503] It helped that some of Francis's actions had alienated the electors, and that some of his supporters had swung over to the side of Charles.

Meanwhile, on the advice of his aunt, Charles managed to retain his friendship with Francis which enabled her to deal with the French king on the subject of Gelderland. To help financially, Margaret assigned to Charles some of the territories she had inherited from Maximilian. In gratefulness he awarded to her Malines and the surrounding area for life.[504] Charles also wrote many thank-you letters which he sent to her to read and then to forward to the King of England, the Cardinal Wolsey of York, ambassadors and others who had been involved. At one time Henry had made a try for the imperial throne.[505]

At the end of May 1520, Charles set sail from Spain, not for the Low Countries, but for England. This had been prearranged, but kept secret from the French, as Charles had decided to resurrect the English alliance. Charles lacked the ebullience of his grandfather, but he had a lot of his

---

501 Quinsonas, Matériaux..., Vol. III, p. 261 ff.
502 The Antwerp merchants were joyous at the defense of Charles's claim to the crown. See Van den Bergh, Vol. II., pp. 203-206, Memorandum of Antoine de Lalaing, Lord of Hoogstraten.
503 Eleanor E. Tremayne, The First Governess of The Netherlands (New York: G.P. Putnam's Sons; London: Methuen & Company, 1980), p, 174.
504 André J.G. Le Glay, Maximilien I, Empereur d'Allemagne, et Marguerite d'Autriche, sa fille, Gouvernante des Pays-Bas (Paris: Chez Jules Renouard et Cie., 1839), p. 61. Also Quinsonas Vol. III p. 267.
505 J.S. Brewer, The Reign of Henry VIII... (London: John Murray, 1884), Vol. I, p. 311.

FORTUNE, MISFORTUNE, FORTIFIES ONE

charm, simplicity, and courtesy.[506] He quite won over his aunt, Queen Catherine, which was to be expected, but also King Henry, whom he had met at Tournai in 1513, and Cardinal Wolsey. The visit was a great success,[507] and further plans for meeting later at Gravelines were made. Charles and Henry set sail the same day for different destinations: Charles for Vlissingen, and Henry for Calais for that famous meeting with Francis at the Field of the Cloth of Gold.

Charles landed at Vlissingen June 1, 1520, and made his way south to Bruges where he was met by his Aunt Margaret, his brother Ferdinand, and a company of nobles and ambassadors. They journeyed on to Brussels where Margaret had convoked the States-General to meet with Charles. When Charles rose to speak, he graciously praised his aunt and her council for their good and devoted management of their affairs, and told them that his heart had always been with them.[508] What ease and contentment he must have felt to be back in a place where the customs and language were familiar. Charles informed them of conditions in Spain, and that he had returned to oversee his dominions in Germany and to claim the crown. He asked for their help and for their financial support. On his aunt's advice, he sent 25,000 of his best troops to Frankfurt to "protect" the electors from possible French pressure.

Meanwhile, at the Field of the Cloth of Gold, relations between Henry and Francis were somewhat strained. Henry had rested at Calais which was under English control, and then had gone out to this palace in the fields which Wolsey had created. It was built of wood and covered with satin, brocades and tapestries, and encircling it were the tents of the nobles. The French camp nearby was equally splendid, and the two camps literally glittered in the warmth of the June sun.

Henry felt unsure of himself against the suave manners and sophistication of the French court. The English women looked plain in contrast to the

---

506 For more on Charles's personality, see the biographers Armstrong, Brandi, and von Habsburg.
507 William Bradford, ed. and trans., Correspondence of The Emperor Charles V... (London: Richard Bentley, 1850), p. 11.
508 Eleanor E. Tremayne, The First Governess of The Netherlands (New York: G.P. Putnam's Sons; London: Methuen & Company, 1908), p. 179.

dazzling French women. His counselors suspected treachery. The days were marked by measured and equal ceremonials, jousts, banquets. Two anecdotes from this medieval meeting live on in history. The Frenchman Rival wrote amusingly:[509]

> Francis displayed less reserve. One fine morning he appeared alone in the English camp, invaded Henry's bedroom and found him in bed. He kissed him, crying: "I am yours, I am your prisoner!" Henry, unable to believe his senses, lay rubbing his little eyes, still puffy with sleep. Francis insisted upon being his valet, hauled him out of bed and put on his shirt. Henry made an effort to impress him by placing on his shoulders a magnificent jeweled collar; but Francis had provided for all emergencies. He drew from his pocket a man's bracelet of equal value and clasped it on to Henry's podgy wrist. At length he departed, saturated with sentiment, brotherly love and romanticism. Henry felt ridiculous. This great lad with his spindle shanks had given him a lesson in courage. He found the pill very bitter.
>
> Henry sought rancorously for a means of humiliating Francis and remembered his own prowess in wrestling. One day, in his salon, in the presence of the Queens, he grasped Francis by the neck, exclaiming: "Brother, let us wrestle!" He had calculated that the long-legged man must give way to his great weight, and Francis, taken unawares, was indeed staggering when he was seized with disgust and sudden fury. Slim legs are agile, and Francis, hooking one of his spindle shanks round one of King Henry's renowned calves, gave a lift and sent the heavy body hurtling into space. King Henry landed upside down among the voluminous skirts of the two Queens. The carpets were soft and so were the portly King's buttocks, but Henry arose gasping with discomfiture and bellowing with fury. The bystanders

---

[509] Paul Rival, The Six Wives of King Henry VIII trans. From the French by Una Lady Traubridge (London: Heinemann, 1971/1937), p. 77.

intervened, Catherine remarked that dinner was served and led the way to the dining hall. That day Henry had little appetite; the next day he was a mass of bruises and at the earliest opportunity he gave the order to strike the tents and departed in a rage.

From there Henry and Catherine went on to Gravelines to meet with Charles and Margaret on July 10. The simplicity of this meeting contrasted sharply with the pomp of the previous one, for this one seemed like a family affair with the reserved and courteous Charles and his two aunts. Charles in his dark suits and with his quiet ways was no threat and Henry felt more at ease. A treaty was concluded in which Charles was to wed the Princess Mary, his cousin. Only a month before, she bad been contracted to marry the Dauphin of France, and Charles was betrothed to Charlotte of France. (Louise had died and Charlotte had been substituted in the agreement growing out of the Treaty of Noyon.) But such deceptions were all part of the game, and no one's conscience seems to have been unduly troubled. Wolsey had managed everything well in the hope of gaining the favor of the King of the Romans, as he fervently aspired to the papacy and knew that he needed Charles's help. They had spent only four days together, but parted affectionately and contentedly. For Margaret and Catherine, who had not seen each other since 1499, it must have been a bittersweet reunion. Margaret had been godmother of a little son Catherine had in 1511 who died soon after, so the years had not dimmed their loyalty to each other. Charles and Margaret then turned toward Aachen (Aix-la-Chapelle) making a slow progress through the cities of the Low Countries. At Maastricht, the last city in the Low Countries before crossing over into Germany, Charles reconfirmed Margaret as Regent, and named Henry of Nassau[510] commander of the army. The lavish and impressive

---

510   Henry of Nassau was the uncle of William "the Silent" of Orange who was instrumental in establishing the United Provinces of the north, now known as The Netherlands. After Henry was widowed, he married Claude, sister of Philibert of Chalons and Prince of Orange. Their son René inherited his uncle Philibert's title, but eventually this passed on to William, son of Count William of Nassau-Dillenburg who had decided Protestant sympathies. Margaret was godmother

ceremony of the coronation took place on October 13, 1520. The crown of Charlemagne[511] was at last his, and Margaret, who never believed in saving money on these occasions, attended as at her own triumph, which indeed it was.[512]

This coronation very nearly did not take place. In 1519 the four-year truce with Gelderland had come to an end, and the Duke, with the help of France, had wasted no time in once again going on the offensive. France was also helping Robert de la Marek wage border warfare in the southeastern part of the Low Countries, and was active in the invasion of Navarre which Spain considered its province. There was internal trouble as well in Spain with open revolt led by several united cities. Valladolid was seized, then Medina de del Campo was burned. Tordesillas was taken, and the leaders offered to Juana the chance to rule in her own right. It was one of her lucid moments, but something made her hesitate and she refused to sign any papers. Adrian, unequal to the task of putting down the rebellion, escaped imprisonment by fleeing.

The slowness of communication (Charles being in the Low Countries at the time) and Charles's nature prevented much interference, but the rebellion eventually burned itself out. Charles appointed two Spaniards, the Constable of Castile, and the Admiral of Castile, to share the regency with Adrian. These men were able and popular, and under their direction troops retook Tordesillas and peace was restored. When Charles eventually returned, he granted amnesty to all but a few of the leaders of the rebellion, and these, in accordance with the laws and customs of the era, were treated with the usual medieval severity. Meanwhile, the Duke of Gelderland

---

to one child of Henry and Claude born in February, and Henry wrote from Breda February 8, 1519 to thank her. The lady who stood in for her was "madame de Hornes" who was probably the former Claude of Savoy, the little sister-in-law whom Margaret raised. See also van den Bergh, Vol. II, p. 149.

511 The coronation was as King of the Romans and Emperor Charles's coronation as Emperor took place in Bologna in 1530.

512 Among the many royal women who attended was Germaine de Foix, niece of Louis XII, who had become the second wife of Ferdinand of Aragon. If their son had lived, Charles's kingdom would have been much smaller. Germaine subsequently married the Margrave Hans of Brandenburg.

had raised an army of seven thousand men and fifteen hundred horsemen by recruiting in the land of Brunswick, and the provinces of Brabant and Holland as well as in his own duchy.[513] Margaret was desperate but determined. She wrote to her ambassador in France and requested him to urge Francis to intervene and extend the truce. Francis sent an elderly commissioner, Philippe de Guyche, who was also esteemed by Charles. Margaret's deputies were Maximilian of Hoorn (de Hornes), Antoine Sucket and Pierre Briquegny. Philip of Burgundy as Bishop of Utrecht was host, and it was in his city that the meetings were held. Continued negotiations to extend the former four-year treaty were always turned down by the Duke's deputies, while the time delay enabled him to build up a sizable army. Margaret had advice from Guillaume Rogendorf, his brother Wolfgang, Floris of Egmond, Henry of Nassau and the Lords of Ravenstein, Hoogstraten, de Berghes, la Roche and Wassenaar, about the importance of fortifying the borders and protecting the Zuiderzee. This Margaret agreed to, though she taxed Wolfgang Rogendorf for raising an army of foot soldiers, fearing it would damage the peace talks still going on.[514] Such delicate considerations did not deter the Duke whose "Black Bands" marauded all over the countryside as far west as Amsterdam and even to the towns and villages in the north. On the Zuiderzee, merchant ships were attacked by a pirate known as "Big Pete" who terrified the sailors and caused "the entire crew of a defeated squadron to walk the plank without quarter."[515]

In all there were some fifty letters exchanged concerning the settlement of claims. At one time The Lord of Guyche, shaking his head and shoulders, said "I have laid bare my charge to the said Duke of Gelderland and they (the deputies) have concluded together as I have written to Madame, I do

---

513 Christopher Hare, The High and Puissant Princess of Austria (London: Harper and Brothers, 1907, p. 265.

514 Van den Bergh, Vol. II, p. 210.

515 Jane de Iongh, Margaret of Austria: Regent of the Netherlands, trans. from the Dutch by M.D. Herter Norton (New York: W.W. Norton & Company, Inc., 1953), p. 208. It seems no one had a good word for the Duke of Gelderland; even Erasmus wrote a story about a shipwrecked crew captured by the Duke. (Mentioned in de Ionghe's work, original Colloquies.)

not know what else to say ... I am not empowered by the king my master to do anything else." In an undertone, he responded that the deputies were not servants of the king (Francis). "I am not able to argue with them, but I will return to their master, and will touch more and plainly on this to learn his intention."[516] Floris of Egmond suggested fortifying with certain special troops just in case something should happen. He also felt this might act to deter the Duke, and "if no adventure occurs, nothing is lost."[517] Jean d'Ostin (always referred to as Hesdin), a steward and diplomat much relied on by Margaret, observed that as the issues were parried back and forth; it was like a game of "passe-passe."[518]

In April, 1519, the Lord of Guyche sent word that because of the plague at Arnhem, their company was going on to Nijmegen. Margaret's deputies noted: "We think it is an excuse not to come to Utrecht."[519] Perhaps they were on their way to join others as Philip of Burgundy wrote on July 3, that the Duke of Gelderland, Duke Eric of Brunswick (not Duke Henry of Brunswick), the Bishop of Munster, the Duke of Mecklenburg, and the Landgrave of Hesse have amassed a great number of troops to march against Frankfurt to be joined by those of Saxony and Brandenburg to impede the election of Charles to the Empire.[520] And then, the whole ominous threat faded away.

In a letter of September 8, Floris of Egmond asked aid for a poor woman, a porteress. It seems that Philips van Zomeren, the traitorous commandant at Hattem, accused the husband of this woman of planning to deliver Hattem to the King Charles and, wishing to make an example of him, cracked his skull open. "And because, Madame, this poor woman has lost her husband for love of the king, I pray you please make her some appropriate gift..."[521] This letter contains so much emotional appeal - it

---

516 Van den Bergh, Vol. II, p. 191.
517 Ibid., Vol. II, p. 167.
518 Ibid., Vol. II, p. 194.
519 Van den Bergh, Vol. II, p. 207. (The Chronique of Arnhem does not mention any "peste" at this time.)
520 Ibid., Vol. II, p. 226.
521 Ibid., Vol. II, p. 232.

reveals the war in all its hideousness and sadness like nothing else. In all, about fifty letters were as the harassed Margaret and her counselors negotiated for peace while, at the same time, countering the military forays of the Duke. In the end, what in part defeated the Duke at this particular time was that his wonderful army had grown too large to feed; and, when Margaret's troops advanced, he retreated in hunger to Wesel,[522] well into his own lands. All of this had been a vendetta with the Duke. If he had, he could have run it with autonomy, so eager was Margaret for peace. On May 19, 1515, the province of Friesland had been sold to Charles by Duke George of Saxony for 100,000 florins. Four years later, on November 6, 1519, an accord was made with the Duke of Saxony on the subject of the artillery he had installed to protect the province Friesland. An inventory was made and a price suggested for the various items.[523] Though the Duke of Gelderland continued his plundering ways until his death in 1538, this purchase, along with the military power of Nassau, tipped the balance of power in Margaret's favor. Charles returned with his aunt to Brussels following his coronation. In January of 1521 he again journeyed to Germany to attend the Diet at Worms. Martin Luther was once more summoned and given a safe conduct. It was at this meeting on April 16 that he made his famous stand. Charles was put off by Luther's proud bearing, his lack of humility. He said to one of his aides, "This man will never make me a Lutheran."[524] Accordingly, Charles submitted his declaration the following day:

> My predecessors...left behind them the holy Catholic rites that I should live and die therein, and so until now with God's aid I have lived as becomes a Christian emperor...A single monk, led astray by private judgment, has set himself against the faith held by all Christians for a thousand years and more, and impudently concludes that all Christians up to now have erred. I have therefore

---
522 Wesel is now just over the border in Germany.
523 Van den Bergh, Vol. II, p. 235.
524 Edward Armstrong; The Emperor Charles V (London: MacMillan and Company, Ltd., 1929/1901), Vol. I, p. 76.

resolved to stake upon this cause all my dominions, my friends, my body and my blood, my life and soul...After Luther's stiff-necked reply in my presence yesterday, I now repent that I have so long delayed proceedings against him and his false doctrines. I have now resolved never again, under any circumstances, to hear him. Under protection of his safe conduct he shall be escorted home, but forbidden to preach and seduce men with his evil doctrines and incite them to rebellion...[525]

Charles's assessment was faulty. This was not the work of a single monk, but the culmination of a large movement of long standing which had finally found its leader. As a result of Luther's stand at Worms, and Charles's reply, public opinion became polarized. Many who had been of moderate persuasion now swung over to Luther. Charles had a young secretary, Alfonso Valdés,[526] a humanist and follower of Erasmus, who conducted several conciliatory talks with Philip Melanchthon. The need for reform was generally acknowledged; the spirit was there, but it was subverted by intransigence on the part of some, and by greed on the part of other highly-placed individuals playing on the ignorance of many. The obdurate and self-righteous position taken by Charles was to set the pattern for many years to come. This would prove to be to the great detriment of the Low Countries which would become awash in the blood of this rebellion. The ferocity of its counter charge is called to this day "The Spanish Fury."

On January 3, 1521, Luther was excommunicated and Charles took measures to enforce the Inquisition. Due to the political situation in Germany, he was not able to enforce these decrees, but he determined to exert all his power in the Low Countries to exterminate "this said sect

---

[525] Edward Armstrong, The Emperor Charles V (London: MacMillan and Company, Ltd., 1929/1901), Vol. I, pp. 77-78. This condensation is from Eleanor E. Tremayne, The First Governess of The Netherlands p. 185.

[526] Carmen Irizarry, The Thirty Thousand: Modern Spain and Protestantism (New York: Harcourt, Brace and World, Inc., 1966), p. 11. Information from Edward Boehmer, Spanish Reformers of Two Centuries: Their Lives and Writings, according to the late Benjamin B. Wiffen's Plans and with the use of his materials (Strasburg: Karl Trubner, 1874), Vol. I, p. 66.

of Lutherans." There was no province immune to Luther's teaching and Antwerp, a cosmopolitan city, had many German merchants who were Lutheran. The city also had many converted Jews called Maranos who were repelled by the hostility of Catholicism.

Up until now, Margaret had maintained a scornful indifference to those zealous and vengeful churchmen who were the inquisitors, while taking strong steps against those equally rabid political provocateurs. But now, as Pirenne relates, Jerome Aleander, a Greek scholar and the papal legate sent by Leo X, arrived in Antwerp September 28, 1520. He and his colleagues became masters of the situation. Aleander secretly organized a campaign against Erasmus, and the Dominicans and Carmelites joined in. Many of Margaret's friends and aides were attacked in inflammatory sermons. Books were burned in the university city of Louvain. Those following a middle way were as good as lost. The Bishop of Cambrai was forced to make a solemn and public retraction within St. Gudule's (St. Michael's) in Brussels. The Inquisitors pursued the Augustinian Henri of Zutphen and the schoolmaster Nicolas de Bois-le-Duc ('s-Hertegenbosch) who were threatened with the stake. The humanist Cornelius de Schryver (latinized Grapheus) and the master Roland van Berchem were charged with heresy. The first was given a chance to make an honorable amendment and the second was released.[527]

Margaret could be described as a reformer with a moderate spirit. She had criticized the "infinite abuses" of the Church and sought to remove or correct these wrongs. Nor did she feel the papacy had any special mystique. As far back as October 22, 1512, Margaret had been informed that the Pope had confiscated the Burgundian property of Augustin Ghisi, a merchant of Sienna and resident of Rome. She wrote her father that the Pope had no rights over these matters within the Low Countries and felt that they should devolve on the Emperor.[528] Maximilian promptly wrote back and gave the property to her "to use as you will."[529]

---

527 Henri Pirenne, Histoire de Belgique, Vol. III, p. 333ff.
528 André J.G. Le Glay, Correspondance ..., Vol. II, p. 54.
529 Ibid., Vol. II, p. 56 .

The intellectual Augustinians had met with such favor in her eyes, that she had asked them to serve the church at Brou, and yet, she sometimes felt they went too far. In a letter to the Prior of Brou, she deplored "these heresies of Martin Luther which are a great scandal to our Holy Mother Church."[530] And so Margaret conformed to Charles's harsh rules. Day by day however, the terror continued. To make a terrible example, the Inquisitors razed the convent of the Augustines of Antwerp, a strong center of Protestantism. Its monks were arrested and two of them, Henri Voes and Jean van Essen, were burned alive at the Grand Place in Brussels on July 1, 1523.[531]

---

530 Max Bruehet, Marguerite d'Autriche, Duchesse de Savoie (Lille: Imprimerie L. Danel, 1927), p. 138.

531 The writer pursued this subject through the helpful mediation of Simonne Moens at the Stadsarchief in Mechelen/Malines. Father Felix De Ceukeleer o.s.a. of the Augustijns Historisch Instituut answered the request for more information with a full reconstruction of events and with scholarly reflection. Through the briefing in English from Mejuvrouw Moens and this writer's translation, the following extract is offered:

After her re-establishment as Regent, Margaret of Austria was confronted with the case of the Augustinian Cloister at Antwerp. By her order, the monks were driven out as she feared this was a center for the spread of Lutheranism. She issued an order for arrest against the Prior Lambrecht Thoren and two others Jan van den Esch (van den Esschen, van Essen) and Hendrik Voes on October 6, 1522, who were then imprisoned at Vilvoorde. The procedure was carried out by Frans van der Hulst, the imperial, papal and civic Inquisitor, assisted by Nicolaas van Egmond, Carmelite and theologian, Joannes Pascha, another Carmelite and Church Inquisitor, and the Dominican Jacobus Hoogstraten acting for the Universities of Keulen (Cologne) and Leuven (Louvain) who coordinated the struggle against Lutheranism in the Low Countries. They were assisted by theologians from Louvain Jacobus Latomus and Ruard Tapper and by an unknown Hodschalk. The entire process lasted nine months. After all the interrogations, it appeared that the accused did not preach the very strict Lutheranism, but more the early teachings of the evangelists and the reform of the community. Even this seemed a danger to the government. Therefore, Van den Esch and Voes were condemned for unorthodox religious preaching, they were deprived of their priestly dignities, and given over to the civic arm of the government to be tried. On July 1, 1523 at the Grand Place in Brussels, they were "desecrated" by Adrien de Bruges, Suffragan Bishop of Cambrai. They refused the help of four priests, and the lighting of the firestake was postponed for one-half hour to increase the moral torture and to set an example for the bystanders. The whole process lasted four hours. Following this, the Prior Lambrecht Thoren renounced the new doctrine; nevertheless he was kept in prison in Brussels. In 1528 he was strangled in Brussels and secretly burned in Vorst (near Brussels). Margaret ordered the Cloister in Antwerp to be demolished, but the city of Antwerp asked if the Cloister Church could be retained as a parish church and Margaret agreed, deciding that it should be dedicated to Sint Andries (Saint Andrew), patron

Their courage inspired admiration and Luther wrote one of his most beautiful hymns in their honor. From that time following, according to Erasmus, "their deaths made very many Lutherans."[532] In spite of warning placards, the Lutheran pamphlets and translations of the Bible continued to multiply.[533]

---

saint of the ducal house of Burgundy. This was to be an example of the "right" learning and believing. Some of the early documents have been lost, but enough remain to indicate that it is unlikely that Margaret signed the death certificates - in any case there was separation of civic and religious jurisdictions. Due to the exceptional situation and the very strong attitude of the Emperor concerning everything which could be a threat the state, Margaret may have confirmed this sentence with her signature, not as a judge, but as the initiator or chief person responsible, but Father De Ceukeleer thinks this improbable. In fact, reckoning with the unlimited might of the Inquisitors and their permission to compel everyone to cooperation, the Augustinians and other scholars are loathe to condemn the Archduchess. Father De Ceukeleer lists these sources for his research:
- Paul Fredericq. Corpus documentorum Inquisitionis haereticae pravitatis Neerlandicae. 4 delen. Gent: 1889-1902.
- Dictionnaire d'histoire et de geographie ecclesiastique, 15 (1963) col. 1007-1008, Esschen, Jean van den (R. Eijenborg).
- M. Picbal, De geschiedenis van het protestantisme in Vlaanderen. Antwerpen-Amsterdam: 1975.
- F. Prims, Antverpiensia, 13° reeks (1939), blz. 77-83
- E. de Moreau, Dictionnaire d'histoire et de geographie ecclesiastique, 3 (1924) col, 889.

532 Henri Pirenne, Histoire de Belgique (Bruxelles: Henri Lamertin, 1907), Vol. III, p. 338.
533 The Low Countries was a hot bed of Lutheran printing. Carmen Irizarry in The Thirty Thousand: Modern Spain and Protestantism (New York: Harcourt, Brace & World, Inc., 1966), p. 23 writes: "The extent to which Lutheran tracts circulated in Spain is evident from a communication sent to the Infante Don Fernando, Charles V's brother, by his retainer at the Emperor's court. This letter, written in Burgos in 1524, informs the prince: 'Your Highness will know that from Flanders came a ship laden with merchandise for Valencia, and that besides this merchandise, it carried two toneles [barrels or casks] of Lutheran books; the ship was captured by the French and, after it had been recovered by ours and brought to San Sebastian, while they were making an inventory of its cargo, the books were found: which (books) were taken to the plaza and burned: but some books could not be taken, and (much) effort is being exerted in their recovery.'" On December 2, 1525, Edward Lee, King Henry VIII's almoner, on a journey to Spain through France, wrote that "a translation of the New Testament, by an Englishman, was completed, and would be sent in a few days to be distributed in England." Sir Henry Ellis, ed., Original Letters ... (London: Richard Bentley, 1846), Vol. II, p. 71. In the same volume on pages 86-87 a letter from the Bishop of Norwich to Archbishop Warham dated June 14, 1527 commending the deed of the Archbishop in purchasing (by Tunstal) all the copies of Tyndale's Testament. Tunstal was at Antwerp at that time. Upon hearing this, Tyndale commented: "I am gladder, for these two benefites shall come therof; I shall get money of hym for these books, to bring my self out of

"By 1523 in Antwerp there were thirty-eight artisans cited by the magistrate for meeting to study the holy evangels; preachers and defrocked monks multiplied; offerings were down significantly."[534]

Margaret prohibited the assemblies of those who met to study the Bible because these "serve to distance the people from the reverence due the sacraments, the honor due to the Mother of God and the saints, of fasting and of other precepts of the Church." Certain penalties were laid down. For a first offense, an amendment of five francs; for the second, forty; and for the third, eighty. When these measures did not have the desired effect, a new edict was made October 14, 1529 to stop the progress of heresy, and it was ordained that all those who had the books of Luther or his adherents were to carry them to the governor of their area under the pain of confiscation of goods or risk of life. Le Glay states that "this was against the character of Margaret, but without doubt, the grave circumstances forced her to take this course...nor should we judge hastily as some of the material coming to light now shows that capital punishment was not being pronounced."[535] It must be remembered that social and political unrest, combined with the religious, presented a terrifying front to the rulers of that era. As with all the governments of this century, and England, France, Germany and Italy were having their troubles too, iron and fire defended the authority of the Church.[536]

---

debt (and the whole worlde shall crie out upon the burnyng of Goddes worde). And the overplus of the money that shall remain [will pay for more printing]"

534   Henri Pirenne, Histoire de Belgique (Bruxelles: Henri Lamertin, 1907), Vol. III, p. 339.

535   André J.G. Le Glay, Maximilien I, Empereur d'Allemagne, et Marguerite d'Autriche, sa fille, Gouvernante des Pays-Bas (Paris: Chez Jules Renouard et Cie., 1839), p. 65. Nevertheless, some did go on Gachard records: "Sentence of Nicolas Coppyn de Montibus, Inquisitor General of the Low Countries against Guillaume de Zwolle, 24 September 1529. By this sentence Guillaume de Zwolle is freed to the secular arm." It was the "secular arm" which carried out the burning. [The Protestant Seminary at Brussels keeps a list of those in the Low Countries who were put to death for their religion.] See L.P. Gachard, editor, Notices et extraits des manuscrits qui concernent l'histoire de Belgique, Academie Royale des Sciences, Lettres et Beaux-Arts, Commission Royale D'Histoire. (Bruxelles: M. Hayez, 1875), Vol. 18, Part 1, p. 369.

536   Even a Dutch historian such as Dr. Jane de Iongh could sympathize with Margaret's and later Mary's plight. In the Low Countries, she writes, "strange disturbances had arisen, caused by social ferment and fanatical religious tensions, showing themselves in a general lack of respect for law and tradition and in the unbalanced excesses of Anabaptists, Melchiorites, and various strange

FORTUNE, MISFORTUNE, FORTIFIES ONE

Erasmus made his escape to Basle, though he wasn't very happy there. In a letter from Maximilian of Transylvania to Alfonso Valdes, this comment was made: "Erasmus would willingly return to Brabant if he were only protected from the 'Fratres cucullati' [hooded brothers] as he dislikes his present residence."[537] In a letter to Mercurino di Gattinara, Erasmus predicted "greater tumults and disturbances after the suppression of the Lutheran heresy; they will be raised by the partisans of discord and enemies of learning."[538] Mercurino received two other letters concerning the arrest of Jacobus Grunenbergius, an old friend of his, who had been taken from the Canary Islands to Spain and accused by the Inquisition "where he is not allowed to defend himself." The Prior of the Carthusian Convent at Schuete near Brussels remarked: "Spaniards are always prone to accuse people, but slow in permitting the accused to defend themselves."[539]

Nevertheless, the Archduchess, as far as she could, protected the innocent and hardworking religious orders and attacked those clergy who by their ignorance, greed and conduct were largely responsible for the progress of this religious unrest. To the extent of her authority, she permitted only "wise" priests to preach, and she forbade the airing in public of those controversies which could only bring agitation to troubled spirits and which could not even be resolved by learned theologians.[540]

---

societies which called themselves "brotherhoods" and proclaimed the arrival of the Millennium... This intoxication raged inside the country... In Groningen a more dangerous sound was heard, preaching reformation and revolution together." See Iongh's Mary of Hungary: Second Regent of The Netherlands (New York: W.W. Norton and Company, 1958), p. 172. (Groningen is in the extreme northeast of the present Netherlands.)

537 Pascual de Gayangos, Calendars of Letters... Vol. III, Part II, p. 431.

538 Ibid., p. 362, September 1, 1527.

539 Ibid., p. 500, December 12, 1527.

540 This is the feeling Erasmus had. In a letter to Luther while they were still friendly, Erasmus objected to the burning of Luther's books at Louvain by "theologians acting so madly... I only warned them not to clamor before the populace in so hateful a manner without yet having read your books... Further I begged them to consider also whether it were expedient to traduce before a mixed multitude views which were more properly refuted in books or discussed between educated persons..." Albert William Levi, Humanism and Politics (Bloomington: University of Indiana Press, 1969), pp. 28-29.

It can be observed from the account of Margaret's first regency that she resented interference in her government, and she had to endure much from Maximilian. With the exception of the Inquisition, she was subject to less of this from Charles. There is a letter to the Emperor from Lope Hurtado de Mendoza in Rome asking that two men may have "the Church preferment which the Pope has conferred on them, but to which Madame Margaret has objected."[541] The result of this is lost in history, but one that is retained is her forceful and strong-willed objection to both Charles's and Pope Adrian's interference in the form the Chief Inquisitor of the Low Countries, Francis van der Hulst. Well aware of her feelings, Van der Hulst tried to escape from her control by fleeing north. Margaret awaited her opportunity; and when she discovered that during a quarrel with the States of Holland he had committed a mistake, she relieved him of his powers. The Archduchess absolutely refused to have this corrupt and cruel man and reproached Charles for not having respect for the privileges of the bourgeoisie. She declared that his conduct had raised everywhere "a marvelous regret" dangerous to the security of the state. She then presented a slate of candidates of good ecclesiastics headed by the Provost of St. Martin at Ypres, Olivier Buedens; Nicolas Houseau the Prior of the Ecoliers at Mons; and the Dean of St. Pierre at Louvain, Nicolas Coppin, (Coppyn) "who I feel to be the most moderate." She advised that they be joined with "counselors of yours, but good moderate men and above all virtuous, who are well known and respected by your subjects."[542] In this she had the strength of the magistrates of the various cities behind her as they had been pleading that this authority be returned to their jurisdiction. She had won a battle, but the war continued. Charles felt the population was inclined to softness, and everywhere Lutheranism seemed to be going from strength to strength.[543] A new Pope, Clement VII, deemed

---

541 Gustav Adolph Bergenroth, Calendar of Letters... Vol. II, p. 547.
542 Karl Lanz, Correspondenz ... Vol. I, p. 86, February 21, 1524.
543 In those polarized times, others agreed. Henri Pirenne, Histoire de Belgique, Vol. III, pp. 300, 313, 339, relates that the Dutch poetess Anna Byns who was passionately religious, attacked the Reformation "in accents moving and sincere" and "reproached the high clergy for neglecting the struggle against Lutheranism." She lamented:

Margaret's prelates soft and negligent and in 1525, new inquisitors were enfranchised and given more power. The Bishop of Liégé, Erard de la Marek, was charged with superintending and exercising the powers of the Inquisition. Now Erard de la Marek was a brother of Robert, who besieged her in the South as the Duke of Gelderland did in the North. Though he had at times sided with Margaret against his brother. He was considered, nevertheless, a dangerous ally. When Margaret adroitly pointed out to Charles that no one should assume his prerogative as head of the commission, this appointment of Erard de la Marek was rendered of no consequence. However, Pirenne believed that the appointment of the Bishop did curb Charles's headlong inflexibility and contributed greatly to the check of the Inquisition.[544] Also, the renewal of war in Italy mitigated Charles's zealous application to heresy, though as the years went by, he became even sterner in his attitudes toward Protestantism. In contrast, his sisters Isabel and Mary (the letter would follow Margaret as Regent) had decided Protestant leanings, testifying to the open-mindedness with which they were reared in their aunt's court. Charles, it is to be recalled, had been under the unbending tutelage of Adrian and Chièvres.

Another facet of Margaret's religious attitude was her lack of rigidity. She was comfortable with different rules for dissimilar churches[545] and in favor of a more regional or national church, because, as she pointed out, "the religions of this country…have their chiefs and provincials in France or in Germany, and during wars, merchants and others under cover of religion pass back and forth as spies."[546] As late as January 18, 1530, Margaret was urging Charles to "dispense with the unreasonable oath which you have required of the country of Brabant concerning the

---

Temmerleiden, metsers sijn ons doctoren nu, Tengieters, pijpers, pinceellekers en schaliedekkers. (Carpenters, butchers are our doctors now, Tinsmiths, pipe layers, painters and roofers.)
The writer's appreciation is given to Bernard J.M. Kemperman for help in translating this old Dutch.
544 Henri Pirenne, Histoire de Belgique (Bruxelles: Henri Lamertin, 1907), Vol. III, p. 157.
545 Karl Lanz; Correspordenz des Kaisers Karl V (Frankfurt/Main: Minerva GmbH, 1966/1844), p. 205, April 22, 1526.
546 Ibid., p. 204.

churches."[547] What Margaret planned to do was manage public opinion by building the quiet confidence of people in their own, well-conducted administration, though she fully intended to maintain her own sovereignty. The Archduchess's policy of moderation in regard to the zeal of the Reformers and the tremendous inroads of Protestantism in her provinces was maintained during her lifetime by her authority and persuasive powers. With her leanings toward humanism, she was able to protect Erasmus, Vives, Cornelius Agrippa and countless others not so well known. After her death, Charles, fearful that the division in religion would destroy the unity of his domains, turned away from the moderation of his aunt (and his sister Mary) and sternly followed the way of the Inquisition. Otto von Habsburg summed up Charles's personality in this way: He was not a Renaissance man. "Both emotionally and intellectually the Gothic Middle Ages and Christianity were still the vital factors in his life, which took precedence over the great revolutionary ideas of his time."[548]

Following Margaret's religious policy in a cohesive way has led us far beyond our account of the other issues and events of her regency, therefore, we must go back to 1521 to pick up the thread of this study.

While Charles was occupied with the business of the German States at Worms, Margaret called together at Mons the States-General of the Low Countries, on February 9, 1521, and made an impassioned plea for help against the French.[549] She had proof of Francis's intrigues to undermine her own dominions as in the case of the Duke of Gelderland, and indeed, he was busy enlisting the support of the Swiss League, the King of Denmark (her niece Isabel's husband),[550] the King of Scotland, and the Dukes of Lorraine, Ferrara, and Savoy, of which she was Dowager Duchess, against

---
547   Ibid., p. 373.
548   Otto von Habsburg, Charles V, trans. from the French by Michael Ross (New York: Praeger Publishers, 1970), p. 68.
549   André J.G. Le Glay, Maximilien I, Empereur d'Allemagne, et Marguerite d'Autriche, sa fille, Gouvernante des Pays-Bas (Paris: Chez Jules Renouard et Cie., 1839), p. 62. Note explains that an extract of this speech may be read "Notice sur Marguerite," by M.J.J. Altmeyer in Revue belge, August 1839, p. 357.
550   Van den Bergh, Vol. II, p. 174. Note states that Sigbritt, mother of Christian II's mistress Duiveke [Little Dove] underhandedly encouraged the Duke of Gelderland.

the Empire. With such plain facts before them so earnestly, they agreed to give their support.

On May 5, 1521, Charles's brother, the loyal and self-effacing Ferdinand, was married to Anne of Hungary. His patience and sense of obligation were rewarded by Charles with the provinces of Austria, Carinthia, Carniola, Styria, and the Tyrol. Later he would receive the German provinces which had been held by their grandfather Maximilian. Several times in Spain, and once, in regard to the imperial crown, Ferdinand had been the favorite and could have succeeded if ambition had overruled family duty. He chose the latter and became the founder of the major branch of the family. Not long after this wedding, Mary was married to Louis of Hungary. It was a happy marriage, but their country was torn by factions and depressed by poverty.

The difficulties with France were exacerbated by its continual involvement in northern Italy, the area the Habsburgs claimed came under their sovereignty. Charles had made a secret agreement with Pope Leo X against the French through his ambassador Don Juan Manuel. This treaty was so shocking to Chièvres, and so against his French policy, that coupled with Charles's independent action, it is said to have hastened his death. There was no love lost between Margaret and Don Juan Manuel, and there must have been a certain sweet satisfaction in the irony of this sharp-witted Spaniard acting against Chièvres, who had supported his defense years before when Margaret wanted to be rid of him.

In order to raise money,[551] Margaret traveled to Ghent, and on July 17 asked the States-General for support. They had failed to take any action

---

551   Karl Brandi, The Emperor Charles V, trans. from the German by C.V. Wedgwood (Oxford: Alfred A. Knopf/Alden Press, 1939), p. 119. writes that the perennial shortage of money was due to the fact that "the government lived not on the revenues which had already been collected, but on the perpetual mortgaging of future income, of domain lands and of mines. This, it is true, is the practice of almost all states at almost all times; but the sixteenth century was still dominated by the old system of private credit. The constant pull between the needs of the Crown and the loans which it had to raise at such short terms, was still felt as an oppressive weight on the personal honour and credit of the prince. Money could be gained from bankers, ministers and war-lords only at the expense of the State. The State itself suffered, for the extravagant journeys and gifts made by the Court immediately devoured all the current yield of the taxes, however high, leaving the demand still unappeased." Knightly life was becoming out of date and "incompatible with

on their vote of support at Mons, but this time, as a result of her speech, sufficient money was granted to allow an army of 22,000 to be raised. The States-General had always been notoriously reluctant, even when it concerned the defense of their own interests, to vote subsidies for armies. They reasoned that no money meant no war. With grateful relief, Margaret saw this army dispatched from Malines to the Ardennes to subdue Robert de la Marek, who had addressed a letter of challenge to her. His audacity and insolence were reinforced by funds from his old playmate Francis, but in this case, the battle went against him so decisively that he was brought to his knees and forced to beg for mercy. From there, the army under the command of Henry of Nassau, turned north to deal with Charles of Gelderland. At the same time, in a three-pronged effort, Charles easily reconquered the powerful city of Tournai in the west.

In the meantime, Cardinal Wolsey had been in Calais trying to arrange a peace between Charles and Francis, but with no success. He then journeyed north to Bruges, where he was met by Charles and Margaret and given a magnificent welcome. He concluded with them on August 25, 1521 a secret treaty against France. It contained the provision that Charles was to marry King Henry's daughter Mary. He was also to visit England on his way back to Spain. It was signed by Margaret and Jean de Berghes, but not by Charles.[552]

While these activities were being carried on in the north, the campaign in Italy was going well, though it was not until November 19 that Milan was taken. It was then Parma and Piacenza surrendered. The jubilation was short-lived, as Pope Leo X suddenly become ill and died on December 1, 1521. He was only forty-six and his death was a shock to everyone, and a blow to Charles's interests in Italy.

---

modern life, with commercial and territorial interests," according to Edward Armstrong, The Emperor Charles V (London: MacMillan and Company, Ltd., 1929/1901)1 Vol. I, p. 204. The knights "relations with their peasants were strained, for they had commuted labour for money rents, and then with rising prices found out their error, and either exacted higher rents or fell back upon the customary services." Thus funding at every level was difficult and ever pressing.

552 Gustav Adolph Bergenroth, ed., Calendar of Letter, Despatches and State Papers, relating to the negotiations between England and Spain, Vol. II, pp. 370-1.

Hostilities ceased while preparations were made to assemble the cardinals for the Conclave. Cardinal Wolsey yearned with all his being for the papacy and had worked and schemed to that end. He was supported by Henry and had Charles's promise to use his influence.[553] This Charles did when Henry withdrew from his halfhearted campaign for the imperial crown and later joined him against the French. It is thought that Charles learned of Pope Leo's death on December 12, and Henry on December 16. After several votes by the cardinals, the Conclave seemed to be deadlocked. The name of Adrian of Utrecht, Cardinal of Tortosa, was them proposed. He gained twenty-six of the thirty-seven votes, which gave him the required two-thirds, and became the new Pope, Adrian VI, on January 9, 1522. Modern historians, in considering all the evidence, believe Charles had nothing to do with the result; but Wolsey never believed that. He considered to his dying day that he had been the object of Charles's treachery. Then there was also gossip that the overzealous Don Juan Manuel had influenced the election, and this made Pope Adrian angry. In a letter to Charles, he asked to know what services had been rendered by Don Juan, and begged "God to preserve him from such friends as Juan Manuel."[554] Following this, Don Juan was recalled from his post as ambassador to Rome.

In March of 1522 the States-General convened again at Brussels to hear Charles bid them farewell. In a carefully prepared address, Chancellor Gattinara, speaking for the Emperor, thanked them for their help during the time he had been in the Low Countries. He praised the Archduchess,

> ...who for so long has shown by her praiseworthy, memorable services and great experience, that she well knows how to honourably acquit herself of the said government and administration. For

---

553 William Bradford, ed. and trans. Correspondence of The Emperor Charles V... (London: Richard Bentley, 1850), pp. 12-47 and 84-93.
554 Gustav Adolph Bergenroth, ed., Calendar of Letters, Despatches and State Papers, Vol. II, p. 532.

which good rule and conduct his Majesty and you are beholden to her through the fervent zeal and natural love she bears you.[555]

"The Chancellor ended his long speech by saying that the Emperor hoped they would live peaceably with each other during his absence 'for their strength lay in unity...'"[556]

Before Charles could leave, he had to have money; so Margaret was to play once again the role of financier. She had helped Maximilian numerous times and had paid to a great extent for the Low Countries' projects and armies from her own dowry. She also had found resources for the bribes to elect Charles. Now she was reduced to pawning her jewelry. The Count of Hoogstraten, her faithful Knight of Honor, and old and trusted friend, extended the funds needed,[557] and graciously permitted her to keep the jewels herself. She was obviously a good risk.

Many stories have been associated with Antoine de Lalaing, Lord of Montigny and Count of Hoogstraten. He first comes into the records of Margaret's life when he went to Strasbourg in 1505 as an emissary of Maximilian and Philip to give her news of the skirmish with the Duke of Gelderland. He then stayed to reassure her. Born in 1480, he was an old friend of her brother Philip, and wrote an account of their trips to Spain in 1501 and 1506.[558] He became a Knight of the Golden Fleece and, in 1524, Margaret's Knight of Honor. He was an ever-present help in the strife with Gelderland. In 1522 he became governor (stadhouder) of Holland, Zeeland and Friesland and in 1528 of Utrecht as well. Gossip down through the

---

555   Eleanor E. Tremayne, The First Governess of The Netherlands (New York: G.P. Putnam's Sons; London: Methuen & Company, 1908), p. 195. Extracted and translated from a manuscript in the Burgundian Library.
556   Ibid.
557   Henri Pireene, Histoire de Belgique (Bruxelles: Henri Lamertin, Libraire-Éditeur, 1907), Vol. III, p. 188.
558   In this he also described a hunt taken with Maximilian and of the Emperor's ability "as he clambered up the rocks after chamois. Glenn Elwood, Waas, The Legendary Character of Kaiser Maximilian (New York: AMP Press, Inc., 1966/1941), p. 49, quoting from Antoine de Lalaing, "Voyage de Philippe le Beau en Espagne, en 1501" in Collection des voyages des Souverains des Pays-Bas, publiée par M. Gachard (Bruxelles, 1876), Vol. I, p. 312.

years has linked them romantically. Paule Henry-Bordeaux in her history of Louise of Savoy refers to him as Margaret's "favorite," and describes her as "the widow always mournful if not always faithful."[559]

The Biographie Nationale de Belgique contains an account of "the love which Antoine de Lalaing had for the princess and for the natural children they had between them, among others Philip de Lalaing."[560] It is assertions such as this which appear in reputable works[561] which set Ghislaine de Boom to the task of sleuthing. In her "Introduction" to the Cambrai Correspondence, she blames it on the Venetians.[562]

> Lalaing, as Knight of Honor, had a post of confidence in which he was privy to all the secrets of the Chancellery. The Venetian ambassadors, those fine observers of international diplomacy,[563] did not fail to point out the role played by the confidant of the Regent "Madame Margaret who, after the Lord of Austria [Charles], has the grandest power and the governing of all."[564] However, they attributed this favor to some secret and Romanesque motive [rather

---

559 Paule Henry-Bordeaux, Louise de Savoie, "Roi" de France, 1476-1531 (Paris: Librairie Académique Perrin, 1971/1954/1943), p. 185.

560 Biographie Nationale de Belgique (Brussels: Établissements Emile Bruylant, 1890-1891), Vol. Eleven, p. 83.

561 Bibliothèque Nationale d'Autriche, Manuscrits et livres imprimés concernant l'histoire des Pays-Bas, 1475-1600 (Brussels: 5 Mai-8 Juillet, 1962), p. 56. According to J. Strelka, Margaret herself composed the "Complainte…" following Maximilian's death in which she renounces her love for an unknown. He noticed that the four letters placed within each frame are the initials of Antoine de Lalaing, Count of Hoogstraten. The editor remarks, however, that the order of the last two is H C and not C H. None of this is evident in the English translation. For more rapport between Margaret and Antoine de Lalaing see Emile Gachet's Introduction to Album et oeuvres poétiques de Marguerite d'Autriche, Bruxelles, 1849; and J. Strelka's Gedichte Margarethes von Österreich, Vienna, 1954, and his Der burgundische Renaissancehof Margarethes von Österreich und seine literarhistorische Bedeutung, Vienna, 1957.

562 Ghislaine de Boom, Correspondance de Marguerite d'Autriche et de ses Ambassadeurs á la cour de France concernant l'Exécution du Traité de Cambrai 1529-1530 (Bruxelles: Maurice Lamertin, Libraire-Éditeur, 1935), pp. vii-ix. Trans. SHB.

563 A note of scorn and sarcasm here?

564 Ghislaine de Boom, Correspondance… Cambrai, p. viii Note: Relation de Contarini, ambassadeur vénitien aux Pays-Bas, du 16 novembre 1525, publie par E. Alberi, Relazione degli ambasciatori veneti. Florence, 1840, série 1, vol II, p. 24.

than to his rank, loyalty, experience or ability. More importantly, the serious historians such as Brassart and Henne are receptive to the legend which makes Margaret of Austria the mother of Philip de Lalaing. This assertion is reduced to nothing by the authentic texts, reposing in the Archives of Lille, and brought to light by the eminent Conservateurs Le Glay and Bruchet.[565] Though the act of legitimation accorded by Charles V in March 1524 does not indicate the name of the mother, this lapse is completed by the amplification conceded by the Emperor, in April 1534, and attributing the motherhood to Ysabeau, illegitimate daughter (bastarde) of Haubourdin.[566] Our manuscript shows us that Philip visited his mother on his return from France. He writes to his father October 14, 1530: "There is the likelihood of good weather and as I departed from the court and from Paris, on my way to Chalons and from there to Chasteau in Portien I stopped to see my mother." For the rest, a simple question of dates suffices to prove the inanity of the legend. The epitaph of Philip de Lalaing states: "After the course of LI (51) years in virtuous conduct, his life was rendered to God the second day of April in the year XVL (1550). He was then born in 1499 while Margaret, widow of Don Juan, still remained in Spain."

Mlle. de Boom was a thorough and meticulous researcher, as librarians at the Bibliothèque Nationale in Brussels will attest to today;[567] but sometimes her respect for the Archduchess amounted to awe and deification, and left Margaret less than human. In her work she avoided altogether any reference to the Duke of Suffolk affair at Tournai, though there is a great deal of material on it about which she must have known. Nevertheless, simple and practical considerations serve to confirm her research. In the first place, it must be suspected that the Italian ambassadors did have a gift for making

---

565   M. Bruchet, Marguerite d'Autriche, duchesse de Savoie (Lille: Imprimerie L. Danel, 1927), p. 61, note 3.
566   Archives du Nord, B 1615. Registre aux Chartes, fol. 150 vo; B 1617, fol. 109 vo.
567   This writer spoke with Mademoiselles Sulzberger and Henry.

their dispatches interesting;[568] and, in the second place, with the public lives they led - hardly alone a minute, not even to sleep - how could such a thing be accomplished with a ruling woman? Or, when Margaret was young, under the watchful eye of Queen Isabella and the entire Spanish court? Further, in marriage negotiations with Henry VII and Louis XII, Margaret is on record as believing she could not have children, and that is not gainsaid in any of the correspondence among the emissaries of the various courts. Another subtle but convincing argument against the case of their being lovers concerns chivalric etiquette. According to the manners of the day, the Archduchess had one dining companion at her table, the wife of the Knight of Honor. With their sense of delicacy honed to the fullest in this regard, it is not likely that they would have carried on a romance under these circumstances as their "honor" would have suffered. In addition, this writer believes that the gossip over the affair with the Duke of Suffolk made her so agitated and fearful that she would be "holden for a fool and light,"[569] that she would not wish to put her reign in jeopardy. Though some noblewomen did bear illegitimate children, as in this case of Philip de Lalaing's mother, and though there were numerous "bâtards" in the houses of Burgundy and Habsburg; a queen or archduchess regnant could not allow herself that liberty.

All the correspondence, however, points to a close, warm and respectful relationship in regard to family and governmental matters between Margaret and Antoine de Lalaing, who maintained a home a few blocks east of Margaret's palace in Mechelen/Malines,[570] but such friendships between men and women are subject in every age to suspicion and mistrust.

And so this loyal friend advanced money from his own funds, without collateral, for Charles's return trip. Towards the end of May 1522, the Emperor left Bruges for a six-week visit in England. While he was there,

---

568 It was a Milanese Italian who wrote that Madame la Grande (Margaret of York) was the mother of Perkin Warbeck.

569 John Gough Nichols, ed. Richard Turpyn's The Chronicle of Calais. (London: The Camden Society by J.B. Nichols and Son, 1846), Vol. XXXV., pp. 71-72.

570 It remains today as "The Court of Hoogstraten." There is also a Hoogstratenplein (square) nearby the Nekkerspoel Train Station.

a messenger from Francis delivered a defiant letter to King Henry which he, in turn, passed on to Charles. This seemed a stroke of luck to Charles because it strengthened the wavering Henry to form a pact with him to join forces against France. They swore eternal friendship, and Charles was made a Knight of the Garter. His workhorse nature chafed at so much leisure and ceremonial,[571] and, as he wrote to his aunt later, "...the six weeks seemed a thousand years."[572] But on July 6, he set sail once more for Spain.

The Archduchess soon had her hands full dealing with the effects of this pact against France. As Brandi relates:

> Unhappily the two Kings, in their courtly festivities and personal conversations, had outrun their ministers. Irritated by the hostility of the Scottish regent, the Duke of Albany, towards their English allies, and encouraged by some measure of military success, the Flemings in the autumn of 1522 threw off the last vestige of disguise from their war on France in Artois and Picardy. English ... and Flemish troops ... after the unsuccessful siege of Hesdin, pressed on ... until winter, cold, hunger and lack of resources forced them to ignominious retreat ... Margaret had her hands full, negotiating for money to wage war; worse was to come when she met the Estates General at Malines in the Spring of 1523.[573]

In February of 1523 Margaret wrote to Charles to inform him of intrigues against the dean of the Cathedral at Utrecht. She also let him

---

571 Lord Somers, A Collection of Scarce and Valuable TRACTS ... Second edition revised by Walter Scott, Esq. Vol. 1. (London: 1809; New York: AMS Press, Inc., 1965), pp. 32-33. Entitled "The Entry of Charles I [so called because Charles the First of Spain] into London. The meeting of the Emperor, his Grace, with the Lord Mayor of London, and his Brethren, with all other Crafts of the said City in their Liveries." Among the many preparations was the "graveling of the streets..."
572 Edward Armstrong, The Emperor Charles V (London: MacMillan and Company, Ltd., 1929/1901), Vol. I, p. 86.
573 Karl Brandi, The Emperor Charles V, trans. from the German by C.V. Wedgwood (Oxford: Alfred A Knopf, 1939; Munich 1937), pp. 194-195.

know that an envoy from Louise of Savoy, the Regent of France, and from the Bastard of Savoy, had come to Liégé to speak with the Cardinal in an effort to make peace between him and the King of France.[574] In this second regency, Margaret's letters are greatly changed from those during the first. Now the correspondence tends to be long, thoughtful cogent and reasoned. She assessed the situations and made tactful suggestions as to strategies to be pursued. In this part of her life, one sees her as the teacher and counselor. For his part, Charles, though very conscious of his own rank, reacted gratefully. In the final paragraph of one letter, he added that this occasion gave him the opportunity to thank her for continually laboring to give order to his affairs in the Low Countries, and prayed that their Creator would keep her always in his guard.[575]

During the year of 1523, there was more trouble with the Duke of Gelderland, no doubt taking advantage of the government's focus elsewhere. But as he approached Leiden, he was overcome by an army from the province of Friesland. Leiden lies in the west in the province of Holland near the North Sea coast, far removed from the Duke's own territory. The purchase of Friesland was proving to be a wise buy. All of this activity tended to obscure the real threat of the Turks in the east. Suleiman the Magnificent had ascended the Ottoman throne about the time of Charles's Coronation, and immediately began his campaigns in the West. On March 3, 1523, Pope Adrian wrote to Charles, and to Francis and Henry urging all the Christian princes to make peace with one another and to wage a common war against the Turks. He was alarmed at their far-reaching progress. They had taken Belgrade, besieged the Island of Rhodes and were menacing Hungary "where the Emperor's sister is Queen." It looked as though nothing would stop them from becoming the masters of Europe unless the three were reconciled.[576] But it was too late, the Knights of St. John, who had occupied Rhodes, were defeated. Charles was so sorrowful

---

574 Ibid., pp 194-195.
575 Ibid., p. 75.
576 Gustav Adolph Bergenroth, ed., Calendar of Letters. (London: 1862), Vol. II, pp. 532-533. Pope Adrian VI to the Emperor. (Belgrade fell August 1521 and Rhodes, December 21, 1522).

at this that he offered the Island of Malta to those Knights who had fought so bravely, as partial recompense to them for the loss of their home.

But still the hostilities in western Europe continued. The Constable of Bourbon, France's great military commander, was suffering under what he considered the unjust persecution of Francis and his mother, Louise of Savoy. The chivalric ideal did not teach men patience when their "honor" was as stake, and thus when he felt he could no longer bear the indignities, the Constable offered his services to the Emperor though either some symbiotic relationship, disquietude, or chivalric loyalty delayed his decision.[577] With so powerful an ally, Charles and Henry renewed their campaign against France. Plans were laid for Charles to cross into France by the Pyrenees, while Henry and Margaret were to unite their forces in the north to invade Picardy. Bourbon was to reinforce Germany. Margaret had to furnish and supply an army[578] of 3,000 horsemen and 4,000 infantrymen with food and transport without any aid from Charles. Despite all her efforts, Margaret was not able to pay her troops in full, which naturally curtailed their thrust. This was a factor in the defeat of the English invasionary forces under the Duke of Suffolk in the north of France, which were driven back while only a few miles (11 leagues) from Paris. There were other factors such as illness, and Armstrong blamed the poor leadership of the Duke.[579] The time was not well chosen "for the transport of artillery and baggage.[580] Margaret had to submit to Henry's and Wolsey's recriminations as they blamed her and Charles for the collapse of their plans. In coming to the aid of Charles, they had neglected and

---

577 Edward Armstrong, The Emperor Charles V, Vol. I, p. 147. William Bradford, Correspondence of the Emperor Charles V... p. 77. J.S. Brewer, The Reign of Henry VIII ... Vol. I, p. 499.

578 Gustav Adolph Bergenroth, ed., Calendar of Letters. (London: 1862), Vol. II, p. 556.

579 Edward Armstrong; The Emperor Charles V, Vol. I, p. 147.

580 William Bradford, Correspondence of The Emperor Charles V...Louis de Praet and Jean de Marnix wrote on June 1, 1523 that they judged the time not favorable and the force required by the English was so large that "the greater part of the Low Countries will be left unprotected and exposed to the enemy." (The season selected by the English was from August to late October.) pp. 67- 68.

postponed their own pressing plans to "reduce the Scotch to obedience."[581] Even the ambassadors in England became the object of their harassment.[582] The secrecy of their correspondence was violated and public attacks were made. While Margaret protested[583] against the injustice of this attitude and the subsequent actions, she still cautioned Charles to remain united with Henry VIII. Dr. William Knight, the English ambassador to the Court at the Low Countries, wrote to Cardinal Wolsey:

> ... my lady Margarete... said she hath bene allwaiys utterly enclyned and determynd to studye for the encrease of honor weale and suerte of the Kinges Highness so she will contynue her life duryng.[584]

Wolsey's treatment of the Archduchess was in many respects disgraceful. Brewer relates:

> To the excuses she had made for disbanding the Imperial contingent of Burgundians, and the irregularity of their pay fatal to their discipline and usefulness, he took the liberty of telling her, they did not expect a lady of her wisdom would have attempted to excuse such notorious wrong "by inventions and compasses, by paraboles and assimulations, interpreting his sayings, mind, and intent otherwise than, by experience of his accustomable manner, she hath found cause or occasion to do." He ended this tart message by repelling the insinuation that his master had ever separated himself from the Emperor, as her favorite minister Hoghstrate had "indiscreetly and otherwise than truly inferred."

---

581 Ibid., p. 59.
582 Karl Lanz, Correspondenz des Kaisers Karl V, Vol. I, p. 90 Margaret to Charles, February 21, 1524. See also Ghislaine de Boom, Marguerite d'Autriche-Savoie... p. 43.
583 Margaret not only protested, she retaliated by having all Englishmen and English ships seized at Nieuwpoort. This was reported by Richard Gresham (who was himself arrested) in a letter to Cardinal Wolsey. Sir Henry Ellis, Original Letters... (London: Richard Bentlye, 1846), Vol. II. pp. 80-82.
584 Ibid., Vol. I, p. 316. Margaret was also involved in delivering to Henry a spy for Richard de la Pole (Yorkist) who "obeying taken and examynd, was put in torture because he varied."

In Wolsey's correspondence with the Regent of Flanders he assumed a freedom and directness of speech to which crowned heads were scarcely accustomed... With consummate and imperturbable tact, not the less galling because it assumed the mask of friendliness, he contrived to place the Emperor's aunt and himself on an equal footing.[585]

Brewer also records this interchange abridged from a letter addressed by De la Sauch to Chiévres on April 7, 1520:

After telling Chièvres how Wolsey had said his master was desirious of having Madame present at the interview (at Calais), that all might urge her to go to Spain, as the only means of reducing that kingdom to quiet, he continues: "On the otherside, the Cardinal urged that, when our master went into Germany, it might be that you (Chièvres) would be desirious of rest, and so would like to have some person in your room [place]; but that you would not wish to be deprived of all authority; reasonably enough." But, he added, they could not see how this could be easily brought about unless Madame were sent into Spain. Wolsey continued to insist on the advisability of his course, and the numerous inconveniences which would follow on rejecting it. "Upon this," continues De la Sauch, "I excused you, and I told him that I thought I knew your intentions well enough to assure him that whenever you made up your mind to retire, which I imagined you would do after the King's coronation at Aix, you would not wish to hold any office, for this would not be retirement (repos). If, on the other hand, you desire to continue your services you would not feel inclined to desert the Emperor; and as to any office or government, you would never become a party to such an exchange as he proposed, and so incur the displeasure of Madame. I told him she was the Emperor's aunt, and there was no reason for supposing that he would deprive her of the government of the Netherlands for any one. Wolsey

---

585 J.S. Brewer, The Reign of Henry VIII... Vol. II, p. 4.

insisted, in reply, that the change was necessary for the Emperor's affairs. 'We will persuade him to this (he said), and that during her absence M. Chièvres shall have her place in Flanders.' 'Certes, Monsieur,' I replied, 'I think that if Madame wished to go into Spain she would be very welcome, and the King would be glad of it; but he would not press her to accept it against her will. And as for M. de Chièvres, I am sure that whenever he retires from the charge he has about the King he will never undertake any other office.' 'Ah! Master Secretary,' he replied to me in Latin, 'if you believe that I perceive well enough that you have no perfect knowledge of the disposition of men in authority.' To this remark I made no reply, but I thought that he fancied all mankind was like himself, and that he would be very sorry if he were deprived of his authority. On the other hand, I could not help wondering at his extravagant (folle) absurdity in supposing that if the King our master wished Madame to go into Spain, she would rather do so at their persuasion than at his. "Chièvres was an old man, whose influence had once been paramount with his master. He must have been more than mortal, if ever he forgave the Cardinal this insult.[586]

Karl Brandi, the German historian, alludes to the same proposal calling it "unwanted advice in Charles's private affairs."[587] Such meddling from so brilliant a minister could be understood, and to some extent forgiven. Unfortunately, as Ellis observes:

> Wolsey's occasional coarseness in his expressions, even toward foreign Princes [jeopardized relations] and it would seem that negotiations sometimes stood a chance of being impeded by the violence of his temper. [Bishop] Tunstall, [Sir Richard] Wingfield, and [Dr. Richard] Sampson... tell jointly the harsh expressions

---

586 J.S. Brewer, The Reign of Henry VIII ... Vol. I, p. 366, note.
587 Karl Brandi, The Emperor Charles V, p. 117.

complained of by Charles the Fifth, which Wolsey had used to his ambassadors. The Emperor himself was "a liar, who observed no manner of faith or promise; my Lady Margaret a ribald; Don Fernando, his brother, a child, and so governed; and the Duke of Bourbon, a creature." The English ambassadors endeavoured to soften the fault, but could not deny the words.[588]

Harsh words, indeed. It should be explained that "ribald" then did not have today's meaning of "coarse," or "characterized by or using broad or indecent humor;" both in Middle English and Middle French (ribaut or ribauld) it carried the connotation of "wanton." [589]

Bishop Tunstall gently reproved the Cardinal by writing, "Your Grace's plainliness is not so well taken…"[590] And, through the ambassador De la Sauch, an oblique apology was transmitted to Margaret on June 30 and to the Emperor on July 4, 1525 which Brewer summarized:

> Wolsey complained that his well-known affection for the Emperor had not been considered as a sufficient atonement for any offence of which he might have been unconsciously guilty. As for the Lady Margaret ... there was not lady in the world, not even the Princess Mary herself, whom he was more willing to serve, so much did he respect her virtues her good sense, her prudent and honourable behavior.[591]

Margaret addressed her letters to him as "my good son" which may have been a Renaissance subtlety to maintain cordial relations while reminding him he was not her equal. Thomas Wolsey actually was five years her senior in age.

---

588 Sir Henry Ellis, Original Letters. Vol. II, pp. 12-13.
589 See Webster's Seventh New Collegiate Dictionary (Chicago: G. & C. Merriam Company), 1971.
590 Sir Henry Ellis, Original Letters, Vol. II, p. 13.
591 J.S. Brewer, The Reign of Henry VIII ... Vol. II, p. 79.

These vignettes of the Cardinal's belligerent expressions and abrasive personality, with which the Archduchess had to cope, have led us somewhat ahead of another important event which occurred in 1523. A family emergency, complicated by political considerations, was occupying a great deal of her time. Jean de Marnix, who sometimes functioned as Margaret's secretary and at other times her treasurer, was now serving as her envoy in London. He, along with Charles's ambassador Louis de Praet, collaborated on this letter to the Emperor on June 1, 1523:

> Sire! The said Madame has written to inform us how the King of Denmark, who with the Queen and his children, is, as we have already made known to your Majesty, in your Low Countries, has demanded of her three things. One, that she should be willing to render sufficient aid and assistance to enable him to reconquer his kingdom; a second, that she should grant a passport to one of his people whom he intends to dispatch to your Majesty, and by him, should write to you in his favor; the third, that you should write to Monseigneur your Majesty's brother Ferdinand, and the Electoral Princes, that right and justice may be rendered to him in his quarrels and contentions against his uncle the Duke of Holstein, who, with the aid of the city of Lubeck, has occasioned his expulsion. To these demands, inasmuch as regards the two letters, Madame has signified her willing acquiescence; but in respect to the first, she begs to be excused, on account of the impossibility of acceding to it; and refers all to the good pleasure of your Majesty.
>
> And further in this matter we have to apprize your Majesty, that the said Seigneur King of Denmark, has sent a herald to demand a permanent safe conduct of the King of England, to enable him to come and go with his navy, into any of the ports of this Kingdom, according to his pleasure either towards friends or against enemies. The Sieur Cardinal has informed us, that a safe conduct has been granted him for six months, on condition of his coming without ships and with a suite of not more than a hundred

followers, and not going into Scotland or elsewhere into an enemy's country; and hence the Cardinal hopes that he will not give them the trouble of coming at all.[592]

Christian had never received all of Isabel's dowry and so he could threaten Margaret and Charles with "pay or make war,"[593] and it was in his power to ruin the shipping trade in the North Sea and Baltic ports and create trouble in Gelderland.[594] Charles was inclined to cooperate, but he still owed a great sum of money which had been borrowed to insure his election to the imperial throne. There was to be no additional revenue from taxation, as the citizens were already overtaxed and rebellious. Up to this time Margaret could see that it was less expensive to give Christian a yearly stipend and preserve the peace of the Low Countries; but, by 1523, when Christian fled from the uprising against him in Denmark, Margaret once more had the upper hand.[595]

Isabel had been made a fool of by two Dutch women: Duiveke, Christian's mistress, and her mother Sigbritt (Siegebritte) Willems who had run a tavern in Holland and had parlayed her talents into running the palace and the throne of Denmark. However, the subjects of the King, known as "the Nero of the North," did not have the unending patience and loyalty of the affronted Isabel, and a revolution in Jutland and Sweden, abetted by Danish nobles, chased him from his kingdoms. Margaret, ever warmly and fiercely maternal, welcomed Isabel and the children, and installed them in a residence at Lier.[596] She loaned her steward Sonastre to bring some order into their household "which seems a thing impossible."[597]

---

592   William Bradford, Correspondence of The Emperor Charles v. pp. 69-70.

593   Dr. Jane de Iongh, Margaret of Austria, trans. from the Dutch by M. D. Herter Norton (New York: W.W. Norton & Company, Inc., 1953), p. 230.

594   Van den Bergh, Vol. II, p. 174. Note states that Sigbritt, mother of Christian II's mistress Duiveke underhandedly encouraged the Duke of Gelderland.

595   Karl Brandi, The Emperor Charles V, p. 190.

596   Lier is not far from Malines. This area is still called the Court of Denmark though only the gate and a few columns remain.

597   Karl Lanz, Correspondez des Kaisers Karl V (Frankfurt/Main: Minerva GmbH, 1966/1844), Vol. I, p. 146.

Isabel was only 22 at the time, but in such ill health and low spirits that Margaret sent her to the baths at Aachen (Aix-la-Chapelle)[598] following a trip she made to the German States to plead for help for her husband.[599] Considering that her nature was more openly affectionate, retiring and passive than the other children, she showed an amazing inner strength considering what she had been through. For Christian, Margaret had no sympathy. Maximilian once had expressed his disgust in a letter to Charles, referring to

> ... the displeasing and shameful life of your brother and my son-in-law, the King of Denmark, with a concubine, to the great mourning and grief of our daughter, your sister, his companion, and the blame of all his kindred.[600]

While Adrian had still been associated with the Court in the Low Countries, he had been sent to remonstrate with the King, but to no avail, and in fact made matters worse for Isabel. Therefore, the Archduchess was not about to subject her own provinces to any military venture for which, in any event, there was no money, for a man she considered debauched.[601] She also did not want to ruin a treaty that favored the commerce of the Low Countries with the new King Frederick of Holstein and his allies, the Hanseatic League. Even when Charles wanted his brother-in-law to reconquer his kingdom, his aunt made clear that this would be a very difficult and dangerous objective. She refused to transmit Charles's letters to Christian and threatened to suspend the exiled King's pension, which she was paying, if he pursued his plans to raise an army and equip a navy. In her report to the Emperor, she firmly concluded: "I am employing all

---

598 Ibid., Vol. I, p. 145.
599 Karl Brandi, The Emperor Charles V, trans. by C.V. Wedgwood (Oxford: Alfred A. Knopf/Alden Press, 1939), p. 189.
600 Van den Bergh, Vol. II, pp. 135-135, January 18, 1516.
601 According to Hare, he had many good qualities as well as bad. See: Christopher Hare, The High and Puissant Princess Marguerite of Austria (London: Harper and Brothers, 1970 pp. 281-282.

of my power to preserve your lands from war."[602] Charles let it rest. He needed the money which came out of the commerce Margaret so zealously protected.

On September 14, 1523, Pope Adrian VI, after a reign of only twenty months, died in Rome following a short illness. A scholarly and good man of simple tastes, he was no match for the shrewd and cynical wits of the Vatican. They hated him and called him the "Dutch saint." Adrian had tried to enlist the help of Erasmus in reforming the church, but Erasmus apparently lacked the commitment to apply himself to such an active and formidable task. After all, he was essentially a thinker, not a doer. Pope Adrian's stern attitude toward the abuses and corruptions of the Church served only to strengthen the Reformation. It was an unhappy and unsuccessful reign.[603]

Again Wolsey thought he had a chance. Although Margaret mourned Adrian whom she had known well for so many years, she had also resented his interference in the religious affairs of the Low Countries. Thus it was with no feeling of disloyalty that she wrote on September 25 to De Praet, Charles's ambassador in England, commanding him -

> ... to repair without delay to the said Cardinal to give him as it may so happen the first intelligence of this event, and to offer him on her part all the favor and assistance in her power towards his promotion to this dignity ...[604]

Charles wrote to De Praet on November 27, 1523:

> ...The principal point is concerning the advancement of the Cardinal to the papal dignity. We have always desired, and with most sincere good feeling and intention have wished to promote

---

602 Ghislaine de Boom, Marguerite d'Autriche-Savoie et la Pré-Renaissance (Bruxelles: La Renaissance du Livre, 1946/1935), pp. 52-53.
603 William Bradford, ed. and trans. Correspondence of The Emperor Charles V... (London: Richard Bentley, 1850), pp. 45-47.
604 William Bradford, Correspondence of The Emperor Charles V ... p. 84.

this to the utmost of our power, having a full recollection how we, and the King our good father and brother, being at Windsor, opened to him our minds on this subject, exhorting him to think of it, and promising our best services in his assistance, because it appeared to us that his promotion and election would be attended with great good to Christendom, and advantage to our common interest... We firmly believe that the Cardinal of Medicis will give his assistance to the Sieur Legate, from the little change, as we are informed, of his own success; and we well know and acknowledge how cordially and sincerely Madame our good aunt is occupied in this affair not only in her own name, but in ours.[605]

Perhaps the cardinals had had their fill of a foreign pope; at any rate Wolsey lost, Cardinal de Medici did win, being elected on November 19, 1523, and taking the name of Clement VII. Cardinal Wolsey believed he had again been the object of deception, and he never forgot.

Because of Isabel's poor health and depression, leading to her death at Ghent in January 1526, Margaret undertook the guardianship of the children Jean (John, Hans) born in 1518, Dorothée, and Christina.[606]

---

605 Ibid., pp. 89-90.
606 The little Jean died in 1532, two years after Margaret's death. Charles wrote a tender letter to the Regent Mary: "I am deeply saddened, for he was the handsomest little boy of his age one can imagine. I am not less affected by his death than by that of my own son, for I knew him better and he was already bigger, and I looked upon him as my own child. But perhaps the little fellow is better off where he is now than here where I wish he were, and perhaps he is laughing heartily at me because I miss him so…"
Jane de Iongh, Mary of Hungary: Second Regent of The Netherlands (New York: W.W. Norton and Company, 1958), pp. 160-161. Dorothée (Dorothea) married Frederick, Count Palatine who had loved her aunt Eleanor. Christina married Francesco Sforza, and after his death, the Duke of Lorraine, then served as regent for her young son when her second husband died a year after their marriage. In 1538, Henry VIII, greatly smitten by her portrait and in the market again for a wife, paid court to her, but she is said to have turned the emissary down by replying "that if she had two heads, she might think of it!"
See Christopher Hare, The High and Puissant Princess Marguerite of Austria (London: Harper and Brothers, 1907), p. 309. Apropos of that, the Regent Mary wrote: "It is to be hoped, if one can hope anything from such a man that if this one (Jane Seymour) bores him he will find a better way of getting rid of her. I believe that most women would not appreciate it very much if this kind of habit became general, and with reason. And although I have no inclination to expose myself to

Christian contested this as he wished them reared in the Lutheran faith, though he later abjured this in an effort to regain his throne. He also knew that this could cause embarrassment and difficulty to Margaret, and the loss of the only income he had. She, for her part, made her moves slowly and quietly so as not to upset the commercial treaty so indispensable economically for her country. She sent an envoy to Spain to ask for Charles's support in taking the children and confided to him her fears as to the bad doctrine taught in Christian's court.[607] The Emperor agreed, but the King of Denmark was not so easily persuaded. Summoned by the Archduchess, he asked for a safe conduct to come and go wherever he wished, the payment of his debts, and above all, to be excused from ratifying the testament by fire, which meant freedom from the Inquisition.[608]

He finally consented to conduct his children to Malines, but arrived there when Margaret was in Antwerp. Perhaps suspecting a trap, he immediately returned to Lier. Christian then decided to place them in safekeeping outside of the Low Countries and hurried to send his furniture and valuables to Antwerp before looking for a refuge in Lutheran Germany. Patient and tenacious, Margaret made one proposal after another, with Christian adding on provisions until at last, he agreed "to turn over his children into my hands." Margaret herself went to Lier for the children and brought them back to Malines "to hold them there and have them nourished." But she signed an agreement to return the children to their father when and if he should conquer the Danish throne. She must have felt that possibility was rather remote.[609]

Having promised to raise them in a royal manner, the Archduchess next had to find a tutor. It is of interest to note that Margaret used the question of "doctrine" in securing Charles's support for her custody suit, but she was

---

dangers of this kind, I do after all belong to the female sex, so I shall also pray God that he may protect us from such perils." Iongh's Mary... p. 182.

607 Ghislaine de Boom, Marguerite d'Autriche-Savoie et la Pré-Renaissance (Bruxelles: La Renaissance du Livre, 1946/1935), p. 65.

608 Ibid., p . 65.

609 For information in above paragraph, see Karl Lanz, Correspondenz des Kaisers Karl V (Frankfurt/Main: Minerva. GmbH, 1966/1844), Vol. I, pp. 193-195, letter from Margaret to Charles, March 6, 1526.

just as enlightened as ever, for she chose the learned Cornelius Agrippa of Nettesheim, Germany, who had been a professor at Dole, then in Savoy. As mentioned in the chapter on Margaret's artistic life, he was a curious mixture of intelligence, erudition in ancient and modern languages, and in contrast to most humanists, an earnest student of the occult. He himself had faced the Inquisition. A man such as this would seem a wise choice to teach children caught between opposing forces.

There was one other little child in this second-generation group. Born in 1522 she was the natural daughter of Charles and Johanna van der Gheenst of Oudenarde, and her name was Margaret in honor of her grand-aunt and godmother.[610] As for the little Margaret, she must have been a child to win hearts. Clothing and presents for her often appear in Margaret's and later Mary's accounts.[611] She must also have been taught to have regard for her mother, as valuable gifts for Johanna and her subsequent children are also listed. The chaplain of St. Gudule's (St. Michael's) Jean Beauvalet, became her tutor. She eventually became known as the second Margaret of Austria, the third of the great women who ruled as Regent of the Low Countries. She married first Alessandro de Medici, Duke of Florence who was murdered a year later in 1537. She next married Ottavio Farnese grandson of Pope Paul III, by whom she had a son Alessandro Farnese who rose to Commander-in-Chief of Philip II's dreaded Spanish armed forces in the Low Countries during the terrible religious wars; in 1581 he was named Governor-General.

The Church at this time still had tremendous strength through its bishops and abbots who wielded great power in their own, autonomous jurisdictions which comprised great territories. Though they expected their principalities to be defended by the civil authorities, they did not feel bound to obey or even cooperate with them. In such troubled times, confrontations were inevitable. Furthermore, countervailing forces were at work as the centrist house of Habsburg was counterposed against local

---

610 Charles had one other natural child, a son called Don Juan of Austria by Barbara Blomberg in 1539. He was way behind his contemporaries in this respect.
611 Ghislaine de Boom, Marguerite d'Autriche-Savoie ... p. 66. See also: Henri Pirenne, Histoire de Belgique, Vol. III, pp. 380-381.

and provincial interests. These were, of course, in addition to the opposing religious beliefs, zealously held.

Besides these internal difficulties, there was the constant strife with Gelderland, the interminable war in Italy and the threat from the Turks in the East. If Margaret at times seemed agitated, she had good cause to be. She had a Privy Council made up of the Knights of the Golden Fleece, combined with leading members of a Council of the States which met at Malines. Though this had a positive and unifying effect over the Low Countries, the populace itself had strongly separatist tendencies which acted against their best interests. As far back as 1522, when they were once again engaged in war with Gelderland, the States of Brabant had refused to pay for the maintenance of troops. De Boom explains:

> However, the nobility, aware of the danger, had voted a subsidy, but the clergy, notably the abbots of the great monasteries, were intractable. Margaret having convoked the deputies of the cities, the third member of the States at her palace in Malines, vainly begged them to not follow "the obstinate and abusive determination of the prelates." Also she held the abbots responsible for her defeat and did not hesitate to make them participate, if not in money, at least in kind, to the maintenance of the troops. With the agreement of the Privy Council, she proposed "to send men of arms to the houses of these abbots of Brabant." She attempted to isolate diplomatically the most intractable, the abbots of Parc and of Tongerloo, and begged the Emperor "to have them called as his chaplains." But when in 1525 the tenacious Abbot of Parc again prevented the vote on the subsidy already approved by the nobility, the towns and a part of the clergy, the Princess went so far as to threaten "to throw him in a boat and send him to Spain."

This was sufficiently terrifying to compel the abbot to desist and he was censured by the Council. But again in 1527 and 1528, they repeated their actions:

The situation became graver as the unpaid police bands began to menace the livelihood of the country. In vain the Chancellor of Brabant presented to the abbots the problems caused to the country by their refusal; in vain the Archduchess herself aided by the principal members of the Privy Council and the Financial Council attempted to persuade them. In the middle of this angry situation, the Abbot of Villiers replied to her in "hard and bitter words" without taking account of the honor of the Emperor or the presence of the Governess. So the outraged Princess decided to seize their worldly goods until they conducted themselves "more decently." In order to completely restrain their political power, she asked her nephew to obtain from the Pope the establishment of new bishoprics, "as much to reduce the men of the Church to reason as for the benefits of your subjects."[612]

As Margaret grew older, she became increasingly assertive which antagonized, provoked and enraged these men. However, her basic nature remained one of geniality, tact and humor which perhaps led them to take advantage of her. Had she been a more severe and haughty woman, they might not have dared their confrontations. There is in these situations just described, an attitude of Margaret's which leads one to observe that the Archduchess meant to have a State Church, in fact, if not in theory, even though she never made any direct statement to that effect. She certainly resisted every attempt at interference with her authority.

In the year 1524, King Emanuel of Portugal died, leaving Eleanor a widow. She had born a son, Carlos, who died in infancy, and a daughter Maria who lived and came to be greatly loved among her people. Joam (Juan) III then ascended the throne, and arrangements were made for him to marry Katherine, now 17, in the autumn of that year. Margaret never knew this last child of her brother Philip, as she had been born to Juana

---

[612] Ghislaine de Boom, Marguerite d'Autriche-Savoie ... p. 55. Trans. SHB.

after his death in Spain. Eleanor, ever devoted to her brother,[613] returned to Spain to be with Charles, and, according to custom, left Maria at the Portuguese court.[614]

Meanwhile, Charles and Francis were still at war. At first the French were driven back following the battle in Lombardy on April 30, 1524 following this great success for the imperial forces under the command of the Duke of Bourbon, there were great difficulties owing to lack of supplies and money. The Duke's plans for taking Marseilles collapsed, and he was forced to retreat across the mountains to Italy. In the fall, Francis rejoined his army in Italy under the command of Bonnivet, the French General who retook Milan. They then laid siege to Pavia which dragged on for four miserable winter months. Finally, on February 24, 1525, - Charles's 25th birthday, the forces were engaged in the battle which has been called the greatest of the sixteenth century. The French were defeated by Charles's forces under the brilliant direction of the Marquess of Pescara and Antonio de Leyva. The French army was annihilated; Bonnivet lay dead; and Francis was taken. Francis, however, had refused to surrender to Bourbon saying "I know no Duke of Bourbon but myself."[615] This battle marks a turning point in the conduct of war, as it showed the superior ability of firearms over pikemen.

Francis was placed under the protection of Charles de Lannoy, to whom he had surrendered. On the following day, Lannoy wrote to Charles:

> ...Sire, we gave battle yesterday, and it pleased God to give you victory, which was so well followed up that you hold the King of France a prisoner in my hands ... I beseech you, earnestly as it is possible to do, to think of your affairs, and to make prompt

---

613 For these observations about Eleanor, see the account of the Emperor's life after his abdication by William H. Prescott in William Robertson's The History of the Reign of the Emperor Charles the Fifth, Vol. III (Philadelphia: J.B. Lippincott Company, 1902/1856).

614 They became estranged, and when they met again during Charles's retirement after 1556, the meeting was not a happy one. Thirty years is a long time, and this encounter proved to be Eleanor's last bitter experience in a life marked by unhappiness. Ibid.

615 William Bradford, ed. and trans. Correspondence of The Emperor Charles V ... (London: Richard Bentley, 1850), p. 108.

execution now that God has sent you such a favorable opportunity; for you will never have a more propitious time than the present to demand restitution of the crowns justly appertaining to you, for you owe no obligation to any prince in Italy; nor can they longer hope for protection from the King of France, as you hold him captive ... Sire, I think you remember the saying of M. de Bersele, "That God sends to men once in their lives a fruitful August, but if they allow it to pass without gathering a harvest; it is a chance whether the opportunity is given them again." I say not this believing that your Majesty is disposed to neglect your advantages, but only because I feel it a duty so to speak...

Sire, M. de Bourbon acquitted himself well, and performed good service...

Sire, the victory which God has given you happened on St. Matthew's Day, which is the day of your Majesty's birth. The 25th day of February 1525. Charles de Lannoy[616]

The outlook had been so gloomy, and the French prospects so glorious, that the anxious Margaret had written to Henry to ask if he could send help to Charles and to suggest that they join forces to harrass the provinces of northern France. She received the astonishing news on March 6, and, in overwhelming relief, proclaimed to the subjects of the Low Countries that they "give thanks to God for the victory ... by fireworks, processions, prayers, and other devout works, and above all to pray for the souls of those who have died."[617]

England received the news on March 9 and rejoiced with bonfires, fountains of wine, and a solemn Mass celebrated at St. Paul's by Wolsey.[618] In remarkable contrast, in Madrid, Charles seemed dazed and retired for

---

616 Extracted from Karl Lanz, Correspondenz des Kaisers Karl V (Frankfurt/Main: Minerva GmbH, 1966/1844), Vol. I, pp. 150-152. See also Eleanor E. Tremayne, The First Governess of The Netherlands (New York: G.P. Putnam's Sons, 1908), pp. 210-211.
617 Ibid, Tremayne, p. 212, taken from MSS in the Bibliothèque de Bourgogne (Burgundian Library).
618 Pascual de Gayangos, ed., Calendar of Letters, Despatches .Vol. III, Part k, pp. 82 and 91.

prayer. All public rejoicings were forbidden as being unsuitable "when a great Christian King had fallen under such great misfortune."[619]

On August 12, 1525 Charles wrote a very polite request to Henry asking to be released from his betrothal to the Princess Mary and explaining that his Cortes had suggested he marry the Infanta Donna Isabel of Portugal, his cousin, who could fill his place during his absences.[620] There is no record that we know of Henry's reply, but Margaret learned that Henry was already negotiating a private alliance with Louise of Savoy. Wolsey, of course, had never become reconciled to what he considered Charles's duplicity in the matter of the papal election. Also, there was the feeling that now the Empire had become too powerful. When Margaret reflected on her information, it seemed that she must again prepare the Low Countries for war. She summoned the States-General, and, though the nobility approved, many of the towns and some of the influential clergy refused to grant money for defense, pleading that their territories had already been drained. This is the time that Margaret delivered her famous threat to the Abbot of Parc "to throw him in a boat and send him to Spain."[621] Antoine de Lalaing, the Count of Hoogstraten, then went from town to town to raise the money needed. Louise of Savoy, acting as Regent during her son's imprisonment, proposed a six-month truce to which Margaret was favorable, perhaps because she knew Charles's popularity had diminished in England, due to his breaking of the marriage agreement with the Princess Mary and Wolsey's disappointment over the loss of the papacy. Being closer to England than Charles was, Margaret was more perceptive than he in this regard, and she realized there would be little or no aid for the Low Countries in their border wars. Representatives of the two Regents worked out the arrangements at Henry of Nassau's palace at Breda, and

---

619 William Bradford, ed., Correspondence of The Emperor Charles V ... p. 111.
620 Gayangos, Vol. III, Part 1, p. 285.
621 Ghislaine de Boom, Marguerite d'Autriche-Savoie ... p. 54. Margaret wrote a lengthy letter to Charles in which she included a discussion of this matter, see Karl Lanz, Correspondenz des Kaisers Karl V (Frankfurt/Main: Minerva GmbH, 1966/1844), Vol. I, pp. 198-204. Henri Pirenne in his Histoire de Belgique, Vol. III, p. 186, states that the clergy constituted a very active and very annoying party of opposition, and exasperated her with their continual difficulties, complaints and rebelliousness.

the Archduchess attended the conference herself, which was presided over by Antoine de Lalaing. In the armistice concluded, the fisheries were to be protected and the seas were declared free for merchant trading. This freed the Burgundian troops to quell riots in Limburg, Brabant and s'-Hertegenbosch,[622] and restored the commercial revenues so necessary to the life of the Low Countries.

However, when Charles learned of this treaty, his usual placid nature was stirred to anger and he wrote:

Madame, my good Aunt!

I have received your letters by Richard, and quite approve what you were able to communicate to him in what your memory served you. I have received also a copy of the treaty of cessation of hostilities, which you have concluded. But I cannot conceal from you, Madam, that I have found it very strange, and very far from satisfactory, that this should have been done without knowing my intentions, and without receiving instructions on this behalf, and powers from me. I have found it convenient both for the advantage of my affairs, and the preservation of my authority as heretofore, to declare to the Ambassadors of England, and still more to those of France, that since the said treaty has been entered into without instructions and powers from me, I shall neither acknowledge it, nor ratify it, nor cause it to be observed ...

Madame! I send you a copy of the cessation of hostilities concluded here, in order that you may cause it to be published duly, and at the time therein declared, and to be strictly kept and performed according to its form and tenor, setting aside your own as null and void, as well as the publications which may have taken place; for it is my express intention, that it should not be held of the smallest force or value; insomuch that if I had not even concluded

---

[622] Jane de Iongh, Margaret of Austria: Regent of the Netherlands (New York: W.W. Norton & Company, Inc., 1953), p. 236.

a treaty, as aforesaid, here, I would not have permitted yours to be carried into effect.

Madam! May our Lord have you in his holy keeping.

Written at Toledo, the 13th of August [1525].[623]

If Margaret replied to this scalding and humiliating letter, there is no record of it. One might surmise, since she was always able to defend herself, that she made a reply so sharp, it could not be preserved; or, she dealt with the matter through an intermediary as the following letter from Perrenot de Granvelle intimates:

> ... Madame! In fulfillment of your wishes, and in accordance with the good pleasure of the Emperor ... I forthwith went to take your letters to the King, and on your part to pay him a visit. I had long audiences with him, at four different times after the fever had subsided, when I found him in a good disposition to receive me, though extremely week from the severity of his malady. He told me, that he and his kingdom were much indebted to you, Madame, for the desire you had manifested for peace ... he must always esteem you, even as a second mother, with whose advice and counsel he should be happy to govern his affairs ...[624]

Perrenot continues later after Charles had been on a short hunting expedition:

> ... and on his return I presented to him your letters. I discussed with him at length the two principal points relative to the peace or truce, and the commercial arrangements in which your country is concerned. The present truce, I observed, such as it was, would not be of long continuance, and was not unattended with dangers and

---

623 William Bradford, ed., Correspondence of The Emperor Charles V ... pp. 151-155.
624 Ibid., pp. 183-184.

inconveniences ... To all this his Majesty gave a willing ear, and seemed to take in good part all that was said ..."[625]

Neither Margaret's nor Charles's fundamental good sense was ever seriously impaired by their occasional outbursts of temperament.[626]

King Francis had been removed to a prison in Spain near Madrid. Though he was treated in accordance with his rank, the inactivity and seclusion began to affect his health. His sister Marguerite, the Duchess of Alenqon, came to visit, and Charles paid several calls. In November, while Margaret's envoy Nicolas Perrenot de Granvelle was in Spain for talks with the Emperor, he also paid a call on Francis on behalf of the Archduchess, and delivered letters from her to Francis. He communicated to her in a lengthy letter[627] that the negotiations for peace had come to a standstill because the Emperor had declared "that nothing less than the Duchy his ancient heritage, the foundation of his order of which he bore the name and arms would satisfy him," and King Francis had "fully made up his mind not to resign the said Duchy ... choosing rather to submit to perpetual imprisonment."[628]

Francis was in such despair over his situation, that he sent word secretly to the Sultan asking for help and suggesting that he attack the King of Hungary.[629] Suleiman's reply is preserved:

> I who am the Sultan of Sultans, the Sovereign of Sovereigns, the distributor of crowns to the monarchs of the surface of the globe, the shadow of God on the earth, the Sultan and Padishaw of the White Sea, the Black Sea, Rumelia, Anatolia, Caramania, Rum, Sulkadr, Diarbekr, Kurdistan, Azerbijan, Persia, Damascus,

---

625 Ibid., p. 188, October 19, 1525.
626 Karl Brandi, The Emperor Charles V, p. 190.
627 William Bradford, ed., Correspondence of The Emperor Charles V ..., pp. 185-186.
628 Christopher Hare, The High and Puissant Princess ..., (London: Harper and Brothers, 1907), p. 294.
629 Paule Henry-Bordeaux, Louise de Savoie ..., (Paris: Libraire Académique Perrin, 1971/1954/1943), p. 326, states that Louise is the one who sent for help to Suleiman.

Aleppo, Cairo, Mecca, Medina, Jerusalem, all Arabia, Yemen, and other countries which my noble ancestors (may God brighten their tombs) conquered and which my august majesty has likewise conquered with my flaming sword, Sultan Sulayman Khan, son of Sultan Selim, son of Sultan Bayazid; you who are Francis, King of France, you have sent a letter to my Porte the refuge of sovereigns night and day our horse is saddled, and our sword girt on.[630]

Suleiman's reply was courageous, bombastic, charming and ambiguous, leaving Francis or Louise no more the wiser about forthcoming aid.

Finally, a peace was concluded in Madrid on January 14, 1526. These were the conditions: Eleanor was to be given in marriage to Francis with the dowry of 200,000 gold crowns and the counties of Mâcon, Auxerre, and Bar-sur-Seine. In Italy Francis was to renounce all claims to Naples, Milan, Genoa and Asti; in Flanders he was to cede to the Low Countries the counties of Charolais and Hesdin, all feudal sovereignty over Flanders and Artois, and to renounce all claims to Tournai and Arras; the Duchy of Burgundy was to be returned to the Emperor; the property of the Duke of Bourbon was to be restored to him; the Prince of Orange was to be set free with no ransom; the Duchy of Gelderland was to be returned to the Emperor, though the Duke Charles of Egmond was permitted to retain his title during his lifetime; and all prisoners were to be set free. In addition, the two eldest sons of Francis were to be held as hostages in Spain until he should fulfill all the clauses; his own freedom would be forfeit if he failed to carry out his promises.[631]

On April 22, 1526 Margaret wrote to Charles to thank him for his gracious letters, "the honor that you do me, and the good will you carry for me," and the copy of the treaty. She reported that the States-General would be convened at Malines to inform them of the treaty. She also

---

630 Cambridge Modern History, "The Ottoman Conquest" by J.B. Bury (Cambridge: 1902), Vol. I, Chapter III, p. 95.
631 William Bradford, ed., Correspondence of The Emperor Charles V ... pp. 206-215, Letter from Charles to De Praet, his ambassador in London, written from Madrid February 19, 1526.

described the mood of the country to be joyful and thankful.[632] This is another long letter filled with official matters large and small: complaints about the French officials increasing the border tolls because of the war so that the merchants have difficulty importing wine; the Governor of Luxemburg maintains that his pecuniary claim must be met before he will submit to removal, and this prevents us from replacing the present incompetent government;[633] differences between the Lords of Herbemont and of Aymeries,[634] the latter claims money owed him "which I believe is due him... I wish the seignory of Derbu in Luxemburg to be under the Lord of Aymeries and reimbursement made to the Lord of Herbemont (Herbeumont)." The Count of Brienne and Robert de la Marek have sent letters concerning restitution of disputed lands; a burgher from Maastricht is appealing a ruling made by their aldermen; foot soldiers and horsemen on the border of Friesland demanding pass-through to embark for Norway; pirates well known as being in the service of Christian II, having ten or twelve boats and trying to get others to join them, have been reported - Margaret has sent word secretly to the cities and ports to be on guard; the Abbot of Parc (Parck, Park) again causing us trouble; the ambassador from Lübeck proposes that the Prince of Denmark (Christian's son)

---

632   Karl Lanz, Correspondenz des Kaisers Karl V (Frankfurt/Main: Minerva GmbH, 1966/1844), Vol. I, pp. 198-207.

633   Ghislaine de Boom, Marguerite d'Autriche-Savoie ... p. 50 explained: "She fought with ardor against the priviléges of the great feudal lords in Luxembourg, Limbourg and the lands across the Meuse (Maas). The Emperor Maximilian had transferred in 1488 the government of the Duchy of Luxembourg to the Marquis Christophe de Bad of whom he was debtor. In consequence the true Lord was unable to obtain any loyalty and the people were burdened with heavy exactions. The madness of Christophe de Bad offered the Governess an occasion for intervention. She entered into negotiations with his sons Philip and Bernard de Bad who refused to submit to her before the complete payment of their trust. In 1527 on the death of Christophe de Bad, she insisted along with Charles V, that the government of Luxembourg should be placed with the Count of Nassau, 'whom I find an honest personage of good intentions and very attached to your service.' Unfortunately the necessary money to liberate the Duchy was not found and Bernard de Bad was named the governor with the same exorbitant powers."

634   Antoine and later Louis Rolin (Rollin), Lords of Aymeries served Maximilian and Margaret faithfully. See Le Glay, Correspondance ... pp. 424 and 434. On September 23, 1528, Margaret wrote to Gilles de Berlaimont (Berlaymont): "... guard your rights as if your husband [Louis] were still living." See Max Bruchet, Marguerite d'Autriche, Duchesse de Savoie (Lille: Imprimerie L. Danel, 1934), p. 398.

succeed Frederick I; there are complications and difficulties concerning the financial settlement of the retaking of the city and castle of Hesdin; and most importantly, concerning Flanders and Artois, Margaret wrote:

> [You] wish me to put in writing the manner in which the King of France ought to make his renunciation of the sovereignty of Flanders and Artois... I have made a memorandum of this and presented it to the Privy Council... which I send to you for your correction ... such is necessary; otherwise, they will offer us disagreements and inconveniences.[635]

Both Margaret and Charles knew with whom they were dealing, and that the written word was more binding than the gentlemen's agreement which Francis gave little intention of keeping. Though he had given his word of honor to Charles, it was with the mental reservation of breaking it as soon as he should be freed. Otto von Habsburg comments:

> German historians have severely condemned Francois I for his perjury at Madrid, which casts such a shadow over his image, There is no doubt, too, that he deserves such criticism, in particular for freely giving his word of honour ... only to break his oath later. However, Francois did find himself in what seemed was an impossible situation; he had been obliged to conclude a peace treaty comprising a number of terms which were quite unacceptable ... for an agreement to be of value and for it to be conscientiously implemented, it must be both reasonable and freely assented to.[636]

Only the year before, Charles had made some notes of assessment in regard to his position with the French, reflecting that "peace is beautiful to

---

[635] This quote and extracts above taken from letter of April 22, 1526 from Margaret to Charles. See Karl Lanz, Correspondenz des Kaisers Karl V (Frankfurt/Main: Minerva GmbH, 1966/1844), Vol. I, pp. 198-207.

[636] Otto von Habsburg, Charles V, trans. from the French by Michael Ross (New York: Praeger Publishers, 1970), p. 113.

talk of but difficult to have, for as everyone knows it cannot be had without the enemy's consent."[637]

Though these weighty international affairs filled their thoughts and absorbed their time, Charles took time out for a matter of domestic importance. On March 10, 1526 in Seville, Charles married his cousin the Infanta Isabel of Portugal who was the daughter of Emanuel and of his second wife Maria, sister of Juana and Charles's mother. In his grave and deliberate way he chose a princess who brought a large dowry and who had "the ripe judgment and the business capacity of a sixteenth-century Portuguese"[638] and the ability to be regent in his absence.[639] But from all reports, he then fell deeply and quietly in love with her, living in serene harmony until her death in 1539.

On March 17, 1526, Francis was released and the two young princes received and taken to Burgos. But Francis, untroubled by fatherly feeling or conscience or knightly codes of honor, considered he was not bound by conditions obtained under duress, and immediately set about implementing the designs he had made while in prison and in undermining the treaty. He found a willing ally in Pope Clement VII who absolved him of his promises. Together they formed the League of Cognac on May 22, 1526. The Republic of Venice was also sympathetic.

During the imprisonment there was much sympathy for Francis and fear of Charles's power. Erasmus wrote to the Emperor:

---

637 Karl Brandi, The Emperor Charles V, trans. from the German by C.V. Wedgwood (Oxford: Alfred A. Knopf Alden Press), 1939/Munich: 1937), p. 219. Memorandum in Vienna Archives dated January 5, 1525.

638 Edward Armstrong, The Emperor Charles V (London: MacMillan and Company, Ltd., 1929/1901), Vol. I, p. 165.

639 Ghislaine de Boom, Marguerite d'Autriche ... p. 58 – Margaret sent a message by her ambassador Pierre de Rosimboz to tell the young Empress with warm words about "this Country which is so beautiful and blessed with good cities who so love their princes and princesses!" And she proposed that one of their young sons should come to the Low Countries to be reared there and eventually rule over them.
Ever delighted by the thoughts of children, she happily relayed the news in 1527 that Maximilian II had been born to Ferdinand and Anne on July 31, sending a courier to the Spanish Court to tell Charles. Eleanor E. Tremayne, The First Governess of The Netherlands (New York: G.P. Putnam's Sons, 1908), p. 251. taken from Calendar of Letters...

If I were conqueror I would thus speak to the conquered: "My brother, fate has made you my prisoner; a like misfortune might have happened to me. Your defeat shows the frailty of all human greatness; receive your freedom, become my friend. Let all rivalry cease between us except that of virtue. In delivering you, I gain more glory than if I had conquered France; in accepting this kindness with gratitude, you achieve more than if you had driven me from Italy."[640]

Margaret had also tried to obtain the release of Francis. In this instance, Charles's intuition did not play him false. Francis's letter to Suleiman may have laid the stage for the next tragedy. On August 29, 1526, the Christian army under the leadership of King Louis of Hungary met the advancing Turks on the plain of Mohacs. The battle was won by the Turks, with twenty thousand slain, and the young king lost his life. Charles's troops arrived too late to help. Ferdinand wrote to inform his aunt and to ask her help, and she replied:

> My good Nephew. I have received your two letters, one of the 18th and the other of the 23rd of September, and by them have heard of the sad and pitiful news of the death of the King of Hungary, the loss of the kingdom, and the state of the poor queen, your sister, my good niece, and above all, the danger which you, your country and subjects are in. I do not know how to express to you the regret and

---

[640] Christopher Hare, The High and Puissant Princess Marguerite of Austria (London: Harper and Brothers, 1907), pp. 291-292. But in the Low Countries, this verse circulated:
    Que ferons nous du roy (What shall we do with the King)
    De nostre prisonnier? (This prisoner of ours?)
    Que feist-on à due Charles (What did they do to Duke Charles)
    Quand fut prins à Nanchy? (When he was taken at Nancy?)
    On ne sceut qu'il devint, (They never knew what became of him,)
    On le scet bien en France; (They know it well in France;)
    Qui lui feroi t ainsy (If the same were done to him)
    Ce seroit la vengeance. (It would be vengeance.)
Jane de Iongh, Margaret of Austria: Regent of The Netherlands, trans. by M.D. Herter Norton (New York: W.W. Norton & Company, Inc., 1953), p.237.

sorrow that I feel, and you can believe that it is not less than if the misfortune had befallen me, and that I was in the position of the queen, your worthy sister, or yourself. In any case it becomes us to conform in all things to the will of God, our Creator, the refuge and consoler of the desolate who never forsakes or abandons those who pray to Him with their whole heart...

I have ordered your courier in Zealand to cross the sea with the first good company that leaves, which is the safest way, and I have written to the emperor reminding him of your conduct and the services you have rendered him, exhorting and imploring him first to assist you in your great and extreme necessity, as I hope he will, and on my part in this and other matters I will do what I can for you and your service. John, Seigneur de Temstel, whom Monseigneur de Bourbon sent to you, and also Messire George de Fronsberg have been to see me and told me that the said Messire George has not been able to raise money from the Fuggers or others on the rings you gave him ... for which I am sorry. I have informed the King of England and the legate [Wolsey] of the loss of Hungary and the death of the king ... Monseigneur, if it should happen that you should see the Queen of Hungary, your sister, or ... that you should send or write to her, I beg you to recommend me to her, and console her for her misfortune as much as is possible, and comfort her and forward a letter which I have written to her ... I beg you, monseigneur, to often send me your news, and I will send you mine from here, and assist you in every way in my power, with the help of our Lord.[641]

While the first part of the letter bestowed conventional sympathy, help and piety, the latter section pours out of an overflowing heart for the young Mary. Margaret was forty-six this year, and had lost her niece Isabel in

---

641 Eleanor E. Tremayne, The First Governess of The Netherlands (New York: G.P. Putnam's Sons; London: Methuen & Company, 1908), p. 244. Taken from Brussels. Archives. See also Andre J.G. Le Glay, Correspondence ... Vol. II, p. 448.

January. These were arid years, so it is not surprising that she took such joy in having Isabel's children and the little Margaret.

On December 17, 1526, Queen Mary of Hungary, who had borne her terror and sorrow with such great bravery, announced that her brother, the Archduke Ferdinand, had been elected to the thrones of Hungary and Bohemia by the Diet. No little influence was due to two women who gathered the forces on his behalf: his sister Mary, and the claim of his wife Anne of Hungary, sister of the dead King Louis.[642]

In spite of such formidable events, the war continued in Italy. However, just as before, strength and attitudes were at work against Francis and Pope Clement VII. Genoa went over to the Imperial side, though there was no money to pay any of these troops; so they ranged half-starved and half-crazed, pillaging and looting wherever they roamed. In an attempt to muster some discipline and offer a focus to this wild army, they were led under the direction of the Duke of Bourbon to march on Rome. Armstrong relates:

> The whole force of 20,000 men or more, mad with hunger and suffering, staggered blindly down through Italy … In vain Lannoy pleaded his convention with the Pope; too late Clement sold Cardinals' hats to provide for the defence … In a thick mist on the morning of May 6, 1527, the attacking force flung itself upon the western walls of Rome. Bourbon, seeing his men waver, sprang upon a ladder to scale the wall; with his foot upon the second rung he was shot down, but his example saved the day… The long-drawn agony of the ensuing weeks needs no fresh description … The horrors of the sack of Rome were but the concentrated essence of the sufferings of Italy for which the first French invasion of 1494 [under Charles VIII] must be held responsible.[643]

---

642 For a full description, read Jane de Iongh, Mary of Hungary: Second Regent of The Netherlands, trans. from the Dutch by M.D. Herter Norton (New York: W.W. Norton and Company, 1958).
643 Edward Armstrong, The Emperor Charles V (London: MacMillan and Company, Ltd., 1929/1901), Vol. I, pp. 177-179.

But just as the battle of Pavia had yielded the King of France into the Emperor's power, so now the sack of Rome delivered up the Pope who was emprisoned at St. Angelo. The news of the taking of Rome reached Spain when the celebrations for the birth of a son, Philip II, born to Charles and Isabel on May 22, 1527, were in full swing.

> It is often said that Charles at once suspended them. On the contrary he gave as an excuse for their continuance the expense which the nobles had incurred therein ... He quickly, however, found that public opinion was deeply stirred by the Pope's misfortunes.[644]

The news of Rome may have been distressing to Margaret; on the other hand, she was realist enough to assess that the policies followed by Clement and Francis had brought them their just due, and that Charles was justified. In any case, events closer to home absorbed her thoughts and energies. It is estimated that the Low Countries at this time had a population of 3,000,000 largely centered in and around 303 cities and 6,579 villages.[645] Visiting strangers noted the density of the population and the highly commercial nature of it. The Low Countries were very dependent upon trade, and their chief trading partner, England, had turned away from the Empire and toward France. It is difficult to assess how much of this defection was wrung from real fear of the size and power of Charles's dominions or how much the bitter end of Henry's marriage to Catherine of Aragon (Charles's aunt), or to Wolsey's animosity influenced decisions. Margaret soon found herself dealing with the unthinkable proposition that England, her long-time ally, might invade the Low Countries. Nevertheless, she assured Charles that "the English will never openly war with us."[646]

---

644 Ibid., p. 182.
645 Henri Pirenne, Histoire de Belgique (Bruxelles: Henri Lamertin, Libraire-Éditeur, 1907), pp. 282-284. Calculations taken from his "Les documents d'archives comme source de la démographie historique" within the Rapports du 11e congrès international d'hygiène et de démographie (Bruxelles, 1903), in the absence of verifiable statistics.
646 Ghislaine de Boom, Marguerite d'Autriche-Savoie et la Pré-Renaissance (Bruxelles: La Renaissance du Livre, 1946/1935), p. 45.

I have some hope of continuing the neutrality of these countries on this side, and I intend to conduct myself this way and address the English.[647]

She proceeded to fortify the frontiers, and, by way of retaliation, made a commercial treaty with James V of Scotland, who was in a very real sense, England's Gelderland. These hostilities were most unpopular in England, as commerce with Spain and the Low Countries had come to a halt. Henry was forced to offer a truce to Margaret in which the Emperor and the King of France were to participate. She wrote to Charles to list the advantages of this proposition, but, without waiting for a response, she sent her ambassadors to negotiate the truce of Hampton Court in 1528.[648] This time Charles offered no rebuke.

During this same period, the Archduchess obtained the submission of her most dangerous and tenacious adversary, the Duke Charles of Gelderland. By the treaty of Gorcum (Gorinchem)[649] in October 1528, he recognized the lordship of Charles V over Utrecht, Overijssel and Gelderland while continuing to hold for hereditary possession the Duchy of Gelderland and the possession for his life of Groningen and the Drenth. Reduced to submission by Imperial forces and lacking money because the defeated French were no longer able to fund his enterprises, Charles of Egmond had no other choice. De Boom exclaimed in humorous exasperation:

> The able Governess had finally and victoriously brought to an end this perpetual gorilla who had for almost half a century desolated Holland and Brabant.[650]

---

647   Ibid.
648   This is outlined in her letter of July 7, 1528. See Karl Lanz, Correspondenz des Kaisers Karl V Frankfurt/Main: Minerva GmbH, 1966/1844), Vol. I. pp. 276-286.
649   L. Ph. C. van den Bergh, Correspondance de Marguerite d'Autriche. Vol. II, pp. 242-248. See also Pascual de Gayangos, ed., Calendar of Letters, Despatches, ... Vol. III, Part II, p. 849.
650   Ghislaine de Boom, Marguerite d'Autriche ... p. 46.

But Charles of Egmond was like a cork, he bobbed up well into the next decade to bedevil the early reign of Mary. For the time being, he was cowed, and even that was a great deal to be thankful for.

On the other side of the Egmond family, "the young lady of Egmond claims she is owed a portion of the revenues of certain villages as well as 400 pounds and requires me to discharge these demands."[651] Margaret wrote to Antoine de Lalaing explaining that she had spoken to the treasurer Ruffault who said there was no basis for the claim. Margaret, however, tended to be very encouraging and sympathetic to the women under her, and suggested that, in view of the fact that her late husband raised the required portion of aids and that she was under heavy debts from rendering the last levies, that she be given a good space of time in which to pay[652] if some settlement could not be made.

According to which history one reads, it was either Margaret or Louise of Savoy who initiated the peace overtures which led to the Treaty of Cambrai, though Wolsey is given credit as early as March in 1528.[653] As these two women were sisters-in-law, they had maintained a personal relationship intermittently through correspondence which could be described as "correct" rather than warm or close, even though each had strong family feeling. Margaret had taken the little Claude of Savoy with her when she returned to govern the Low Countries, and Louise had taken under her protection the lovely Philiberte.[654] Neither one admired the brother Charles who became Duke when Margaret's husband died. Paule Henry-Bordeaux comments that he was called "the Good" when he

---

651 Van den Bergh, Vol, II, p. 238.

652 Van den Bergh, Vol. II, p. 238.

653 Eleanor E. Tremayne; The First Governess of The Netherlands (New York: G.P. Putnam's Sons, 1908), p. 251.

654 Philiberte was the half-sister of Louise who protected her and saw to her marriage to Pope Leo's brother. She was the daughter of Claudine de Brosse who died in 1513, the step-mother-in-law of whom Margaret was so fond. She assumed the title Duchess of Nemours in connection with her dowry, though this was only for life. It is thought that she is the one who posed for the "Mona Lisa." See Paule Henry-Bordeaux, Louise de Savoie, "Roi" de France (Paris: Librairie Académique Perrin, 1971/1954/1943), p. 123.

better merited the title "the Feeble."[655] René remained a bone of contention until his death at Pavia. On April 24, 1515 Louise wrote from Melun to Margaret about the restitution of the County of Villars to René, but Margaret refused saying it was given to her by her "very dear husband."[656] Later, he and Louise led the French bid for the Empire in 1519.[657] In 1521, at Louise's home at Romorantin, they met with Francis, Robert de la Marek, the Duke of Lunebourg and their ally the Duke of Gelderland, along with Andre de Foix of Navarre to make plans for a concerted attack on the Low Countries.[658] Margaret, whose sources of information rarely failed her, wrote to Louise to ask for the neutrality of Burgundy in case of trouble between opposing forces,[659] and, on June 5, 1522, a treaty for three years of peace was arranged between the two Burgundies[660] - the one, the county in France; the other, the domains of the Low Countries ruled by the House of Burgundy. Thus the avenues of communication remained open, and this led to the treaty of peace at Breda in 1525 over which Charles became so incensed, but later backed down.

In October 1528, Guillaume des Barres, an emissary of Margaret traveled to Paris to secure the French ratification of the treaty of Hampton Court. While he was there, Louise tried to sound him out as to the possibilities of something more firm and longstanding between France and the Empire. Des Barres replied guardedly that he was not empowered to pursue such a topic, so Louise then sent her secretary Gilbert Bayard, Bishop of Avranches, to Malines.[661] Upon his arrival, Bayard asked to be received in an audience alone because he had a matter of the greatest importance to communicate. Margaret treated him with

---

655 Ibid., p. 89.
656 Paule Henry-Bordeaux, Louise de Savoie, "Roi" de France (Paris: Librairie Académique Perrin, 1971/1954/1943), p. 124. Considering Margaret's near imprisonment there for two years long before, it may not have been a good place from which to ask a favor.
657 Ibid., p. 188.
658 Ibid., p. 211.
659 Ibid., p. 223.
660 Ibid., p. 328.
661 Ibid., p. 420.

courtesy and invited him to her garde-robe for private conversation. Though she listened attentively, she replied that unless he had something concrete to offer, "she had no wish to meddle in any way."[662] In order to give the Archduchess time to reflect, Bayard announced he was going to Antwerp for a little vacation. Here "he wandered along the Scheldt River, visited the city, bought a horse, and saw the ships and tapestries."[663] Her suspicions somewhat allayed, she explained to him on his return, that in order to persuade the Emperor, she must have honest and reasonable propositions.[664] Five weeks later, Louise supplied these, which Margaret decided to transmit to Charles after examination by her Privy Council. Following this, Margaret wrote her reasons for suggesting that she and Louise try to arrange a peace to her Chief Steward and financial officer, Pierre de Rosimbos, on January 3, 1529 from Malines. The guidelines she gave her envoys in presenting her case before Charles are freely translated by Bradford:

> First, she observes, such had been the bitterness of the reproaches written and spoken on either side, that ill-will and hatred were the inevitable consequences. The hostilities which ensued were of a character so fierce and exasperated, that neither of the two Sovereigns could compromise his dignity by being the first to talk of reconciliation, a challenge having been given and accepted for settling the differences and disputes by single combat. On the other hand, how easy for ladies, natural as it would appear, and unsolicited, to concur in some endeavours for warding off the general ruin of Christendom, and to make the first advances in such an undertaking. Secondly, that it is only by a mutual forgiveness of all offences, and the total oblivion of the causes of the war, and of everything that had passed in writing concerning them, that the idea of peace could be entertained. This could

---
[662] Paule Henry-Bordeaux, Louise de Savoie, Louise de France (Paris: Librairie Académique Perrin, 1971/1954/1943), p. 421.
[663] Ibid.
[664] Ibid.

not be thought of, or proposed by the Princes without a sacrifice of what they held most precious, their honour; but ladies might well come forward in a measure for submitting the gratification of private hatred and revenge to the far nobler principle of the welfare of nations. Thirdly, were the King of France to conduct negotiations with the Emperor, it would be necessary for him to act with especial reference to allies and co-operators, the Venetians, Florentines, etc.: and here a difficulty would arise in effecting a reconciliation with the Emperor, not to be surmounted without the probability of some stain upon his honour; but the act of the Lady of Angoulême, his mother, [Louise] would in such case take away all responsibility on the part of the King, whilst a similar advantage would present itself to the Emperor, in silencing the complaints of his friends, who might make objections to the terms of the peace. Again in the event of any of the great powers being called in as mediators in a negotiation, such as England, or the Pope, their own particular interest it is probable would be too much considered, and something perhaps required in little territorial concessions as the price of their interference; whilst the intervention proposed could be subject to no such inconvenience; as the mother of the King and the Aunt of the Emperor who regarded him as her son as well as heir, would keep in view one sole object which they had mutually at heart, the general good of Europe, in the reconciliation of these two great Princes.[665]

Margaret's envoys, Pierre de Rosimbos and Guillaume des Barres, traveled through France and met with the King and his mother the Regent. Louise argued over several points, but they were "mistrustful and willfully 'obtruse,'"[666] leaving Margaret's proposal well intact. They then continued towards Spain where they reported their instructions to the Emperor.

---

665 William Bradford, ed. and trans., Correspondence ... (London: Richard Bentley/AMS Edition, 1850/1971), pp. 224-225.
666 Paule Henry-Bordeaux, Louise de Savoie, "Roi" de France (Paris: Librairie Académique Perrin, 1971/1954/1943), p. 424.

He listened most willingly, and perhaps even with relief, as even Spain's rich resources were also being depleted in this constant warfare. Charles ordered that the Archduchess was to be given full powers.[667]

On May 26, 1529, Margaret wrote from Brussels a full memorandum to Charles that she had agreed to meet Louise at Cambrai on June 15 and felt the peace was assured if Francis would be as reasonable as Charles. She also said she had dispatched Jehan de le Sauch to King Henry to advise him that she did not intend to do anything repugnant to the good and long-standing friendship between his country and the Empire. She suggested as well that Charles put off his coronation until the meeting was over, as he could carry out his plans at less cost and with more chance of success. She added, as well, the sad news that a gentlemen from Queen Catherine's household had just given her the message that King Henry had recommended divorce proceedings, and that Catherine needed two qualified persons to counsel and help her. She continued that she intended

> ... sending to Malines to obtain the opinion of experienced lawyers in that place; and if the personage appointed by the Emperor to replace Don Inigo [de Mendoza, Bishop of Burgos, former ambassador to English court] had not yet left Spain, his departure should be hastened, for the poor Queen is very perplexed, and there is no one in England who dares take up her defense against the King's will.[668]

It is easy to understand Margaret's concern, because the two had remained close ever since the days in Spain when she had taught her young

---

667 Karl Lanz, Correspondenz des Kaisers Karl V (Frankfurt/Main: Minerva GmbH, 1966/1844), Vol. I, pp. 300-308, Margaret's letter of May 26, 1529 to Charles acknowledging full powers. Translation is in Pascual de Gayangos, ed., Calendar of Letters ... Vol IV, Part I, pp. 37-43.
668 Karl Lanz, Corresondenz des Kaisers Karl V (Frankfurt/Main: Minerva GmbH, 1966/1844), Vol. I, pp. 300-308. Translation in Pascual de Gayangos, ed., Calendar of Letters ... Vol. IV, Part I, pp. 37-43. In Gayangos Vol., III, Part II, p. 848, Henry stipulated on November 18, 1528 that any foreign lawyers for Catherine should be Flemish not Spanish, giving as he reason that Spain was so far away and England not easily accessible from there.

sister-in-law French. In 1511, she had been godmother to a little son of Catherine's who unfortunately did not live long. Certainly Catherine would not have found herself in this position if he had lived.

Margaret's envoy in all these pre-negotiations in England and in France was her secretary Le Sauch who gave complete and detailed accounts of all the conversations he had, and of his replies, and of what Madame Margaret thought. One is conscious of a certain "touchiness" in Louise's comments as can be expected from one dealing from a position of weakness.[669] From Margaret there was veiled warning. Le Sauch relates to Francis and Louise that courtiers had warned the Archduchess not to go to Cambrai since Francis might take her prisoner. Madame's answer to such warnings and admonitions had been that she had no mistrust or fear of any sort as regarded Madame Louise or the King, her son, and that if any of her councilors or courtiers were afraid they might remain at home."[670] And further, "if there was one single armed man in her suite, people might imagine that she were going on a warlike enterprise, not on a work of peace…"[671] Francis must have caught Le Sauch's meaning very well. Louise's last message for Margaret is very candid:

> I depart upon this journey frankly and full of confidence in my sister, sincerely hoping that our meeting and conference will turn out as I wish, and that whatever is agreed upon between us the Emperor will approve and ratify. I know not whether you are aware that some of the conditions have already been settled between Madame and myself by letter, and that I hardly think Madame would like me to undertake this journey for nothing, though I confess that I would have taken even a much longer one for her sake, and to have the pleasure of seeing her.[672]

---

669 Pascual de Gayangos, ed., Calendar of Letters … Vol. IV, Part I. p. 107. June 22, 1529.
670 Ibid. , p. 103.
671 Ibid., p. 104.
672 Ibid., p. 107.

There was some feeling on both sides that the English should be excluded, to avoid Wolsey's intrigues or possible loss of territory as payment; but this proved impossible, unrealistic, and even unhelpful. Louise continued:

> …you may confidently write to Madame, my sister, that she need not be jealous of the English, or imagine that they can prevent my Journey to Cambray, for in no case would I miss the appointment, or make less concessions than I am prepared for.[673]

Le Sauch answered:

> Madame… I am inclined to think that the Emperor will raise no difficulty to having the King of England comprised in the treaty about to be made, for it is now more than a month since I, myself, took the offer to him on Madame's behalf.[674]

Louise then acknowledged that she knew he had been in England and performed well his post as he had refused to name the place of meeting. She then asked if the Cardinal of Liégé were coming, and if he were useful, and "a man to aim at good?" Le Sauch then replied:

> Yes, he is coming. He has been useful ever since he entered the Emperor's service, that I calculate he has been worth of 4,000,000 of crowns to him, and intends still more, as he is determined to devote his whole fortune and talents to the cause of the Empire. He is consequently the most important person in the estates of Flanders after Madame…You may believe me when I say that he is strongly attached to peace, and would like to see others share his opinion.[675]

---

673 Pascual de Gayangos, ed., Calendar of Letters… Vol. IV, Part I, p. 108.
674 Ibid.
675 Ibid.

At that Louise concluded:

You may write this to my sister and tell her what my plans are, and that I hope we may hear of each other daily. Of women, I only take with me those of my own chamber, who are numerous enough, for when Queen [Claude] died we kept them all in our service... Write also to her boldly that we must necessarily contend and argue, but that I sincerely hope it will be without anger or ill-will. I will tell her things which she will be astonished to hear. She thinks that the Pope is the Emperor's friend, but I can assure her that he is very far from being such, for he is evidently trying to prevent the Emperor's journey to Italy before the treaty is concluded between the parties, and in all other matters he will be found very different from what you think. I do not mean to imply thereby that he (the Pope) acts any better towards us; such is, however, his condition, that he is of no good to us, nor to you, nor to the Church itself.

And so these two skillful women laid the background for their talks in the neutral Bishopric of Cambrai. Louise sent to request the keys to the city which angered the citizens. A demand for hostages on the part of Francis was received no better. Cambrai intended to be fair, and the entire event was well orchestrated. On June 13, 1529 the Prince-Bishop of Cambrai led a procession followed by his three brothers, then the Knights of the Golden Fleece, soldiers, the representatives of the corporations with their bright ensigns punctuating the entertainment. They were followed by banks, the advance couriers of Margaret and Louise, and Cardinal Salivate, the Pope's legate. Where to put all these people? The Magistrate began to sort it out. Those who did not pass muster were not admitted, or ushered away. On July 4, the Prince-Bishop of Liége arrived. Margaret entered Cambrai by the Notre Dame port on Monday, the fifth of July, 1529, accompanied by her council, the state deputies and all of her court in great pomp, and her guards and servers all "honestly dressed" in new doublets and hose and bonnets. Even the female dwarf Neuteken had a new costume. Margaret herself made the trip in a sumptuous litter. She arrived at three in the afternoon and was escorted into the Abbey of St. Aubert. The anonymous chronicler, whose manuscript is preserved at Lille, describes the Archduchess as dressed in black velour and still beautiful, with an entourage of ladies infinitely agreeable to see. The Lord of Hoogstraten, gentlemen and prelates arrived on horses covered with velvets, silk and gold. Two hours later, Louise of Savoy with her daughter Marguerite, Queen of Navarre, and Marie of Luxemburg, Countess of Vendôme arrived and were conducted into the Abbey where they spent two hours in conversation with Margaret. Then they retired to their own apartments nearby at the Hotel St. Paul and the residence d'Anchin. The three habitations were united by covered galleries for the privacy and convenience of the ladies in going back and forth for meetings.

Such brilliant royal assemblies brought forth throngs of people. The noble families feasted and took part in ceremonies, games and dances; the children scrambled for coins; wine flowed in place of water; and shops did a thriving business with all the attendants and those who had come to see. Outside the taverns, piglets and birds turned on spits, and inside were crowds booming in the rowdy and robust atmosphere of the day.[676]

Amidst all this noise and activity, Margaret and Louise met quietly. Their lives had been difficult and painful. Their positions prevented them from having friends as equals. But as they discussed all aspects of their situation, they gradually hammered out an agreement which was as fair as possible given those circumstances.

There is little testimony concerning the talks themselves, but the thin, nervous and passionate Louise was seen to return to her hotel at night "exhausted, twisted in sadness, sustaining pain, retiring to her chamber, her bed - far from curious eyes." On other nights, Margaret, more mistress of herself, calm, imperturbable, serene, was observed pensively looking out the window as the rain fell into the garden of the Abbey.[677] Margaret was,

---

[676] Such riotous scenes have been preserved for us by artists, such as a painting by Jan van Hemessen (1500-1575) entitled "A Rowdy Party" in which even the bird's cage is tilting crazily. Original at Berlin-Dahlem, Staatliche Museum, Stiftung Preussischer Kulturbesitz.

[677] Paule Henry-Bordeaux, Louise de Savoie, "Roi" de France (Paris: Librairie Académique Perrin, 1971/1954/1943), pp. 439-440. Taken from the anonymous author of the description and

after all, on the winning side and was not as engaged emotionally as Louise with her two emprisoned grandsons.

By July 29, they had reconciled their differences, and, on August 1 after dinner, Margaret, Louise and her daughter attended vespers at the Abbey "taking each others hands, a beautiful thing to see."[678] On August J the treaty was ratified. The terms were a softer version of the Treaty of Madrid. Francis's sons were to be freed on the payment of 2,000,000 crowns; the marriage between Francis and Eleanor was to be concluded; Charles's claim to Burgundy was still maintained though it was to remain under France's jurisdiction; and Francis was to give up all his claims in Italy, Flanders and Artois, and to desist from his aid to the Duke of Gelderland and Robert de la Marek, Charolais was to remain with Margaret for her lifetime, and then devolve upon Charles at her death. Following his death, it was to revert to France. The possessions of the Duke of Bourbon and the Prince of Orange were given to Francis. This Treaty of Cambrai known as "The Ladies' Peace," was celebrated by a mass in the Cathedral on August 5, 1529, as the two princesses solemnly swore to uphold it by oaths taken before the altar of our Lady of Cambrai. With a choir chanting a Te Deum, a blare of trumpets and the clashing of cymbals, the peace was made known to the crowds. On the same day, English ambassadors Thomas More, William Knight and John Hacket signed with Margaret a treaty of alliance and friendship, re-establishing commercial relations.[679]

---

account of this assembly in the summer of 1529 at Cambrai. Original in the Bibliothèque at Lille, France. André J.G. Le Glay, Correspondance ... Vol. III, p. 451. footnote, suggests Notice sur les principales fêtes et cérémonies publiques... in Carpentier, Estate de Cambray et du Cambrésis, I, 148, Cambrai, 1827.

678   Ibid.

679   This information is put together from several sources:
Edward Armstrong, The Emperor Charles V, Vol. I, pp. 196-197.
Ghislaine de Boom, Marguerite d'Autriche ... pp. 46-47.
Christopher Hare, The High and Puissant Princess ... pp. 303-307.
Paule Henry-Bordeaux, Louise de Savoie ... pp. 429-448.
Henri Pirenne, Histoire de Belgique Vol. III, pp. 98-99.
Eleanor E. Tremayne, The First Governess ... pp. 242-267.
See also Pascual de Gayangos, Calendar of Letters ... Vol. IV, Part I.

FORTUNE, MISFORTUNE, FORTIFIES ONE

Francis hurried the sixty miles north to Cambrai from Compiègne where, it was noted, the Duke of Suffolk remained.[680] He was well received and the festivities increased. This great public joy has been immortalized by poets and artists. The Belgian humanists Jean Second and Cornelius Grapheus (de Schrijver) celebrated it in Latin verse while the French poet Jean Marot composed a rondo comparing the three princesses, Margaret, Louise and her daughter Marguerite, to the ancient goddesses Venus, Pallas and Juno. In honor of Margaret, the Low Countries issued a medal with the quotation: "Pacis ego studiosa quater bella horrida pressi,"[681] while the city of Cambrai consecrated a token to her, on the reverse of which was the beaming Margaret and her famous motto: "Fortune, infortune, fort une."[682] Medals such as these were very popular among the nobility as they harkened back to those made for the Roman emperors and for that reason were thought to insure fame and immortality.[683]

Brandi gives an interesting sidelight to "The Ladies' Peace:"

> About this time the great Hall of Justice at Bruges was nearing completion. To celebrate the occasion, medallions of Eleanor and her husband, supported by cupids, were added to the main pillars of the gigantic and elaborately carved three-tiered chimney-piece. To the right and left the founders of the Habsburg-Burgundian-Spanish dynasty were represented - life-size figures of the Emperor Maximilian, the Duchess Mary of Burgundy, King Ferdinand of Aragon and Queen Isabella of Castile. In the background, seated on a throne, were Philip the Handsome and Joanna (Juana); in front of them, their son, the youthful Emperor, in the robes of the Golden Fleece, the Sword of Justice drawn in his hand, and lifted

---

680 Paule Henry-Bordeaux, Louise de Savoie ... p. 442.
681 'Pacis ego studiosa quater bella horrida pressi' can be translated: I, zealous of peace, have four times restrained savage wars. The writer's deepest appreciation is extended to Mr. Harry Goldby of Chatham College in Pittsburgh for a true and poetic translation.
682 'Fortune, infortune, fort une' is translated: fortune, misfortune, strengthens a woman.
683 Hannelore Sachs, The Renaissance Woman, trans. Marianne Herzfeld (New York: McGraw-Hill Book Company, 1971), p. 12.

as if to Heaven. Behind the figures, the arms of all his countries over which he ruled decorated the wall, and among them the busts of Lannoy and the Archduchess Margaret - his representatives in Naples and the Low Countries. The whole is a proud symbol of triumphant power, of the elation which all must have felt on thinking of the victory at Pavia and the peace at Cambrai.[684]

Margaret was quite taken by the dashing Francis. Though she adored the quiet and thoughtful Charles, Francis was nearer the Renaissance idea of manly perfection. He was like her gay and irresponsible brother Philip and much-loved husband Philibert - or even Charles Brandon, the Duke of Suffolk. He had the charm of Maximilian, without, however, his sense of honor. The Italian ambassadors manifested a nervousness, as well they might, for Cambrai had been known as "the purgatory of Venetians" since 1508,[685] when Margaret carried out her first major treaty. For the time, Francis hid his chagrin, but according to the historian Paul Jove,

> Francis regretted the deed carried out by the two princesses, who according to the character and genius of women, accommodated themselves better to peace than to war...[686]

In response to a sorrowful plea from Francis, she wrote to Charles on October 11, 1529, and, in a postscript of her own handwriting, requested the release of the two young princes.

> My lord, God has given you the blessing of beautiful children, so that you may better feel what a father's love is worth, and can sympathize with the sorrow of the said king. Wherefore I beg of

---

684 Karl Brandi, The Emperor Charles V, trans. by C.V. Wedgwood (Oxford: Alfred A. Knopf/Alden Press, 1939), pp. 280-281.
685 André J.G. Le Glay, Correspondance ... Vol. II, p. 453.
686 Paule Henry-Bordeaux, Louise de Savoie, "Roi" de France (Paris: Libraire Académique Perrin, 1971/1954/1943), p. 448.

you, as I always have written to you to keep the friendship of the said king ... and grant his request which is so honest and reasonable...

Your very humble aunt, Margaret.[687]

By an act of August 8, 1529, Margaret and the principal lords of the Low Countries agreed to pay Francis a million gold coins if the children of France were not liberated in accordance with the Treaty of Cambrai. But it was not until a year later, in July 1530, that the transfer took place at Bayonne, when Eleanor, exasperated at the many delays, took the matter into her own hands. They were exchanged in the "middle of the night, in the middle of the water" near Bayonne, where Francis received his sons from the hands of his bride Eleanor.[688]

Following Margaret's return home, she appointed Philippe de Lalaing, legitimized son of Antoine, and Francois de Bonvalot, brother-in-law of Nicolas Perrenot de Granvelle, to be her ambassadors at the French court, in order to work out the provisions of the treaty. And to Malines came Gilles de la Pommeraye sent by Louise. There were largely missions of courtesy to maintain amicable relations and no less important for that. She counseled her emissaries to proceed with prudence and leave to the Regent [Louise] the task of making some good overture ... nevertheless I have confidence in you."[689] They had the aid as well of Jehan de le Sauch and Guillaume des Barres, two experienced diplomats and long-time ministers of Margaret. The topics of their correspondence encompassed such disparate matters as: the claims of the nobles caught in the middle by the French and Imperial forces concerning border or disputed lands; the protests of French merchants of the pirating at sea by Spanish and Dutch merchant raiders;

---

687 Karl Lanz, Correspondenz des Kaisers Karl V (Frankfurt/Main: Minerva GmbH, 1966/1844), Vol, I, p. 348.
688 Ghislaine de Boom, Correspondance de Marguerite d'Autriche et de ses ambassadeurs à la cour de France concernant l'exécution du Traité de Cambrai (1529-1530) (Bruxelles: Maurice Lamertin, Libraire-Éditeur/Commission Royale d'Histoire, 1935), pp. 113-115. See notes on those pages as well.
689 Ghislaine de Boom, Correspondance ... concernant ... Traité de Cambrai, pp. 33-35.

continuing problems over sovereignty and reparations in Flanders and Artois; suggestions for prelates to serve in border areas and supply convents and sees ministering to both peoples;[690] assurances necessary before the French princes (Francois and Henri) should be released; and a financial settlement for the Princess La Roche-sur-Yon, sister of the late Duke of Bourbon. As the French considered the Duke a traitor, they protracted these negotiations, delayed arrangements; and, following the return of the princes, it seemed unlikely the Princess would receive anything as Francis was no longer constrained to hold to his promises or the terms of the agreement.[691] Marriages were proposed between the children of Charles and Francis.[692] Perhaps of greatest interest was Margaret's concern about "the great disorder of moneys of France and England" which made trading difficult. To institute the necessary reforms, she proposed establishing a general council of representatives from their kingdoms as well as the Low Countries.[693]

Of all the ninety letters in the Cambraian correspondence between Margaret and her ambassadors, the matter which caused her the most anxiety, and which is alluded to at least twenty times, was the divorce of Queen Catherine. While Margaret was relieved that trade between England and the Low Countries had been resumed, she was deeply troubled over Henry's continuation of divorce proceedings. In September of 1529, Eustace Chapuys had written to her of an audience he had with Henry and later with Queen Catherine. On September 27, he wrote with more news of the divorce,[694] and Margaret took up the cause. She wrote to Philippe de Lalaing and Guillaume des Barres "to speak to my sister [Louise] and show her that in order to guard the honor of ladies and princesses, this is

---

690 Ibid., p. 25. One Margaret put forward was an Augustinian brother and doctor of theology, Jehan Wanderer for the post of Suffragan to the Bishop of Clermont (in northern France) - she remained all her life inclined to that Order.

691 Ibid., p. 116.

692 Ibid., p. 149.

693 Ghislaine de Boom, Correspondance ... Traité de Cambrai, pp. 133-137.

694 Eleanor E. Tremayne, The First Governess ... p. 266. See also Pascual de Gayangos, Calendar of Letters... Vol. IV, Part I. p. 42.

not an honest and favorable act."[695] She also wrote to Charles to enlist the aid of the Pope.[696] But Louise considered it no concern of hers, and Francis was unwilling to alienate the goodwill of Henry since he was under the yoke of Charles. In fact he allowed the English to subvert the faculty of the University of Paris in their favor.[697] Margaret wrote plainly, however, that she was angered for the honor of the French King as these matters be decided freely and without constraint.[698] But, in the end, it availed her nothing but Henry's ill will. One consequence of the negotiations was the strong bond it forged between Margaret and Louise, two great and able women. The warm collaboration between the two led the ailing Louise to write on October 13, 1530 to "Madame, my good sister" to thank her for "her good mediation," and at the end of a task well done, reaping the fruit "of our labor together." Signed: "The best of everything, your good sister, Louise."[699]

During this year, Charles was on a triumphal tour to Bologna, having left Barcelona on July 27, 1529 and traveled through Genoa, Piacenza, Parma and Reggio. He had made peace with the Pope, though Margaret thought at too great a cost. She had written on October 2, 1529:

> Although God has been pleased to give Your Majesty peace with all your neighbours, there are still many causes for anxiety, both as regards politics in general, and the critical circumstances in which your brother of Hungary finds himself, owing to this invasion of the Turk. I may, therefore, perhaps, be excused if I presume to offer my advice on this occasion...
>
> I do not pretend to say that the alliance with the Pope is not a good and desirable thing; but Your Majesty must bear in mind the character of His Holiness, his inconstant humour and fickle disposition, and that he must be greatly changed in temper and general

---

695 Ghislaine de Boom, Correspondance... Traité de Cambrai, p. 42.
696 Ibid., p. 55.
697 Ibid., pp. 108-111.
698 Ibid, , p. 66.
699 Ghislaine de Boom, Correspondance ... Traité de Cambrai, p. 193.

condition if he does not try now, as he did last time, to expel you from Italy after he has got all he wants from you...

Respecting Milan, my opinion is that, considering the expense hitherto incurred, Your Majesty ought by all means to endeavor to remain master of it by investing your son with it, and treating with Maximilian Sforza [mistake for Francesco Sforza evidently] ... to allow him to retain the towns he now holds in the Duchy ... This being done, great care should be taken that Milan be not again lost, for it is the key of Italy...[700]

Your Majesty ought likewise to profit by the situation of the Florentines and Ferrarese without driving them to extremities ... .And if you cannot at present entirely do your will in Italy, time will come ...

The King, your brother, in the meanwhile must be fully provided with the means of defence, and money procured for him to carry on a good enterprize against the Turk...

Meanwhile, Your Majesty might attend to your own affairs in Italy, and everything being settled there, depart for Germany at the head of all your forces, leaving only in Italy those strictly required for the defence of Milan and Naples. This would naturally result in great honour and reputation to your army, which might be paid out of the money collected for the intended expedition, and then you could not only succour your brother, repulse the Turk, and perhaps also follow him up to his own dominions, but also increase our Faith, which will be by far a greater honour and merit than losing your precious time in the recovery of a few towns in Italy...[701]

On February 24, 1530, Charles's thirtieth birthday, he received the crown which had eluded his grandfather Maximilian (the Emperor-Elect),

---

[700] Pascual de Gayangos, Calendar of Letters ... Vol. IV, Part I, pp. 260-261.
[701] Pascual de Gayangos, Calendar of Letters... Vol. IV, Part I, pp. 262-263. This is translation of letter also included in Karl Lanz, Correspondenz des Kaisers Karl V (Frankfurt/Main: Minerva GmbH, 1966/1844), Vol. I, pp. 341-347 - a lengthy memorandum, only parts of which are given here.

the Imperial Crown of Charlemagne. Charles was at a high point in his life with peace in Spain, peace with France, and peace with Clement VII and all Italy. In Austria more territory had been added by his brother Ferdinand and in the Low Countries prosperity was returning.

Charles journeyed north passing through Trent, Bötzen and Innsbruck, until he reached Augsburg where the Diet was scheduled for June 20, 1530. He remained there for five months trying to conciliate the Electors and bring some harmony to the divisive religious arguments. Though the title King of the Romans was secured for Ferdinand, who was already King of Hungary and Bohemia, the Diet was largely a failure with both sides suspicious of Charles. His quiet attitude probably kept further quarrels from erupting, however, and a stalemate appeared preferable to outright battles. The main issue of this meeting was the Augsburg Confession, which was a central Protestant document whose content was intended to bridge the doctrinal gap between Catholics and Lutherans.

Margaret was growing weary of the unceasing duties of ruling in such troubled times in a country divided many times within itself. In later years in England, Elizabeth at least had received the love and respect of a homogeneous English people for all her work and worry. In the Low Countries with their quarrelsome, uncompromising ways, there was no such reinforcement or encouragement for Margaret.

Her private life offered little comfort. She was the supreme recourse among the members of her court. If they were sick or wounded or grieving or in debt, she said the kind words, wrote the letters, sent the doctor and paid the bills. She saw to it that orphan children were educated or learned some trade.[702] It is said of her that even her dwarfs, who were shabbily treated in the courts of that day, received her respect and were well-dressed and fed.[703]

Her continuing suffering from a festering puncture wound in her foot supposedly caused in 1527 when she accidentally stepped on a piece of shattered goblet further brought her distress since such wounds are always

---
702 Ghislaiene Boom, Marguerite d'Autriche-Savoie... p. 68.
703 Ghislaiene Boom, Marguerite d'Autriche-Savoie... p. 68.

difficult to treat. A flare-up of infection during the negotiations at Cambrai had forced the doctor Pierre Dismaîtres to come post haste from Bruges.[704] Margaret, like her father, never complained of ill health. There is only one reference to sickness in all the literature concerning her, and that is in the Spring of 1514 when she wrote her father that she would write him in her own hand, but had at present "a catarrh [probably a cold] and toothache which disturbs me."[705]

The on-and-off nature of the illness slowed her down, and during the last year kept her entirely in Malines, most unusual for the Archduchess.[706] It did not seem to interfere with her correspondence which continued as before, or her duties,[707] but did lead her to yearn for retirement, even to make plans for it. In a letter of 1527 to the Mother Superior of a Convent at Bruges, Margaret confided: "The time approaches when the Emperor will come, to whom with the aid of God I will render the charge and government which he pleased to give me; and this fact, I render to the will of God and our good mistress, his glorious mother."[708]

The place Margaret had chosen was the Convent of the Annonciades in Bruges, and the successor she had in mind was that youngest and most irrepressible niece, now the widowed Queen Mary of Hungary.

Two documents detailing her wishes have been preserved. The first to the Mother Superior of the Convent of the Annonciades in Bruges, written in 1527, reads:

---

704 Paule Henry-Bordeaux, Louise de Savoie ... p. 441.

705 André, J.G. Le Glay, Correspondance... Vol. II, p. 241.

706 Max Bruchet and E. Lancien, L'Itinéraire de Marguerite d'Autriche (Lille: Imprimerie L. Danel. 1934).

707 Pascual de Gayangos, Calendar of Letters ... Vol. IV, Part I,: Margaret began the task of collating all "inventories, deeds, obligations, contracts and so forth entered into with England, having them examined and copies made." p. 458; she continued to work for Catherine against the divorce (in which she had the aid of Mercurino di Gattinara, p. 465) "at which, as may be supposed, the King was highly displeased." p. 464. Margaret wrote to Charles dealing with complaints of the inhabitants of Utrecht and Overijssel against the Duke of Gelderland whose ambitions never ceased. Further, she was kept abreast of all the news - Eustace Chapuys wrote to Charles that he "informed Madame" of all he learned, p. 706.

708 Ghislaine de Boom, Marguerite d'Autriche-Savoie ... p. 93.

My Mother, I have ordered the bearer [Etienne Lullier, valet of the chamber] of this, whom you know well, to give you news of me, and tell you of my good resolution for some days past, and also inquire how you are, which I hope is as well as you could wish for me. My hope is in the good God and his glorious Mother, who will help and keep you for better things. I have given him (the bearer) a memorandum for you, and the Pater, your good father, which is from my own hand; from this you will learn my intention. I desire that it shall not get talked about, and for good reason, and with this I will end, begging you to recommend me to our good father's prayers, and also to all my good daughters, praying the Creator and His blessed Mother to give His grace to you and also to me. Your good daughter, Margaret.[709]

The second is a memorandum to Etienne Lullier instructing him what to say during the conversation with the Mother Superior and the priest:

First, that I wish above all to put my religious (community) in such a state they will never be in great poverty, but will be able to live without begging; and I wish to know ... if more money is needed, and if so, how much, that they not be stinted; for with God's help I will see to all; and every other thing that they desire, they must let me know, for I intend to make there a good end, with the help of God and our good Mistress, His glorious Mother.

Amongst other things say to the Mother Ancille (Ancelle)[710] my good mother, that I beg her to make all my good daughters pray for the purpose which I have always told her...[711]

---

709 This translation is from Eleanor E. Tremayne, The First Governess, pp. 285-286. See also Le Glay, Correspondance ... Vol. II, p. 455 from La Serna Santander, Memoir sur la Bibliothèque de Bourgogne, p. 135; A.C. De Schrevel, "Marguerite d'Autriche et le convent des Annonciades à Bruges" in Annales de la Société d'Émulation de Bruges, Tome 67, 1924.
710 A term of humility from "ancilla," servant.
711 Ibid.

Even then, Bruges was an old city and the center of art in the Low Countries. Much of the business activity had been lost to Ghent and Antwerp because of the silting up of the River Zwin, their outlet to the port, and the increase of larger ships. Bruges had been a favorite residence of the Dukes of Burgundy since the beginning of the fifteenth century, when the great and wealthy Bruges families had built their palatial homes. Her grandfather Charles the Bold and her mother, Mary of Burgundy were buried there in the Church of our Lady.[712] The Holy Blood Procession which takes place around the first of May on Ascension Day each year to commemorate the gift of the Patriarch of Jerusalem[713] to Derrick of Alsace, Count of Flanders, for his bravery during the Second Crusade, was even then an old celebration. As long ago as 1516, during Margaret's semi-retirement, she had established this convent in the north end of the city outside the Porte des Anes (Ezelpoort) near the Ostend Gate, and had charged the nuns to pray for the prosperity and safety of the Princess of the House of Austria-Burgundy. She became more and more attached to this foundation and began making plans for eventual retirement from public life. The contemplation of spending her last years in the tranquil, intellectual and religious atmosphere of this lovely old city, contented her.

But this was not to be. On November 23, Charles set out for the Low Countries, arriving in Cologne where he learned of his Aunt Margaret's illness and sudden death during the night of November 30-December 1. The strength and swiftness of Margaret's illness may have surprised even her.

The following account of Le Glay from an old manuscript in the Archives at Brou, written by an Augustinian monk, outlines the tragic details leading to the events which swiftly took place in Margaret's life during November 1530:

---

712   However, Maximilian had been emprisoned here in the Cranenburg House from February 5 to 22, 1488. Henri Pirenne, Histoire de Belgique, Vol. III, pp. 45-46.

713   The gift was a precious relic believed to contain drops of the blood of Christ. The writer saw this procession in May, 1978 - it is faithful to antiquity, well-run and most awesome, magnificent and spectacular.

Early on the morning of November 15, the Archduchess, not feeling well, remained in bed but asked one of her ladies, Magdalen Rochester,[714] for a glass of water. The glass slipped out of the lady's hands, fell and shattered. Though they cleaned the floor, one fragment had dropped into Margaret's slipper, and when she finally rose and put her feet into her slippers, she suffered a sharp wound. This wound became infected and subsequently the doctors were called. A week later they decided on amputation because the leg had become so inflamed. Margaret took the news calmly and asked for several days to get her affairs in order and to offer prayers. On November 30, in preparation for the operation, Margaret was given a large dose of opium in order to spare her pain, but it was too much for her already fevered body, and she died in her sleep.[715]

At the tomb in Brou, a mark has been made in the marble on Margaret's foot to indicate a cut; however, it is not known if this is true. One piece of information was gained, nevertheless. When the graves were opened in 1856, it could be seen that Margaret's leg had not been amputated.[716] There is no way to know for certain the cause of Margaret's death,[717] but of

---

714 This must be the same Magdalen Rochester who, as ward of the Duke of Suffolk, came to live with the Archduchess in 1513 at about age eight.

715 André J.G. Le Glay, Correspondance ... Vol. II, p. 456. Le Glay quotes from Histoire et description de l'église royale de Brou by Father Rousselet, Bourt, 1826, p. 59. See also M. Gachard, Analectes Belgique, Bruxelles, 1830 which has an authentique account of the "Maladie el mort de Marguerite d'Autriche" also in the collection de documents inédits concernant l'histoire de Belgique, Bruxelles, 1833, Tome I. Further concerning the death of Margaret and the funeral ceremonies and speeches, consult H. Coninckx, "Margaret d'Autriche commémorée" in the Bulletin du Cercle archéologique de Malines, Tome 17-18; and Le Comte Emmanuel de Quinsonas, Matériaux pour servir a l'histoire de Marguerite d'Autriche, (Paris: Chez Delaroque Freres, 1860), Volume I, pp. 388-404.

716 Le Comte Emmanuel de Quinsonas, Matériaux ... , Vol. II, p. 262.

717 However, since it appears she had suffered from an infection for some time, perhaps this accident with the glass is true, but happened long before the monk relates. In Margaret's era, this kind of wound might have drained, healed over, then suppurated again causing chronic infection of the bone and a great deal of discomfort. This might have alternated with acute phases of the infection where she became feverish and bedridden. Another possibility is phlebitis, or thrombosis of a vein. This can be caused by a tight garter, or a blow or injury which leads to inflammation. A clot of blood forms which restricts the normal flow of blood; there is swelling below the clot

the circumstances surrounding it we can be more knowledgeable because of the letters and literature left to us.

The eminent archivist Ghislaine de Boom is inclined to think that the account by the monk at Brou is largely a "picturesque legend." According to her research, the Archduchess was taken by an attack of fever on the twentieth of November, 1530 "so that the humors of her leg mounted in height."

> Despite the science of seven doctors surrounding her bed, and the prayers of the sad crowd which followed the procession of the Holy Sacrament around the streets of Malines, the disease made terrible progress. On November 28, Antoine de Lalaing, the faithful Knight of Honor, warned the Emperor then at Speyer, of the worrisome illness... Two days later he virote to Charles 'that the doubt [possibility] of her death exceeds the hope of her life.' After having turned over the government of the Low Countries to the Count of Hoogstraten November 30, 1530, between midnight and 1 o'clock Margaret of Austria succumbed, probably due to gangrene because 'the fire was put on her leg and at once rose to her body.'[718]

Jean de Carondelet, the Bishop of Palermo, and Antoine de Lalaing sent an account of her death to Charles:

> Madame has indeed shown in her end the virtue that was in her, for she died as good a Christian as it seems to us possible to be. She is a great loss, Sire, to your Majesty, and to all your countries over here.[719]

---

which causes pain, tenderness and swelling in the leg. Above the clot is a secondary, softer and non-adherent clot which makes its way back to the heart and lungs. This is called an embolism and can lead to shortness of breath and death. Also, there may have been some congenital weakness, as Maximilian's father had a leg amputated. It is, of course, almost impossible to diagnose 500 years later, but I am grateful to my sister-in-law Mary Pauline Bonner Miller, B.S., R.N. for going over the literature with me and making these suggestions as to what might have happened.

718 Ghislaine de Boom, Marguerite d'Autriche ... p. 93.
719 Eleanor E. Tremayne, The First Governess ... p. 289. See M. Gachard, Analectes Belgique (Bruxelles: 1830), p. 380; also Le Glay, Correspondance ... Vol. III, p. 458.

Her surgeon, Philip Savoien, was given thirty philippus "for having treated Madame as well as he could, and for having embalmed her body."[720]

On the last day, Margaret, still lucid, dictated a letter to Charles:

> My lord, the hour is come when I can no longer write to you with my own hand because I find myself in such a disposition to believe my life to be brief. Happy and content in my conscience and of full resolve to receive that which pleases God to send me without any regret, except the privation of your presence and to be unable to see you and talk to you one more time before my death, that is why I write you this letter of mine which I fear will be the last you receive from me. I appoint you my sole universal inheritor and for all to be used in whatever manner you recommend. You are left your countries on this side, which during your absence were not only guarded, but greatly augmented, and I render the government of those in which I have loyally acquitted myself, to the extent that I hope from it divine remuneration, contentment for you, my lord, and the pleasure of your subjects; you are also recommended to peace and especially with the kings of France and of England. Finally, I beg you, my lord, for the love that you bear to this poor body, that you will keep in memory the salvation of the soul, and regard for my poor servants, for the love of God to whom I pray, my lord, that you be given prosperity and long life.
>
> From Malines, the last day of November 1530.
>
> Your very humble aunt, Marguerite[721]

---

720 Eleanor E. Tremayne, The First Governess ... p. 289. See also Le Comte Emmanuel de Quinsonas, Matériaux ... Vol. III, p. 397. for a list of several doctors to whom Margaret made bequests in her will.

721 Karl Lanz, Correspondenz des Kaisers Karl V, Vol. I, p. 408. See also footnote in Le Glay, Correspondance ... p. 457 taken from GA chard's Analectes Belgique, p. 378.

Only two days before, in a codicil to her will of 1508, she had pleaded that Charles not abolish the name of the House of Burgundy, and that at his death it should remain with the inheritors of the Low Countries.[722] The same yearning to unite all these provinces which had motivated her grandfather Charles the Bold had remained with Margaret and had been strengthened and realized by her government.

The bells tolled for forty-five days in the compellingly mournful ways of that epoch. Margaret's body was placed first in her own chapel across the passageway from her palace at Mechelen/Malines. After six weeks she was moved across the street to the church of Sts. Peter and Paul. The funeral was held in the Cathedral of St. Romboud whose vast naves were draped with yards and yards of black cloth. The mourning was led by her grandnephew, child of the unhappy Isabel and the King of Denmark, whose own death would follow in two years. Cornelius Agrippa gave the funeral sermon to the family, the nobility, members of State, the Knights of the Golden Fleece, foreign ambassadors, and all the clergy plus crowds of people, saying in part:

> We have lost the anchor on which our hopes rested. We are weighed down with this great affliction, for no greater loss could have befallen us and our country. What consolation can we find in the death of the very saintly Princess Margaret? We all weep, we all lament her! All the provinces, all the cities, all the towns, all the villages, all the hamlets are plunged in grief, sorrow, and mourning.[723]

Earlier in the Cathedral at Cologne Jean Fabri had given a funeral oration to Charles and his court in the flowery fashion of the day. However, Charles wrote very simply to his sister, Mary of Hungary, who was at Krems

---

722 André J.G. Le Glay, Correspondance ... p. 458.
723 Eleanor E. Tremayne, The First Governess ... p. 290. The original copy of the Elegy is in the Imperial Library in Vienna; see Manuscrits et Livres Imprimés Concernant L'Histoire des Pays-Bas 1475-1600 (Bruxelles: l962), p. 56.

on the Danube, of "the loss we have suffered ... who considered her mother as well as Governess over these countries."[724]

In fulfilling the provisions of her will, Margaret's heart was given to the Convent of the Annonciades at Bruges where her body remained for two years until the tombs at Brou were completed. Her intestines were placed in a leaden urn and laid under the pavement of the choir at St. Peter and Paul in Mechelen/Malines.[725]

Among the provisions of her will were legacies to churches, hospitals and a plague-house, her officers and servants, Claude of Savoy,[726] and dowries for a hundred young girls.[727] A final bequest to the church at Brou allowed for its completion, and at long last in 1532, her body amidst a company of nobles and servants led by Antoine de Lalaing, was solemnly transported to Brou.

Once again over the meadows and hills of France and into the Jura mountains of Savoy, a May-June journey far different from the one she had undertaken years before over the same route in the late fall and winter - a reluctant bride on the way to her third marriage. Now with mild spring's gentle presence, Margaret came back to Brou. For three days, June 10, 11 and 12, 1532, funeral masses were celebrated in this beautiful gothic church

---

724 Karl Lanz, Correspondenz des Kaisers Karl V, Vol. I, p. 416. (Krems is about 50 miles northwest of Vienna.)

725 A marble stone, four times the size of the other stones surrounding it, and with a brass ring which lies flat within it, marks the place between the first step of the high altar and the lateral wall on the gospel side where the urn is buried. A "new" church was built around 1778 during the reign of Maria Theresa of Austria. Revolutionary turmoil had taken its toil and the old one had to be demolished. One of the highlights of research for this writer was a visit to Sts. Peter and Paul where an old nun speaking through the translation of a helpful young cleaning woman, showed me the marble block and gave me some of the history of the church. They appeared amazed and touched that an American would care.

726 According to Le Glay, Correspondance... Vol. I, p. 475. Claude died in 1528. The testament was written in 1508 and Margaret never changed that provision.

727 André J.G. Le Glay, Correspondance ... gives provisions of her will in Vol. II, pp. 458-459. Dowering was a very common form of charity as "a girl insufficiently dowered might have to suffer that disparagement in marriage which was so much dreaded and so carefully guarded against." See Eileen Power's Medieval Women, ed. By M.M. Postan (Cambridge: University Press, 1975), p. 41.

of such luminous and exuberant splendor that death truly had become a homecoming feast. Her years of longing were expressed in these lines:

> Time is long for me and I know why,
> Because for me one day is longer than a week
> And I pray to God that my body will be returned
> To my heart which is no longer with me.[728]

Brother Antoine de Saix, Commander of the Abbey of St. Anthony of Bourg spoke eloquently to the crowds in both Latin and French so that everyone would understand. It was a simple sermon of praise and honor in which he spoke of Margaret's qualities and talents.[729]

Margaret had never altered her arrangements for her final resting place. Ever since Philibert's death, she had continued to plan and supervise, though from afar, the building of this monument to that early love, and to her mother-in-law's unfulfilled vow.[730] She was wholly committed to the project, and against the best financial advice from the kindest of counselors Mercurino di Gattinara,[731] she never wavered from this goal. The constant

---

728 Ghislaine de Boom, Marguerite d'Autriche... p. 97, trans. by JEB and SHB.

729 Ibid. See also Le Comte Emmanuel de Quinsonas, Matériaux ... Vol. I, pp. 388-404, "Oraison funèbre de Marguerite d'Autriche, prononcée à Brou par A. Du Saix, 1532."

730 The prior of the monastery of Brou, Louis de Gleyrens, wrote to Margaret on September 2, 1521: "To our much-honoured Lady and very gracious Mother, - God grant you a good and long life. You will be pleased to know that the day of the feast of Saint Augustine Monseigneur Marnix came to visit your church of Brou, with the gentlemen of your Council of Bourg, and saw the progress of the same, and found that your two chapels in the aisle of the choir are roofed over, as well as the higher and lower aisles and oratories above and below, on the side of the belfry, and that the pipes and gargoyles for carrying off water falling from the roofs are fixed on the said aisles. And the belfry has grown this year to the height of twenty-three to twenty-five feet ..." (He goes on to say that the workmen have plenty of materials, wood, etc., to finish the work - but that money is running short, and that only about fifteen or sixteen florins are left, which will hardly last till All Saints Day, and unless more is supplied, the work must be interrupted) ... "but at present it is in the best state and appearance possible, and ought shortly to be finished, as those will tell you who have seen it ..." Eleanor E. Tremayne, The First Governess ... p. 191 - her translation of a letter in J. Baux, L'Église de Brou.

731 This able first counselor of Margaret's died on June 5, 1530 at Innsbruck pre-deceasing her by only six months. Years before he had predicted that his "very formidable lady would lose her last chemise over it." Eleanor E. Tremayne, The First Governess ... p. 279. On a trip through France, the writer and her family stopped one sunny-rainy summer day to make a tour, and

FORTUNE, MISFORTUNE, FORTIFIES ONE

drain on her finances that governing the Low Countries entailed also slowed the progress of the monument. So much so, that at her sudden death in 1530, much work remained to be completed, and it was two years before her body could be moved to Brou.

As the years went by Margaret became a legend and the truths of her life and death became embroidered. She was immortalized because of her love. All the strain and work of governing, the glory, success, sorrow and failure was forgotten, until today, one can read many histories of the times and never learn that there was a Margaret of Austria and Burgundy who governed the Low Countries for almost twenty-four years. One reads only of Maximilian and Charles - but the art historians remembered, and the monks cherished her memory and cared for the monument until a better day.

> All for the best, I dare to say,
> Though sorrow must be borne and pain,
> If thus I reach the better way,
> To suffer is not loss, but gain.
> My heart in simple faith doth rest
> And clings to nothing here below,
> All for the best
> For my part I will nought desire,
> Let come what may, my fate fulfill,
> For I will say and still maintain
> That God disposeth at his will
>   All for the best.[732]

---

fortunately there were very few in the group which gave them the opportunity to observe, and the quiet to contemplate. The chapel itself is light and spacious, and the focal points are the three marble tombs. The detail work is exquisite, and the marvel is that after so many years, very little is disturbed. In poorer, unsettled times, it endured the wars of religion and revolution, and had been consecutively an army post, a refuge for beggars, and a stable for pigs. The French government has done much to restore Brou, but the town's secluded location was its best protection. The money which in the early years of building had been slow in forthcoming and painfully collected, began to be returned in later years as the monks realized the tourist value of their shrine. It is now run by the French government.

732 Translation of poem in Margaret's Album, Christopher Hare (Mrs. Marian Andrews), The High and Puissant Princess Marguerite of Austria (London: Harper and Brothers, 1907), p. 326.

So rest, for ever rest, O princely pair!
In your high church, amid the still mountain air,
Where horn, and hound, and vassals never come.
Only the blessed Saints are smiling dumb,
From the rich painted windows of the nave,
On aisle, and transept, and your marble grave...

The moon through the clere-story windows shines,
And the wind washes through the mountain-pines...

And, in the sweeping of the wind, your ear
The passage of the angels' wings will hear,
And on the lichen-crusted leads above
The rustle of the eternal rain of love.[733]

In her summation of Anne of Brittany's life, the Countess De La Warr concluded that "the education of princes thus went on all their lives."[734] This was the humanist ideal, and the same statement could also describe the life of Anne's contemporary, Margaret of Austria.

The intent of this biography was to research the life of the Archduchess Margaret with a view to understanding those formative educational values, processes and forces which shaped this remarkable woman whose life spanned the final decades of the fifteenth century and the early decades of the sixteenth century known as the High Renaissance. Special emphasis was given to Margaret's childhood and formal education, her years in the other courts of Europe brought about by her marriages, her involvement in the arts and humanities which enriched her life, and the practical

---

[733] Excerpts from "The Church of Brou" by Matthew Arnold. See Arnold, Poetical Works, editors C.B. Tinker and H.F. Lowry (London: Oxford University Press, 1966), pp. 17-18. Poem written about 1850. Arnold became dissatisfied with this poem when he learned some parts were incorrect descriptively or historically. The church and tombs were a favorite theme in the nineteenth century with French poets as well. See Le Comte Emmanuel Quinsonas, Matériaux ... , Vol. II, pp. 131-138.

[734] Constance Mary Elizabeth Sackville, Countess De La Warr, A Twice Crowned Queen: Anne of Brittany (London: Eveleigh Nash, 1906), p. 220.

knowledge she gained as Regent of the Low Countries from the stern lessons of war, religious unrest, domestic and international particularism, all of which developed her talent and skills in diplomacy.

The Archduchess's reign has been largely overlooked in general histories, the effects of her regency being attributed to her father Maximilian I, or her nephew Charles V. It is to be hoped that this study will serve to illustrate the fulfillment of an educational ideal and the process by which it was accomplished, and to restore Margaret of Austria and Burgundy to her rightful place in history.

EPILOGUE

With the passing of Margaret, conditions in the Low Countries steadily worsened. While letters of condolence were sent, and expressions of sympathy made following the death of Margaret, Henry VIII's wrath was not appeased by her passing. His embittered feelings are related in correspondence sent by the Imperial ambassadors Eustace Chapuys and Micer Mai to Charles:

> The death of Madame whom may God receive into His glory, has been much felt by the merchants of this city most of whom carry on business with Flanders. As to the King, not only has he, as I am informed, shewn pleasure at her demise; but he was heard to say, when he first received the news, that the death of the Princess was certainly no great loss for the world, and to make use of other similar expressions indicating that he was no wise affected by it. And I am not surprised, for it is a general rule with him to consider anything turning to Your Majesty's personal disadvantage as good fortune, whereas your prosperity and success are gall and wormwood to him. But as Your Majesty very wisely and magnanimously remarks in one of your letters to me, these are not things to be taken into account, inasmuch as it is only the mere impulse of his

blind, detestable, and wretched passion [for the Lady] that makes him speak in so inconsiderate a manner. I fancy, however, that in future he will be more cautious and guarded in the expression of his sentiments towards Your Majesty ... Among other causes that most likely make the King glad of Madame's death, one is that he knows very well with what warmth and zeal the said Princess had taken up the affairs of the Queen, and also that she was supposed to be the principal instrument through whom the friendship of France would be maintained, which he (the King) would like to see shaken to its very foundations. Indeed one of the things which most attracted his attention and excited his curiosity, as well as that of the members of his Privy Council some time ago, was the occasional arrival of French agents at Madame's court, for when that happened they never failed to inquire of me what their mission could be, and for what purpose they went thither.[735]

...but before he (the King) read the letters, he inquired of me who was likely to succeed Madame in the Government of the Low Countries? ... Then he began to open and read the letters, and observing that the date fixed for the funeral was so near, said that he could not possibly on so short a notice send a personage of his Court to assist at the ceremony, but that ... he would send his instructions to Master Johan Acquet (John Racket) to represent him at the funeral ...[736]

It is sad to reflect that such a long personal, business and political relationship had so deteriorated that it threatened to create ill will between the two countries, for the Low Countries were in such a state as to require optimal conditions for their improvement. The religious controversy everywhere was growing more heated. Jane de Iongh observed that the treasury was empty, there were high debts, and total lack of credit.[737]

---

735 Pascual de Gayangos, Calendar of Letters... Vol. IV, Part II, pp. 1-2.
736 Ibid., p. 12.
737 Jane de Iongh, Mary of Hungary: Second Regent of The Netherlands, trans. by M.D. Herter Norton (New York: W.W. Norton and Company, 1958), p. 147.

... the representatives of Holland had given [to Charles] a poignant description of the misery in their province. Holland, they said, had been ruined by the recent wars. It was too poor to mend its dikes and therefore was continually exposed to floods. There was much unemployment, trade was paralyzed by oppressive taxes and high export licenses. Flourishing cities like Delft and Gouda were practically depopulated. Holland was living in a state of emergency ... [738]

... demobilized mercenaries of the two armies [France and the Empire], no longer held in check by any sort of discipline, could only support themselves by robbery and plunder ... [739]

... plague, epidemics and crop failures, the ruin of commerce and industry, continually rising prices and pinching shortages reduced large groups of the population of the Low Countries to despair.[740]

Many blamed the Emperor's policies. Margaret herself had warned of an emergency, "exhausted as Europe must be and is by the last wars."[741]

Under such circumstances, it seemed to Charles that the person most qualified to take the place of their aunt as Regent, was his sister Mary. On the third of January, 1531, Charles wrote from Cologne to his sister, "I pray you to accept this charge."[742] Mary was twenty-six years old. The little tomboy grown up was now the self-reliant dowager Queen of Hungary who had already proved herself as wife and widow of King Louis.

For some time Mary had been reading and reflecting on Luther's teachings and her court had decided Protestant leanings. Her brother Ferdinand had implored her to stop reading Luther's books. Charles, however, never doubted. He held Mary in high esteem and asked only that

---

738 Ibid.
739 Ibid., p. 145.
740 Ibid.
741 Pascual de Gayangos, Calendar of Letters ... Vol. IV, Part I, p. 262.
742 Karl Lanz, Correspondenz ... Vol. I, pp. 416-418. It also appears in English translation in Pascual de Gayangos, Calendar of Letters ... Vol. IV, Part II, pp. 4-6.

she dismiss her Protestant-minded servants. For her part, Mary required that she not be forced into any new marriage. Having contrasted the misery of Eleanor's and Isabel's lives with the independent state of her Aunt Margaret, Mary opted for the latter. Many years later, Charles's daughter Juana described her as "ambitious of power."[743] Perhaps, but she served forcefully and well during the next twenty-five difficult years as conditions continued to worsen in the Low Countries. Mary followed the policies of her aunt in trying to keep the provinces neutral, in attempting to moderate religious zealotry, and in encouraging industry and commerce. She too was against helping Christian of Denmark when Charles wavered, and she urgently argued for peace in Germany.

During this epoch, never ceasing wars,[744] conflicts with France and the Turks, and between Catholic and Protestant forces, had brought Charles's frail body to the breaking point. Death had interrupted Margaret's retirement plans, but Charles determined that his little remaining time should be spent in peace. On October 25, 1555, he entered the great hall of the palace at Brussels, his hand leaning on the shoulder of the 22-year-old Prince William of Orange, to make his abdication speech. Some days later he received the new French ambassador Admiral Coligny. Eventually these men would become prominent in the Protestant revolt; the former in the northern provinces of the Low Countries, the latter with the Huguenots in France. In that year, the Admiral's daughter Louise was born. She was to become the fourth wife of Prince William. Their son Henry Frederick would in 1625 succeed his brother and father as Stadholder of Holland.

In 1556, when Charles had completed the task of abdication, Mary resigned, and, accompanied by the widowed Eleanor, sailed with their

---

743 William Robertson, The History of the Reign of the Emperor Charles the Fifth with an account of the Emperor's life after his abdication by William H. Prescott in Vol. III. (Philadelphia: J.B. Lippincott Company, 1902/1856/1769), Vol. III, p. 407. It is true, however, that Mary did not have Maximilian's or Margaret's easy geniality.

744 Henry W. Littlefield, History of Europe 1500-1848, Barnes and Noble Books, 5th ed. (New York: Harper & Row, 1939), p. 34, observes that Europe was distracted by a series of international and civil wars until 1648 in practically all of which the religious issue was prominent.

brother from Zeeland for Spain - Charles to his retirement in the monastery at Yuste.

With the accession of Charles's son Philip II, the delicate fabric of the Low Countries began to tear apart. Margaret had ruled firmly as the rightful princess of the Low Countries; Mary as widowed Queen of Hungary and sister of the Emperor. Age and experience, in addition to their intellectual gifts, had taught them how to temper their goals for a strong central government with conciliatory measures and beneficences. They had an authority that was unassailable and wise counselors. Their policies were designed to protect the Low Countries and encourage industry and commerce. Humanists to the core, they pursued a middle path in regard to religion.

Now the presence of a young and inexperienced king who spoke only Spanish exacerbated the hatred the people felt for the Spanish soldiers quartered among them. The imposition of a new ecclesiastical hierarchy deprived the nobility and the local church leaders of power. Pervasively in all classes, the people of the Low Countries began to feel like an adjunct to Spain and the papacy.

Margaret of Parma, Charles's natural daughter, was appointed regent in 1559, but she had neither the power, the ability of her predecessors, nor the support of the nobles, who were divided politically and religiously and unable to cooperate among themselves. The lower nobility took matters into their own hands. Dressed as beggars (geuzen), and maintaining their loyalty to the government, they petitioned Margaret of Parma, in 1566, to relax the religious ordinances. She was of a mind to do this, but her advisers, who were of an inflexible and arrogant nature, were against it. They prevailed. Margaret, not having the strength of her convictions and opposed by forces too strong for amelioration, found the situation worsening. Later, in 1566, radical elements among the Calvinists, called, the "iconoclasts," looted churches and broke images. These campaigns were so violent and damage so extensive, that Philip sent his general the Duke of Alba to quell the riots. To the great horror of the people, the counts of Hoorn (Hornes) and Egmond were beheaded in the Grand Place at Brussels in 1568. Reasonable and loyal men who had served Charles faithfully, they had sought to establish an order not to the severe Philip's liking. On November 4, 1576, 7000 people lost their lives in what is known as "The Spanish Fury." (Later, the Duke of Anjou tried to seize Antwerp, and this culminated in "The French Fury" of January 16-17, 1583.)

These events precipitated one of the fiercest and bloodiest revolts of all time. The seventeen provinces which had been united under Margaret of Austria became, by an agreement concluded on January 23, 1579 at Utrecht, partitioned. This became the foundation for the United Provinces of the Netherlands, or the Dutch Republic, or Holland in the north, while the lower provinces were known as the Spanish Netherlands, comprising what is now largely Belgium and Luxemburg. This latter section was ruled once again by a woman, Isabella of Spain from 1598 to 1633, her husband, the co-regent Archduke Albert of Austria, dying in 1621.

History has not been kind to these lands. They have been invaded and fought over by France and Austria. In 1713 the Treaty of Utrecht terminated the War of the Spanish Succession and brought the lower section under the rule of Austria. Then Napoleon had his turn, and Belgium and Holland became parts of his empire. After Napoleon's defeat in 1814 by allied forces under the English Duke of Wellington at a beautiful little place just south of Brussels called Waterloo, all the provinces were once again united under Prince William of the House of Orange-Nassau, and the Kingdom of the Netherlands was created. But the breach between north and south was too extensive to be overcome at this time. Cultural and religious differences were too marked. Politically the Belgians were not fairly represented. They revolted in 1830 and with the help of England established the independent Kingdom of Belgium - this old Roman name which re-emerged during Margaret's reign is used in modern times to transcend the Walloon and Fleming languages.

Overrun by the Germans in both world wars[745] these nations decided in 1947 to overcome their regional diversities to some degree by creating

---

745 The Battle of the Bulge in the Ardennes was fought in Belgium and Luxemburg; "A Bridge Too Far" occurred around Arnhem in The Netherlands.

an economic union which is called Benelux. In 1949 they joined other nations in the NATO Agreement. In addition, Brussels is now the seat of the European Economic Community. Centuries of self-defeating factionalism have at last been transcended by a measure of cooperation. The Archduchess Margaret would be content.

BIBLIOGRAPHY

Abbagnano, Nicola. "Humanism." Translated by Nino Langiulli. The Encyclopedia of Philosophy. New York: The Macmillan Company, 1967. Vol. IV.

Adams, Robert P. The Better Part of Valor: More, Erasmus, Colet, and Vives, on Humanism; War, and Peace, 1495-1535. Seattle: University of Washington Press, 1962.

Allen, P. S. ed. Opus Epistolarum Des. Erasmi Roterodami. Oxford: MCMVI (1906).

Alpern, Mildred. "Images of Women in European History" in Social Education 42: 3; March 1978, 220-4.

Anne of France (Anne de Beaujeu), Duchess of Bourbon. Les Enseignements d'Anne de France... à sa fille Suzanne de Bourbon. Moulins, C. Desrosiers, 1878.

Appelbaum, Stanley. The Triumph of Maximilian I. New York: Dover Publications, Inc., 1964. (With 137 woodcuts by Hans Burgkmair, Albrecht Dürer and others.)

Armstrong, C.A. J. "The Burgundian Netherlands 1477-1521." New Cambridge Modern History, 1957. (pp. 228-32).

Armstrong, Edward. The Emperor Charles V. 2 vols. London: MacMillan and Company, Ltd., 1929/1901.

Arnold, Matthew. Poetical Works. Edited by C.B. Tinker and H.F. Lowry. London: Oxford University Press, 1966.

Bainton, Roland H. Women of the Reformation in France and England. Boston: Beacon Press, 1975.

Baudson, Françoise, conservateur de Musée de Bourg-en-Bresse. "A history and description of the church and tombs at Brou" From La France Illustrée. Paris: 1977.

Becker, Philipp August. Jean Lemaire, Der Erste Humanistische Dichter Frankreichs. Réimpression de l'édition de Strasbourg, 1893. Genève: Slatkine Reprints, 1970.

Bergenroth, Gustav Adolph, ed. Calendar of Letters, Despatches and State Papers, relating to the negotiations between England and Spain, preserved in the Archives at Simancas and elsewhere. 17 vols. Vols. I and II, also Supplements to each volume, 1862, apply to this study. See also Gayangos, Pascual de.

Bergh, L. Ph. C. van den. Correspondance de Marguerite d'Autriche, Gouvernante des Pays-Bas, avec ses amis. Sur les affaires des Pays-Bas de 1506-1528. Tirée des Archives de Lille et publiée par ordre du Gouvernement. Tome I - 1506-1511; Tome II - 1511-1528. Utrecht: Chez J. de Kruijff, 1849.

Best, Michael R. and Brightman, Frank H. ed. The Book of Secrets of Albertus Magnus of the Virtues of Herbs, Stones and Certain Beasts. Oxford: Clarendon Press, 1973.

La Bibliothèque de Marguerite d'Autriche. Bruxelles: Ministère de L'Instruction Publique; Bibliothèque Royale de Belgique, Rue du Musée, 5, Mai-juillet, 1940.

Bibliothèque Nationale D'Autriche. Manuscrits et livres imprimés concernant l'histoire des Pays-Bas, 1475-1600. A composite work by the Bibliothèque nationale d'Autriche à Vienne and the Bibliothèque royale de Belgique. Editor of the catalogue is Dr. F. Unterkircher of Vienna, the translators into French are M. Wittek and M.-Th. Lenger of Brussels.

Boom, Ghislaine de. Correspondance de Marguerite d'Autriche et de ses ambassadeurs à la cour de France concernant l'exécution du Traite de Cambrai (1529-1530). Bruxelles: Maurice Lamertin, Libraire-Éditeur, Rue Coudenberg, 58-62, 1935. (Commission Royale d'Histoire).

_____. Marguerite d'Autriche-Savoie et la Pré-Renaissance. Bruxelles: La Renaissance du Livre, 12 Place du Petit Sablon, 1946/1935.

Born, Lester K. The Education of a Christian Prince by Erasmus. See Erasmus.

Bornate, Carlo. "Historia vite et gestorum per domimun magnum cancellarium" (Mercurino di Gattinara), con note, aggiunte e documenti, from Miscellanea di storia italiana. Torino: Regia deputazione di storia patria per le antiche provincie e la Lombardia, 1915. Toma 17, Serie 3, pp. 231-585.

Boulger, Demetrius Charles de Kavanagh. Belgian Life in Town and Country. New York: G.P. Putnam's Sons, The Knickerbocker Press, 1904.

Boyd, William. The History of Western Education. 8th ed. New York: Barnes & Noble, 1966.

Bradford, William, editor and translator. Correspondence of The Emperor Charles V and his ambassadors at the courts of England and France, from the original letters in the Imperial Family Archives at Vienna; with a connecting narrative and biographical notices. ANS Edition, 1971. London: Richard Bentley, New Burlington Street, Publishers in Ordinary to Her Majesty, 1850.

Bladley, Carolyn G. Western World Costume. New York: Appleton-Century-Crafts, Inc., 1954.

Brandi, Karl. The Emperor Charles V. Translated from the German by C.V. Wedgwood. Oxford: Alfred A. Knopf/Alden Press, 1939; Munich, 1937.

Brehier, Emile. The Middle Ages and the Renaissance. Translated from the French by Wade Baskin. Phoenix Books. Chicago: The University of Chicago Press, 1967.

Brewer, J. S. The Reign of Henry VIII from his Accession to the Death of Wolsey. Reviewed and Illustrated from Original Documents, ed. James Gairdner, 2 vols. London: John Murray, 1884.

Bruchet, Max and Lancien, E. L'Itinéraire de Marguerite d'Autriche. Lille: Imprimerie L. Danel., 1934.

Bruchet, Max. Marguerite d'Autriche, Duchesse de Savoie. Lille: Imprimerie L. Danel, 1927.

Bruges, City of Art. Illustrated guide with explanations and map of the city. Gidsenbond Brugge. Tenth edition.

Bullard, Melissa Meriam. "The Roots of Higher Education for Women." Graduate Women: AAUW Journal (May-June 1979), pp. 23-27.

Bury, J.B. "The Ottoman Conquest." Cambridge Modern History. Cambridge: 1902, Vol. I, Chap. III, p. 95.

Cammaerts, Emile. A History of Belgium. New York; D. Appleton and Company, 1921.

Castiglioni, Dr. Arturo. A History of Medicine. Translated from the Italian and edited by E.B. Krumbhaar, M.D., Ph.D. New York: Alfred A. Knopf, 1941.

Chamberlin, E.R. Marguerite of Navarre. New York: The Dial Press, 1974.

Chamberlin, Frederick. The Private Character of Henry the Eighth, New York: Ives Washburn, 1931.

Champion, Pierre. Louis XI. Paris: Librairie Ancienne Honore Champion, 1927.

Clark, Sydney. All the Best in Belgium and Luxembourg. New York: Dodd, Mead and Company, 1956.

Comines, Philippe de, Sieur d'Argenton, 1455?-1511. The Memoirs of Philippe de Commynes. Edited by Samuel Kinser; translated by Isabelle Cazeaux. Vol. II contains Books Six, Seven and Eight, 1477-1498. Columbia: University of South Carolina Press, 1973.

Cuyler, Louise. The Emperor Maximilian I and Music. London: Oxford University Press, 1973.

De La Warr, Constance Mary Elizabeth Sackville, Countess. A Twice Crowned Queen, Anne of Brittany. London: Eveleigh Nash, 1906.

Dickens, A.G. Reformation and Society in Sixteenth-Century Europe. London: Thames and Hudson, 1977/1966.

Ellis, Sir Henry, ed. Original Letters, Illustrative of English History: including numerous royal letters: from autographs in the British Museum, The State Paper Office, with notes and illustrations. London: Richard Bentley, New Burlington Street, Publishers in Ordinary to Her Majesty, MDCCCXLVI (1846). 2 vols.

Elton, G.R., ed. "The Reformation 1520-1559." The New Cambridge Modern History, Vol. II, 1958.

Ensor, Robert Charles Kirkwood. Belgium. New York: Henry Holt & Company, 1951-18(?).

Erasmus, Desiderius. The Education of a Christian Prince. Translated and edited by Lester K. Born. New York: Columbia University Press, 1936.

Erasmus Epistles, see Allen, P.S. or Nichols, Francis Morgan.

Festival van Vlaanderen - Mechelen (Program and Catalogue). "De Muziek... en Herdenkingsstelling van Margareta van Oostenrijk, 1480-1980."

Forbush, Frances Lawhon. "The Patronage of Margaret of Austria: Taste in Transition." Unpublished M.A. thesis, University of Virginia, May 1977.

Gachard, L. P. Analectes Belgique, Bruxelles, 1830; Collection de documents inédits concernant l'historie de Belgique, 1833; Rapport sur différentes séries de documents qui sont conservés dans l'ancienne Chambre des Comptes à Lille, 1841; Analectes historiques, Bruxelles, 1856-1871.

Garraty, John A. Unemployment in History: Economic Thought and Public Policy. New York: Harper & Row, Publishers, 1978.

Gayangos, Pascual de, ed. Calendar of Letters, Despatches and State Papers, relating to the negotiations between England and Spain, preserved in the Archives at Simancas and elsewhere. 17 vols. Vols. III, Parts I and II; and IV, Parts I and II apply to this study. See also Bergenroth, Gustav Adolph.

Godefroy, Jean ed. Lettres du roy Louis XII et du cardinal d'Amboise, avec plusieurs lettres, mémoires et instructions écrites depuis 1506 jusques et y compris 1514. Bruxelles: Chez François Foppens, 1712. Four volumes contain almost 200 letters between Margaret and her ambassadors at the French court.

Gomez de Fuensalida, Gutierre. Correspondencia de Guiterre Gomez de Fuensalida, Embajador en Alemania, Flandes e Inglaterra, 1496-1509. Madrid: Published by the Duque de Berwick y de Alba, Conde de Siruela, 1907.

Green, Lowell. "The Education of Women in the Reformation." History of Education Quarterly, Spring 1979, pp. 93-116.

Green, Mary Anne Everett (Wood) 1818-1895. Letters of Royal and Illustrious Ladies of Great Britain. London: H. Colburn, 1846.

Guicciardini, Francesco. The History of Italy. Translated, edited, with notes and an introduction by Sidney Alexander. New York: The Macmillan Company, 1969. (First published 1561, twenty-one years after Guicciardini's death.

Habsburg, Otto van. Charles V. translated from the French by Michael Ross. New York: Praeger Publishers, 1970.

Hackett, Francis. Francis the First. New York: The Literary Guild, 1934.

Henry the Eighth. New York: Horace Liveright, Inc., 1929.

Hale, J.R. Renaissance Europe 1480-1520. 7th ed. London: Fontana/Collins, 1977.

Renaissance Exploration. New York W.W. Norton and Company, Inc., 1968.

Hare, Christopher. (Mrs. Marian Andrews). The High and Puissant Princess Marguerite of Austria. London: Harper and Brothers, 1907.

Haring, C.G. The Spanish Empire in America. A Harbinger Book. New York: Harcourt, Brace and World, Inc., 1963/1952/1947.

Henry-Bordeaux, Paule. Louise de Savoie, "Roi" de France. (1476- 1531). Paris: Librairie Académique Perrin, 1971/1954/1943.

Hill, Pamela. Here Lies Margot. New York: G.P. Putnam's Sons, 1958.

Hillgarth, J.N. The Spanish Kingdoms 1250-1516. Oxford: Clarendon Press, 1978, Vol. II.

Hughes, Muriel J. "The Library of Philip the Bold and Margaret of Flanders, First Valois Duke and Duchess of Burgundy." Journal of Medieval History 4, No. 2. North Holland Publishing Company. (June 1978), pp. 145-188.

Huizinga, J. The Waning of the Middle Ages. Doubleday Anchor Books/St. Martins Press, 1949. New York: Doubleday and Company, Inc., 1954. Translated by F. Hopman; first published in Dutch in 1924.

Hume, Martin. Queens of Old Spain. London: G. Richards, 1906.

_____. The Wives of Henry the Eighth and the Parts They Played in History. New York: McClure, Phillips and Company, 1905.

International Exhibitions Foundation. Old Master Paintings from The Collection of Baron Thyssen-Bornemisza. Introduction by John Walker. Catalogue by Allen Rosenbaum. Washington, D.C. 1979-1981.

Iongh, Jane de. Margaret of Austria: Regent of the Netherlands. Translated from the Dutch by M.D. Herter Norton. New York: W.W. Norton & Company, Inc., 1953.

Iongh, Dr. Jane de. Margaretha van Oostenrijk, Regentessen der Nederlanden. Amsterdam: N.V. EM. Querido's UitgeversMaatschappij, 1946, (Dutch edition of above).

_____. Mary of Hungary: Second Regent of the Netherlands. Translated by M.D. Herter Norton. New York: W.W. Norton and Company, 1958.

Irizarry, Carmen. The Thirty Thousand: Modern Spain and Protestantism. New York: Harcourt, Brace and World, Inc., 1966.

John, Eric, ed. The Popes: A Concise Biographical History. Tenbury Wells, Worcester, England: Fowler Wright Books, Ltds., 1964.

Kelso, Ruth. Doctrine for the Lady of the Renaissance. Urbana: University of Illinois Press, 1956.

Kendall, Paul Murray. Louis XI. New York: W.W. Norton and Company, 1971.

Keniston, Hayward. Francisco de los Cobos, Secretary of the Emperor Charles V. Pittsburgh: University of Pittsburgh Press, 1958.

Kirchner, Walther. Western Civilization to 1500. Barnes & Noble Books. New York: Harper & Row, 1960.

Labande-Mailfert, Yvonne. Charles VIII et Son Milieu (1470-1498). Paris: Librairie C. Klincksieck, 1975.

Lanz, Dr. Karl. Corresondenz des Kaisers Karl V. Aus dem königlichen Archiv und der Bibliothèque de Bourgogne zu Brüssel. First published 1844. Frankfurt/Main: Minerva GmbH, Unveränderter Nachdruck (unchanged printing), 1966.

Le Glay, André J. G. Correspondance de l'Empereur Maximilien I et de Marguerite d'Autriche. Paris: Chez Jules Renouard et Cie. 1839.

_____. Collection de Documents Inédits sur l'Histoire de France. Paris: Imprimerie Royale, MDCCCXLV (1845), Tomes I and II.

_____. Maximilien I, Empereur d'Allemagne, et Marguerite d'Autriche, sa fille, Gouvernante des Pays-Bas. Paris: Chez Jules Renouard et Cie., 1839. The contents of this book also appear under "Notices" of Vol. II following the correspondence in Le Glay's Correspondance ... (See above). Page numbering is different, however.

Lemaire de Belges, Jean. Les Épîtres de l'Amant Vert. Édition critique publiée par Jean Frappier, Professeur à l'Université de Strasbourg. Lille: Librairie Giard; Genève: Librairie Droz, 1948.

Lemaire de Belges, Jean. Oeuvres. Publiées par J. Stecher, Tome IV. Réimpression de l'édition de Louvain, 1882-1885. Genève: Slatkine Reprints, 1969. (Contains La Couronne Margaritique, poems and letters.)

Levi, Albert William. Humanism and Politics. Bloomington: University of Indiana Press, 1969.

Lewis, D.B. Wyndham. Charles of Europe. New York: Coward-Mccann, Inc., 1931.

Lewis, Paul. The Gentle Fury. New York: Holt, Rinehart and Winston, 1961.

Littlefield, Henry W. History of Europe 1500-1848. 5th ed. Barnes & Noble Books. New York: Harper & Row, 1939.

Lockyer, Roger. Henry VII. London: Longman/Harper & Row Publishers, Inc., 1968.

Marygrove College, Detroit. Into Her Own: The Status of Women from Ancient Times to the End of the Middle Ages. Sirois, Marcia. "Medieval Woman's Influence on Social and Political Life." Freeport, New York: Books for Libraries Press, 1972/1946.

Nichols, Jean. Chroniques de Jean Molinet. Publiées par Georges Doutrepont et Oilier Jodogue. Bruxelles: Palais des Academies, 1935. Tome I - 1474-1488; Tome II - 1488-1506.

Nichols, John Gough, ed. The Chronicle of Calais in the Reigns of Henry VII and Henry VIII to the Year 1540. Richard Turpyn, reputed author. Camden Society, Vol. XXXV.) London: J.B. Nichols and Son, 1846.

Nichols, Francis Morgan, ed. and trans. The Epistles of Erasmus. 3 vols. New York: Russell and Russell, 1962/1918.

O'Faolain, Julia and Martines, Lauro, ed. Not in God's Image: Women in History from the Greeks to the Victorians. Colophon Books, New York: Harper & Row, 1973.

Pirenne, Henri. Early Democracies in the Low Countries. Translated from the French by J.V. Saunders. Harper Torchbooks. New York: Harper & Row, 1963. (First published by Longmans, London: 1915).

_____. Economic and Social History of Medieval Europe. Translated by I.E. Clegg. 9th ed. London: Routledge & Kegan Paul, Ltd., 1972.

_____. Histoire de Belgique. 3 vols. Bruxelles: Henri Lamertin, Libraire-Éditeur, 1907.

_____. Geschiedenis van België. Vertaald door Richard Delbecq. Gent: Samenwerkende Maatschappij "Volksdrukker J," Hoogpoort 29, 1908. (Dutch version of Histoire ...)

_____. A History of Europe. Vol. II, From the Thirteenth Century to the Renaissance and Reformation. Translated by Bernard Miall, Anchor Books. New York: Doubleday & Company, Inc., 1958.

_____. Medieval Cities: Their Origins and the Revival of Trade. Translated from the French by Frank D. Halsey. Princeton, New Jersey: Princeton University Press, 1952/1925.

Plowden, Alison. The House of Tudor. New York: Stein and Day, 1976.

Pollard, A.F., ed. The Reign of Henry VII. 3 vols. London: Longmans, Green and Company, Ltd., 1913. New York: AMS Press 1967.

Potter, G.R., ed. "The Renaissance 1493-1520." The New Cambridge Modern History. Vol. 1, 1957.

Power, Eileen. Medieval Women. Edited by M.M. Postan. Cambridge: Cambridge University Press, 1975.

Prescott, William H. History of the Reign of Ferdinand and Isabella the Catholic. 3 vols. Philadelphia: J.B. Lippincott & Co., 1880, Vol. 22. (Prescott also wrote an account of Charles V's life after his abdication, see Robertson, William.)

Quinsonas, Le Comte Emmanuel de. Matériaux pour servir à l'histoire de Marguerite d'Autriche. 3 vols. Paris: Chez Delaroque Freres, MDCCCLX (1860).

Rabb, Theodore K. The Struggle for Stability in Early Modern Europe. New York: Oxford University, 1975.

Reiffenberg, Le Baron de. Histoire de l'Ordre de la Toison d'Or. Brussels: Fonderie et Imprimerie Normales, M DCCC XXX (1830).

Richardson, Walter C. Mary Tudor: The White Queen. London: Peter Owen, 1970.

Rival, Paul. The Six Wives of King Henry VIII. Translated from the French by Una Lacy Traubridge. London: Heinemann, 1971/1937.

Robertson, William. The History of the Reign of the Emperor Charles the Fifth with an account of the Emperor's life after his abdication by William H. Prescott. 3 vols. Philadelphia: J.B. Lippincott Company, 1902/1856. Robertson's work was first published in 1769.

Russell, Joycelyne G. The Field of Cloth of Gold. London: Routledge & Kegan Paul, 1969.

Sachs, Hannelore. The Renaissance Woman. Translated from the German by Marianne Herzfeld. New York: McGraw-Hill Book Company, 1971.

Schrijver, Elka. "The Life of Jan van Scorel." History Today. London: February, 1978, pp. 121-125.

Scott, Sir Walter. Quentin Durward. (A fictional account of Louis XI of France and the Lord de la Marek, the "Wild Boar of the Ardennes.") Boston: Houghton, Mifflin and Company, 1900 (?).

Seward, Desmond. Prince of the Renaissance, The Life of Francois I. London: Constable, 1973.

Somers, Lord. A Collection of Scarce and Valuable TRACTS… Second edition revised by Walter Scott, Esq. Vol. 1. London: 1809. AMS Press, Inc., New York, 1965.

Steenackers, Chan. Em. La Grande École à Malines (1450-1630). Malines: Imprimerie L. Godenne, 1921.

Thompson, James Westfall. Economic and Social History of Europe in the Later Middle Ages (1300-1530). New York: The Century Company, 1931.

Tuchman, Barbara W. A Distant Mirror, The Calamitous 14th Century. New York: Ballantyne Books, 1978.

Tremayne, Eleanor E. The First Governess of The Netherlands. New York: G.P. Putnam's Sons; London: Methuen & Company, 1908.

Van Doorslaer, Dr. G. Coup d'Oeil sur la Ville durant la régence de Marguerite d'Autriche. Malines: L & A Godenne, Imprimeurs-Éditeurs, 1907.

Vives, Juan Luis. Instrucción de la Mujer Christiana. Translated by Juan Justiniano from Latin to Spanish. Madrid: Signo, 1936.

Voet, Leon. Antwerp: The Golden Age. Antwerp: Mercatorfonds, 1973.

Waas, Glenn Elwood. The Legendary Character of Kaiser Maximilian. New York: AMS Press, Inc., 1966. (1941 Columbia University Press.)

Walsh, Richard J. "Charles the Bold and the Crusade: Politics and Propaganda." Journal of Medieval History 3, No. 1, North-Holland Publishing Company, (March 1977), pp. 53-86.

Weiss, R. "The Renaissance 1493-1520." The New Cambridge Modern History. Vol. II, 1958.

Willis, F. Roy. Western Civilization, an Urban Perspective. Vol. I. Lexington, Massachusetts: D.C. Heath & Company, 1973.

Winker, Elsa. Margarete Von Österreich, Grande Dame der Renaissance. München: Verlag Georg D.W. Callwey, 1966.

Woodward, William Harrison. Desiderius Erasmus concerning the Aim and Method of Education. New York: Columbia University Teachers College Bureau of Publications, 1964. First published in 1904, reprinted by permission of the Cambridge University Press.

_____. Studies in Education During the Age of the Renaissance, 1400-1600. New York: Columbia University Teachers College Press, 1967. First published in 1906, reprinted by permission of the Cambridge University Press.

_____. Vittorino da Feltre and Other Humanist Educators. New York: Columbia University Teachers College Bureau of Publications, 1963. First published in 1897, reprinted by permission of the Cambridge University Press.

Yarwood, Doreen. The Encyclopedia of World Costume. New York: Charles Scribner's Sons, 1978.

Made in the USA
Middletown, DE
03 April 2015